Multinational Firms and International Relocation

NEW HORIZONS IN INTERNATIONAL BUSINESS

General Editor: Peter J. Buckley
Centre for International Business,
University of Leeds (CIBUL), UK

This series is aimed at the frontiers of international business research. The study of international business is important not least because it gives researchers the opportunity to innovate in theory, technique, empirical investigation and interpretation. The area is fruitful for interdisciplinary and comparative research. This series is established as a central forum for the presentation of new ideas in international business.

Titles in the series include:

Transnational Corporations in Southeast Asia
An Institutional Approach to Industrial Organization
Hans Jansson

European Integration and Competitiveness
Acquisitions and Alliances in Industry
Edited by Frédérique Sachwald

The State and Transnational Corporations
A Network Approach to Industrial Policy in India
Hans Jansson, M. Saqib and D. Deo Sharma

Competitive and Cooperative Macromanagement
The Challenges of Structural Interdependence
Edited by Gavin Boyd

Foreign Direct Investment in Japan
Edited by Masaru Yoshitomi and Edward M. Graham

Structural Competitiveness in the Pacific
Corporate and State Rivalries
Edited by Gavin Boyd

Euro-Pacific Investment and Trade
Strategies and Structural Interdependencies
Edited by Gavin Boyd and Alan M. Rugman

Multinational Firms and International Relocation
Edited by Peter J. Buckley and Jean-Louis Mucchielli

Current Issues in International Business
Edited by Iyanatul Islam and William Shepherd

The Struggle for World Markets
Edited by Gavin Boyd

Multinational Firms and International Relocation

Edited by

Peter J. Buckley

Professor of International Business and Director of the Centre for International Business, University of Leeds, UK

and

Jean-Louis Mucchielli

CESSEFI, University of Paris 1 Panthéon-Sorbonne, France

NEW HORIZONS IN INTERNATIONAL BUSINESS

Edward Elgar
Cheltenham, UK • Brookfield, US

Published by
Edward Elgar Publishing Limited
8 Lansdown Place
Cheltenham
Glos GL50 2HU
UK

Edward Elgar Publishing Company
Old Post Road
Brookfield
Vermont 05036
US

British Library Cataloguing in Publication Data
Multinational Firms and International
Relocation. – (New Horizons in
International Business Series)
    I. Buckley, Peter J.   II. Mucchielli, J.
    L.   III. Series
    338.6042

Library of Congress Cataloging-in-Publication Data
Multinational firms and international relocation / edited by Peter J.
    Buckley and Jean-Louis Mucchielli.
        — (New horizons in international business)
        Includes bibliographical references and index.
        1. International business enterprises—Management.
    2. International business enterprises—Location—Decision making.
    3. Business relocation—Decision making.   I. Buckley, Peter J.,
    1949–   .   II. Mucchielli, Jean Louis.   III. Series
    HD62.4.M843   1996
    658.3'83—dc20   95–25263
                                                                        CIP

ISBN 1 85898 302 9

Typeset by Manton Typesetters, 5–7 Eastfield Road, Louth, Lincolnshire LN11 7AJ, UK.
Printed and bound in Great Britain by Bookcraft (Bath) Ltd.

Contents

v

Figures

Tables

Contributors

Giovanni Balcet is at the Department of Economics, University of Turin, Italy.

Pierre-André Buigues is Head of Unit and Advisor in the Directorate-General for Economic and Financial Affairs of the European Commission.

Peter J. Buckley is Professor of International Business and Director of the Centre for International Business, University of Leeds, UK.

Wong Yu Ching is at the Department of Economics, Keio University, Japan.

John H. Dunning is Professor of International Business, Rutgers University, US and Professor of Economics Emeritus, University of Reading, UK.

Edward M. Graham is a Senior Fellow, Institute for International Economics, US.

Farid Harianto is with the PPM Graduate School of Management and the University of Indonesia and is Visiting Professor at the Center for International Studies, University of Toronto, Canada.

Thomas Hatzichronoglou is at the Organisation for Economic Co-operation and Development.

Alexis Jacquemin is Advisor in the Forward Studies Unit of the European Commission.

Jean-Louis Mucchielli is at CESSEFI, University of Paris 1 Panthéon-Sorbonne, France.

Terutomo Ozawa is Professor of Economics, Colorado State University, US.

A. Edward Safarian is a Senior Fellow of the Center for International Studies, University of Toronto, Canada and an Associate of the Canadian Institute of Advanced Research.

Philippe Saucier is at IOF, University of Orléans, France.

Yoko Sazanami is Professor of Economics at Keio University, Japan.

Hideki Yamawaki is at the Anderson School of Management, University College of Los Angeles, California, US.

Preface

This volume is the result of the Colloque en Sorbonne 'Stratégies des firmes Multinationales et Impacts des Délocalisations' held in June 1994 under the patronage of the Ministère de l'Enseignement Supérieur et de la Recherche, the Commissariat Général du Plan and the University of Paris I (Panthéon-Sorbonne). The Conference was organized by the Centre for International Economy and Business Strategy (CESSEFI), University of Paris 1, directed by Jean-Louis Mucchielli.

The editors would particularly like to thank Ambassador Jean-Daniel Tordjman, the head of the Invest in France Mission, M. Franck Borota, Président de la Commission Parlementaire sur les Délocalisations and Professor Yves Jegouzo, President of the University of Paris 1. Thanks go also to all our colleagues who participated in the debate, particularly those who acted as discussants.

Peter J. Buckley
Jean-Louis Mucchielli

1. Introduction

Peter J. Buckley and Jean-Louis Mucchielli

The chapters in this book address two issues of crucial importance for the future of the world economy – the extent to which foreign direct investment replaces jobs in the home economy and the impact on the host country of inward foreign direct investment. These were the subjects of the Colloque at the Sorbonne in June 1994 at which the first versions of these chapters were presented (Colloque en Sorbonne, Stratégies des Firmes Multinationales et Impacts des Délocalisations). It is entirely appropriate that these deliberations took place in Paris, because it is in France that the *délocalisation* debate is at its fiercest.

The relocation debate has focused on the transfer abroad of manufacturing production to lower wage countries at a time when Europe, and France in particular, was experiencing rising unemployment at home. The Senate Report (Arthuis, 1993) suggested a connection between French outward direct foreign investment and relocation of jobs, estimating that over one million jobs are threatened in France by the process of delocalization. The report brings together three key factors: (1) technological progress which allows a wide swathe of industrial production to become more footloose (particularly textiles, electronics and toys), (2) the opening of many new countries to international trade and therefore to becoming potential sites for relocation – this includes Eastern and Central Europe and China – and (3) the recession itself which forces companies to cut costs. The report identifies three successive phases of relocations: traditional consumer products, services and intangibles (the last of these potentially occurring in all sectors) (UNCTAD Division on Transnational Corporations, 1994). This report suggests that many of the relocation platforms (particularly those in Asia) are not playing to the same rules as the European nations and that their exports represent 'social dumping' in that labour standards are not being met, and also that many European countries do not have open markets to foreign (European) products. These assertions are challenged in this book on both empirical and theoretical grounds.

We have chosen the term 'relocation' to express the production transfer notion captured by *délocalisation*. Our term is also less loaded and includes the impact on the recipient economy. The chapters represent an attempt to bring to bear concepts deriving from international and industrial economies, business strategy and international business theory to address the concept and the practice of international industrial relocation. Chapter 2, by Mucchielli and Saucier, addresses the issue directly and brings in the crucial matter of technological change. The authors find static equilibrium analyses unconvincing in the modern world economy and bring a Schumpeterian approach to bear on the relocation problem. In addition to a careful study of the meaning of comparative advantage and its development over time, they conclude that defending declining industries risks slowing down the innovation process and is therefore likely to be self-defeating.

Buckley's chapter concentrates on decision making at the level of the firm and suggests that a relocation decision can only be considered in the context of the firm's overall foreign market servicing strategy. This is a dynamic process which evolves over time in response to a wide variety of stimuli and is dependent on internal decision-making processes. It is by no means clear within this framework that domestic investments are feasible alternatives to foreign direct investments in situations of increasing international competitiveness.

In Chapter 4, Buigues and Jacquemin address the issue of industries faced by low-wage competition. A varied and variable picture emerges across the European Union (EU) and the authors are able to suggest policies which will improve European competitiveness. These include the encouragement of greater investment per worker, increased training expenditure with the specific goal of skill improvement and strengthening the Single European Market, which should develop economies of scale.

Giovanni Balcet examines the relocation strategies of Italian firms and again finds a multiplicity of causal effects at work. Much of Italian foreign direct investment is market-oriented and so has had largely complementary effects on exports. A new strand is technology-exporting foreign direct investment, largely aimed at Central and Eastern Europe. As Balcet points out, cost-oriented outward investment often evolves into market-oriented or global strategies. Interestingly, Balcet also alludes to some structural difficulties in the Italian domestic economic structure and to potential problems arising from *inward* direct foreign investment – notably on technological development.

In Chapter 6, Graham provides a cross-sectional analysis of US foreign direct investment abroad and its impact on exports – and therefore, of course, on employment. The overall result is that US outward investment and exports are generally complements, not substitutes. Sazanami and Wong take an overview of the strategies of Japanese multinationals in Asia, the EU and North America. Just like Graham for the USA, the authors find a positive relationship between (the share of) Japanese exports and Japanese foreign direct investment.

Chapter 8, by Thomas Hatzichronoglou, takes a wide-ranging view of the impact of foreign direct investment on domestic manufacturing employment in the Organization for Economic Cooperation and Development (OECD). He points out that much foreign direct investment takes the form of acquisitions and that it is often difficult to attribute differences in employment before and after the acquisition to the change because of difficulties in calculating the number of jobs which would have been maintained in the absence of take-over. The key virtue of inward direct foreign investment in Hatzichronoglou's view is its ability to mobilize domestic resources, particularly manpower.

Terutomo Ozawa takes the Japanese motor industry as a case study of the move into the world class manufacturing sector and as a model for many would-be followers (Chapter 9). He regards the 'protected competition' phase of Japanese industry as a protectionist scheme moderated by the intense domestic competition between Keiretsu groups. The innovations (such as team production methods) brought about by the car makers were eminently transferable abroad and laid the basis for the ability to take on foreign competitors in their own domestic market. The rate of diffusion of these innovations is a crucial variable in determining the future structure of global trade in the motor (and comparable) sectors.

In Chapter 10, Harianto and Safarian examine the Southeast Asia experience of multinationals and technology diffusion. This diffusion follows the upgrading of production: simple production units add value and diverse activities as they become more established; inter-firm linkages grow and technology and skills spill over to the local economy. In Chapter 11, Hideki Yamawaki examines the exit behaviour of Japanese multinationals from European and US manufacturing industries. This is found to be related to entry mode, with diversifying acquisitions and joint ventures most likely to result in exit. This chapter suggests some intriguing possibilities for further research on exit behaviour.

John Dunning provides concluding comments in Chapter 12. He takes us beyond the confines of relocation decisions towards notions of 'alliance capitalism', where cooperation as well as competition is increasingly required to survive in an increasingly interdependent world economy.

It is the hope of the editors of this volume that light has been shed on the nature of international relocation and on the *délocalisation* debate. However, our authors have shown that relocation can only be understood in a wide context which examines not only business strategy and government policy but also the feasible alternatives for governments and multinational firms. We should also remember that foreign direct investment and relocation is not a one-way phenomenon, in that all countries investing abroad are also recipients of inward investment.

REFERENCES

Arthuis, J. (rapporteur) (1993), *Délocalisations hors du territoire national des activités industrielles et de services*, Paris: Rapport du Sénat, No. 337.
UNCTAD Division on Transnational Corporations (1994), *World Investment Report 1994*, Geneva: UNCTAD.

2. European industrial relocations in low-wage countries: policy and theory debates

Jean-Louis Mucchielli and Philippe Saucier

In June 1993, a report presented to the French Senate (Arthuis, 1993) launched a national debate on industrial relocations to third world countries. Those relocations were considered to be responsible for an impressive part of French unemployment (three million jobs were supposed to have been lost and up to 80 per cent of jobs in French industries and services were likely to be sooner or later relocated in low-wage countries). A few months later the French National Assembly issued its own report, taking a more moderate view (Chavanes, 1993). Although they were based on facts and attempted rough theoretical interpretations of case studies, these reports selected ad hoc arguments and neglected important evidence. The debate itself meant that protectionist action and impediments to outward foreign direct investment (FDI) in developing countries were being considered, although these policy instruments were obviously outmoded. During the same period, in the European Commission, the same debate was going on.

The phenomenon of relocations requires careful analysis. The first part of this chapter will assess its importance. Determinants and impacts will also be traced in the intricate puzzle of multinational firms' strategies. The second part will attempt to find which of a so-called international equilibrium approach and of a neo-Schumpeterian approach gives the relevant theoretical answers and policy indications.

ASSESSMENT OF THE RELOCATION PHENOMENON

Survey and Scale of Relocations

Definition of relocations
The definition of relocations has to be clarified. To relocate means to move a manufacturing process from one place to another. As far as the multinational

activity of a firm is concerned, relocation involves the closing down of a manufacturing unit in the home country to replace it with a new unit in a foreign country. The most common type of relocation is followed by re-imports of goods previously manufactured in the home country. Such reloca-tion does not necessarily concern the whole production process: only a seg-ment may be relocated, for instance the assembly base. Moreover, a reloca-tion does not always imply a fully owned subsidiary; it can arise through different types of agreements between partner firms, and as joint ventures or even original equipment manufacturing (OEM).

There is a danger in giving a very extensive definition of relocation. All kinds of international subcontracting and even any import that has a substi-tute within national boundaries, such as Moroccan tomatoes, could be defined as relocation ('in agriculture, relocations mainly take the form of imports', Arthuis, 1993, p. 85). With such an extension of the concept, international business itself is considered as a relocation.

Should one retain this broad definition, all international trade with third world countries, notably with Asian countries and the Maghreb countries, will have to be reassessed. This raises another question: should we reduce, maintain or reinforce our trade protection against imports from those coun-tries? Indeed, those who adopt such a broad definition very often reach the conclusion that we must reduce our trade with host countries of relocations accused of social dumping.

Data on foreign direct investments and on multinational firms

To assess the importance of relocations one should first look at data on foreign direct investments and on multinational firms. They refer to a broad view of relocation since only part of FDI implies relocation of domestic activities, but it shows the upper limit of the phenomenon. FDI flows can partly be studied through the balance of payments. Usually, we have international direct invest-ments when the investment flow studied gives a minimum control of the firm located abroad which receives the investment (usually at least 10 per cent of the firm's capital). The OECD data (Table 2.1) shows that world international invest-ment reached 191 billion dollars in 1994 (270 in 1995) compared to the 4090 billion dollars in 1994 for the international trade (GATT, 1995). After following an upward trend until the end of the 1980s foreign direct investment flows have been stabilized between 1991 and 1994. But a new upsurge is observed in 1995.

It therefore seems excessive to claim we are experiencing an extension of relocations. In terms of stocks, world international investments in 1993 were worth 2 125 billion dollars. Investment stocks mostly belong to American firms (539 billion); French firms are only in fifth position (with foreign stocks of 182 billion), behind the United States, the United Kingdom, Japan and Germany (Table 2.2).

Table 2.1 FDI flows for OECD countries, 1981–93 (billions of US dollars)

	Annual average (billions of dollars)							Annual average share in total (percentage)					Annual growth rate (percentage)ᵇ					
	1981–1985	1986–1990	1991	1992	1993ᵃ	1994	1995	1981–1985	1986–1990	1991	1993	1995	1981–1985	1986–1990	1991	1992	1993	1995
Developed countries																		
Inflows	37	130	121	102	109	133	203	74	84	74	62	65	1	24	-32	-5	7	53
Outflows	47	163	185	162	181	191	270	98	96	96	85	85	3	24	-17	-12	12	42
Developing countries																		
Inflows	13	25	39	51	80	87	99	26	16	24	35	32	-4	17	25	32	54	15
Outflows	1	6	7	9	14	38	47	2	4	4	15	15	33	49	-28	33	55	22
Central and Eastern Europeᶜ																		
Inflows	0.02	0.1	2	4	5	58	120	0.04	0.1	1	27	3.8	1	90	716	85	25	106
Outflows	0.004	0.02	0.01	0.03	—	550	301	0.01	0.01	0.005	0.09	0.09	-11	20	-74	172	—	-45
All countries																		
Inflows	50	155	162	158	194	225	315	100	100	100	100	100	-0.1	23	-22	-2	23	40
Outflows	48	168	192	171	195	230	317	100	100	100	100	100	3	24	-17	-11	14	38

Notes: The levels of worldwide inward and outward FDI flows and stocks should balance; however, in practice, they do not. The causes of the discrepancy include differences between countries in the definition and valuation of FDI; the treatment of unremitted branch profits in inward and outward direct investment; treatment of unrealized capital gains and losses; the recording of transactions of 'offshore' enterprises; the recording of reinvested earnings in inward and outward direct investment; the treatment of real estate and construction investment; and the share-in-equity threshold in inward and outward investment.

a Based on preliminary estimates.

b Compounded growth rate estimates, based on a semi-logarithmic regression equation.

c Former Yugoslavia is included in developing countries.

Source: UNO World Investment Report, 1993.

Table 2.2   *FDI stock by country and region, 1980–95 (billions of US dollars)*

Region/country	1980	1985	1990	1995[a]
A. Outward				
Developed countries	*507*	*664*	*16 145*	*25 143*
United States[c]	2 201	2 510	4 352	7 055[b]
United Kingdom	804	1 003	2 308	3 190[b]
Japan	188	443	2 046	3 055[b]
Germany	431	599	1 515	2 350[d]
France	236	371	1 101	2 009[d]
Developing countries	*61*	*212*	*693*	*2 144*
World	514	685	1 684	27 301
B. Inward				
Developed countries	*373*	*538*	*1 373*	*19 327*
Western Europe	200	245	758	10 875
North America	137	249	508	681
Other developed countries	36	44	106	1 637
Developing economies	*108*	*196*	*341*	*693*
Africa	21	27	41	59
Latin America and the Caribean	48	76	121	226
Asia	38	92	176	403
Central and Eastern Europe	*0.87*	*1.8*	*18*	*318*
World	482	735	1 716	26 578

Notes:
a   Estimates
b   Estimates by adding flows to the stock of 1994.
c   Excluding FDI in the financial sector of the Netherlands' Antilles, except for 1995.
d   Estimates by adding flows to the stock of 1993.

Source: UNO, *World Investment Report, Investment, Trade and International Policy Arrangements*, Geneva, 1996.

One can also try to identify relocations through the evolution of the number of multinational firms. To summarize, a multinational firm is a firm that controls at least one production unit in a foreign country and at least 10 per cent of the firm's capital. For the year 1995, the United Nations estimates (1995) that 39 000 multinational firms owned 270 000 subsidiaries: 90 per cent of them from developed countries, 1 per cent from East European countries and the others from developing countries (mostly from Singapore,

China, Taiwan, Mexico and Brazil). Multinational firms originating in Japan, France, the United States, Great Britain and Germany represent more than half of all multinationals.

French foreign direct investment versus direct investment in France

According to the DREE data (French Department of Foreign Economic Relations, Ministry of Economy, February, 1994), 160 000 subsidiaries of French companies existed throughout the world in 1992. They accounted for almost 2.4 million jobs. These figures should be treated with caution, since they may include jobs in foreign firms that are only partly owned by French firms (participation above 10 per cent). The top ten French multinationals accounted for 685 000 jobs abroad, that is 28.5 per cent of the total. The top 27 accounted for half of total employment in foreign subsidiaries of French companies. As Table 2.3 shows, some French multinationals achieve 70 per cent or more of their turnover abroad (Michelin, Rhône-Poulenc, Saint-Gobain).

Table 2.3   The top ten French groups by numbers employed abroad

Groups	Numbers employed abroad	Percentage employed abroad	Turnover abroad (%)
Alcatel-Alsthom	124 000	58	68
Michelin	94 900	70	80.5
Saint-Gobain	70 400	67	72.5
Gale des Eaux	68 500	34	27
Cie de Suez	63 000	80	50
Accor	60 100	73	53
Thomson	57 100	54	68.6
Lyonnaise des Eaux	50 000	45	—
Rhône-Poulenc	49 600	56	77.5
Schneider	47 500	47	50
Total	685 100	56	—

Source: DREE (1994).

It is to be noted (Table 2.4) that French firms mostly settle in OECD developed countries, which hosted 67.6 per cent of French subsidiaries' total employment in 1994. Germany, Spain, the United States, Great Britain and Sweden are the main host countries. The European Union accounts for 43 per cent of employment of French companies abroad.

Table 2.4   Main host countries for French multinational firms

Rank (1992)	Rank (1991)	Countries	Number of Affiliates	Number of Employees	Share (%)
1	1	USA	1 700	375	16.6
2	2	GB	1 340	259	11.4
3	3	Germany	1 330	226	10
4	4	Spain	870	201	8.9
5	5	Belgium–Luxemburg	960	152	6.7
6	6	Italy	670	116	5.1
7	7	Brazil	350	109	4.8
8	10	Morocco	270	54	2.4
9	8	Canada	170	51	2.2
10	33	Sweden	110	46	2
		Total of above countries	7 770	1 589	70.1

Source: DREE (1994).

Foreign direct investment (and probably relocation) is a two-way process. Over 70 per cent of international investment flows take place between developed countries. France is also a host country as well as a country that relocates its industry abroad. Taking into account profits reinvested in the country, France stood first in the world as a host country for foreign investments in 1992. In that same year, French outward foreign investment exceeded inward foreign investment, but the deficit was a mere 15 billion francs, compared to 95 billion two or three years earlier. Flows were completely balanced in 1993 and inflows were higher than outflows in 1995 (Table 2.5).

Table 2.5   French FDI outflows and inflows (billions of francs)

	1988	1989	1990	1991	1992	1993	1994	1995
Inflows	42.9	60.9	49.3	62.7	84.3	68.8	58	66.6
Outflows	76	115.7	147.5	115.7	99.4	68.8	60.4	53.3

Source: DREE (1994).

There was a French foreign investment boom over the second half of the 1980s, but only a small part of it went to developing countries, which received an average annual flow of 4.4 billion francs between 1980 and 1985, and 5 billions between 1986 and 1991 (Detape and Quélennec, 1993). According to the SESSI analysis, OECD countries represented more than 90 per cent of the

French stock of industrial direct investment abroad. The EEC hosted more than 53 per cent and North America more than 27 per cent. More impressive is the declining share of LDCs in this French foreign direct investment stock: its global importance, which stood at 24 per cent in 1980, was only of 5.5 per cent in 1990.

Determinants of Relocations

Labour cost is not the main determinant of relocations

Labour costs differences are often pointed to as an explanation for relocations. For instance, for a total wage cost of 100 francs in France, a company would pay approximately only 2 francs in China, 5 francs in Malaysia, 11 francs in Poland, between six and 12 francs in Mexico, and so on. In fact, this has of course to be adjusted for productivity differences – otherwise the whole world industrial activity would have moved to Madagascar, which offers the lowest wage costs in the world.

Despite high labour costs, developed countries with high rates of productivity (quantity produced per hour of work) remain significant production locations. Moreover, it is wrong to believe that the cost of labour represents a major part of manufacturing expenses. Even in some segments of the textile industry, production is located in France because of the small share of labour cost in total cost. Hence CEF (Compagnie Européenne de Fils) started production in 1993 in Partenay: 'the choice of setting up a spinning mill on French territory relies on the availability of highly qualified labour, and on the low share of labour cost in this type of manufacturing; it represents only 10 per cent of the finished good cost price' (*Les Echos*, 8 March 1993).

More generally, as is underlined by Jungnickel (1994) (see Figure 2.1), even if the labour costs ratio between the most developed countries and developing countries is sometimes as high as 20:1, this disadvantage narrows to 1 if unit costs are considered. Viewed thus, the hourly wage is an inappropriate yardstick for competitiveness and decisions as to locations, but also wage costs in direct manufacturing often represent less than 50 per cent of the production costs even for labour-intensive goods.

A main determinant: foreign market penetration

The preceding analysis does not take into account an important determinant of relocations: opportunities to develop sales (including exports) on the local market in which the firm is setting up. Recently, Southeast Asian countries experienced 8 to 10 per cent increases in their GDP, whereas Europe had negative or near zero growth rates. Asian Pacific markets offer great opportunities for French exports and local expansion of French firms. This mainly concerns technology-intensive industries, rather than labour-intensive

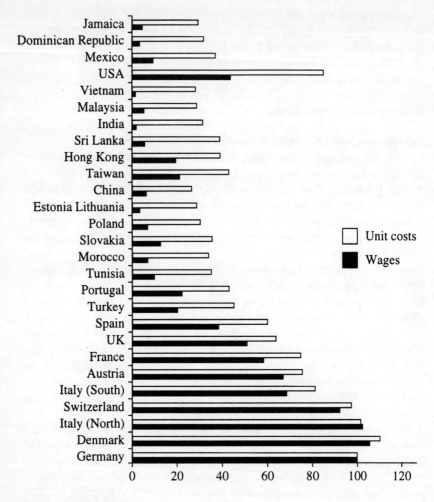

Source: Jungnickel (1994).

*Figure 2.1   Index of wages and costs in the international clothing indus-
tries, 1987 and 1992*

industries whose importance is stressed in the debate on relocation. Fast-
growth Asian developing countries are a major market for European aero-
nautics, telecommunications and other high-technology industries.

According to the GATT data from 1991 (published in 1993), South Korea,
Malaysia, Thailand, the Philippines and India had a trade deficit. In Asia,
only China, Taiwan and Indonesia have trade surpluses. However, Taiwan

showed a trade deficit with Europe during the first half of 1993. Such deficits reflect a rising demand in those countries. Hence this aspect of relocation should not be neglected, even though it mostly concerns assembly-based manufacturing. Here again the example of Japan is worth mentioning: its highest trade surpluses are now with Southeast Asian countries, where its firms have widely relocated. Southeast Asia has to be seen as providing new markets and not only low-cost location opportunities. Compared to the NICs, or Japanese and US firms, French and European companies have been slow to recognize Southeast Asia as a new market to exploit. For example, for China (first host country for FDI in 1993), between 1979 and 1992 French FDI represented 1 per cent of the total flows and the European Union 6 per cent, whereas Asian NICs represented 66 per cent, Japan 13 per cent and the United States 10 per cent.

Apart from Southeast Asian countries, other dynamic regions should be considered. Renault has invested two billion francs in Turkey in three years. Turkey has become the fourth largest world outlet for the French motor manufacturer, ahead of Spain. The Turkish market for private cars is increasing sharply: by more than 30 per cent per year since 1991. In 1971, the Oyak-Renault plant in Bursa produced its first car, the R12. From 20 000 motor vehicles per year, the manufacturing capacity of the plant rose to 105 000 in 1992 and should reach 150 000 in 1994. 'In order to keep its *rank* as second local car producer, Renault has to invest' (*La Tribune*, 20 September 1993). Renault would only get a small share of this market through exports if it was not supported by local investments.

A growing constraint: flexible response and 'lean' production
Flexible response as quick response is increasingly prevalent as a means of competition, especially in cases of short product cycles and competitive advantages gained by 'first movers'; the substantial reduction of delivery times is important in this respect. Jungnickel (1993), estimates for products to be sold on the US market the total time in process and transit to be 66 days for integrated production in the Far East, 35 days for integrated production between the USA and Jamaica. It takes only 36 days for integrated production in the USA, using the best technology available in 1987 and less than 15 days, using the most advanced present robot technology.

Global trends: the technological race and strategic alliances
The last few years have witnessed an increase in the number of cooperation agreements, of setting up joint subsidiaries between multinational firms – so-called new forms of FDI. However, this cooperation is mostly to be seen among firms of developed countries. They are especially found in high-technology industries, such as electronics, computers and aerospace, or in

industries that have reached maturity but show new technological capabilities (the car industry, for example). In oligopolistic markets, cooperation or competition strategies resemble races between competitors. This strategic race can be seen in R&D, in manufacturing, in marketing and in the adoption of technical standards.

R&D competition is crucial in technology-intensive industries. This explains why the strategic race is studied in relation to R&D and cooperation agreements. Most of the time, there are international agreements since big firms adopt strategies that are more and more global. They make it possible for firms to acquire different types of advantages: scale or learning economies, a minimum amount for R&D investment, a lower shared risk, improvements in market power. Alliances can also drive competing firms out of the technological race. In this oligopolistic competition and strategic race framework, a firm's multinationalization, relocation and search for foreign partnership are essential to the survival of the company and to the expansion of its competitive advantages (Mucchielli, 1991).

Impacts of Relocations on Employment and International Trade Dynamics

Previous developments already give an idea of the impact of relocations. The current French debate was already going on in the United States in the 1970s. The United States was then the leading international investor.

The multinational firms versus domestic employment debate in the United States

In 1970, American trade unions were stirred by the consequences for employment of US firms' foreign investments. From a survey ordered by the trade unions, the AFL-CIO asserted that foreign activities of American firms resulted in a loss of 500 000 jobs in the United States between 1966 and 1969, or even of 900 000 between 1966 and 1971. It claimed that those jobs were mainly in labour-intensive activities abroad (Ruttenberg, 1971). The AFL-CIO summarized thus the trade unions' position: 'the decline of the American position in the world is linked to the activity of multinational firms... They have exported American technology, thus reducing American production and employment to the sole benefit of firms. They are responsible for the rapid and considerable drop in the American production of rather sophisticated goods such as radios, TV sets and other electric goods, shoes and garments.'

This report inspired the so-called Burke-Hartke Bill of 1972. This bill, which was not ratified, aimed both at restricting imports and at deterring American investments abroad, by imposing a tax on goods produced abroad by US firms and on the overall value of goods first exported to be reimported (after being partly manufactured or assembled in a foreign subsidiary). It was also planned to restrict licence and patent transfers abroad, so as to avoid competition with domestic production. Yet later reports by academic circles and government bodies found the impact on employment to be positive. Job creation was estimated at between 89 000 and 600 000. Only one study found a loss, of 32 000 jobs, with debatable assumptions. As a result of these reports, the campaign for restrictive law was cancelled.

This debate is now partly over: from 1985, the United States had more capital inflows than capital outflows, and it is now the leading international investment host country. However, a similar kind of worry arose during the NAFTA (North Atlantic Free Trade Agreement) negotiation and ratification. Some Americans feared a massive relocation of firms to Mexico. Studies of the impact on global employment of this agreement showed the same discrepancies in assessments as those of the reports carried out 20 years earlier (see Table 2.6). The AFL-CIO once again estimated that 500 000 jobs would be lost because of this agreement, whereas other institutions evaluated the net improvement to be between 64 000 and 130 000 jobs (Hufbauer and Schott, 1992).

The overall effect of relocations on unemployment
The optimistic result found in most reports can be explained as follows: effects of relocations on employment depend widely on the complementarity or substitutability of foreign production compared to domestic production. There are four main types of direct or indirect effects (in the short, medium or long run).

1. Foreign production can replace domestic production to start with (substitutability); there is then *a direct effect of loss of employment.*
2. Parent firms or firms from the home country can supply foreign subsidiaries with parts or with manufacturing materials and equipment. This raises exports and generates the creation of new production in the home country (complementarity): there is *an indirect effect of job creation by stimulation of exports.*
3. Within the parent company, foreign relocation of production of standardized goods may increase management staff and surveillance personnel concerned with this production. Relocation can also be accompanied by more R&D in the parent company and production of more sophisticated goods, intensive in skilled labour. There is *an indirect effect of increasing a job's qualification requirements.*
4. Last, relocation of production can stimulate, within the firm's national boundaries, a rise in related jobs in banking, consultancy and advice services: it will create *jobs related to international business.*

Table 2.6 Impacts of US multinationals firms on US employment: a summary of studies

Study	Source of data	Estimate of % of foreign markets retained by US firms in the absence of foreign investment	Employment effect (number of jobs)[1]			
			US production displacement effect	Export stimulus effect	Home office and supporting firm employment effect	Net employment
1. Ruttenberg, AFL-CIO study, 1971. (Ruttenberg, 1971)	Aggregate official data	Inferred to be high	−500 000 jobs during 1966–9 owing to adverse trade movements, of which MNEs account for an 'important part'[1]	n.a.	n.a.	'Important part' of −500 000
2. Stobaugh and associates, 1971. (Stobaugh and associates, 1976)	Nine case studies and aggregate data	Low or zero in the long run		+250 000	+350 000	+600 000
3. Emergency Committee for American Trade, 1972. (US Tariff Commission, 1973)	Sample survey of 74 companies	Inferred to be low	n.a.	+300 000	+250 000	Substantially positive
4. US Chamber of Commerce, 1972. (US Department of Commerce, 1972)	Sample survey of 158 companies	Inferred to be low or zero	n.a.	+311 345[2]	n.a.	Positive
5. R.G. Hawkins, 1972.[3] (Hawkins, 1972)	Aggregate data	Assumption 1 (5% of production of US affiliates retained in the USA	−190 000			+279 000
		Assumption 2 (10% of production retained)	−381 000	+260 000	+209 000	+89 000
		Assumption 3 (25% of production retained)	−791 000			−322 000

| 6. US Tariff Commission, 1973. (US Tariff Commission, 1973) | Unpublished statistics on operations of US firms with foreign operations | Assumption 1 (average share of foreign markets actually held by US exports during period 1960–61)[5] | −603 100 | +286 000 | +321 000 | +488 000[4] |

Notes:
1. Negligible.
2. Based on net trade.
3. Apart from the assumptions of US production displacement, Hawkins made other assumptions: (a) 47 per cent of exports to affiliates would not have occurred in the absence of the affiliates; (b) 63.7 workers were required per million dollars of manufacturing output in US exports.
4. The net result includes 629 000 jobs created in the USA by foreign-based MNEs. It is doubtful whether, in fact, this should be brought into the calculation.
5. Calculations were also undertaken on the basis of two other assumptions: (a) that 100 per cent of the markets held by US exports were displaced by MNEs; (b) that 50 per cent of the markets held by US exports were displaced. The net domestic employment impact in the two cases was −1 297 000 jobs and −417 800 jobs respectively.

Sources: US Tariff Commission, 1973; Hawkins, 1972.

Thus the AFL-CIO report of 1971 did not take into account the positive indirect effects of relocations on employment. It had merely registered jobs of American firms abroad and assumed them to be losses for the United States (perfect substitution effect); similar arguments were used in France when the debate on relocations began. They deserve the same criticisms.

Japanese fears regarding foreign investment

The Japanese case followed the same pattern. In the 1960s and 1970s, the first relocation wave struck the Japanese textile industry. A debate on the 'boomerang effect' of FDI in low-wage countries was launched (Shinohara, 1979). Within a decade Japan, which was the leading exporter of textile goods, became a net importer. Yet has employment decreased? A second wave of investments abroad developed with appreciation of the yen in 1985. This time, it was directed towards developed countries, notably the United States, to avoid trade barriers, the so-called 'tariff jumping'. Did this lead to a

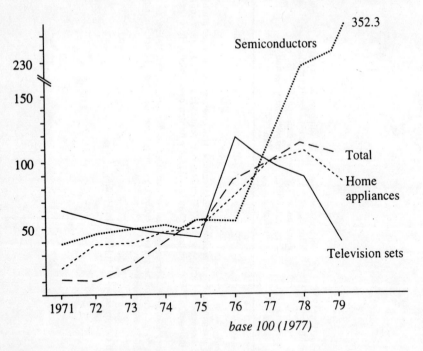

Source: Ministry of International Trade and Industry, *White Paper on International Trade and Industry*, various years.

Figure 2.2   Export index of Japanese-made electrical machines exported to the USA, 1971–9

decrease in employment in Japan? The 'hollowing out effect', like the 'boomerang effect' of the 1970s, had no significant impact on employment, although Japan relocated markedly to developing countries. (See Figure 2.2). On the other hand, international trade flows increased. We can clarify this phenomenon. As low-standard goods were relocated to developing or developed countries, Japanese firms reshaped their domestic production units to manufacture more sophisticated goods or to build segments able to produce goods complementary to relocated products (parts-intensive in technology, with high added value).

The Japanese example illustrates the Schumpeterian creative destruction process (Figure 2.3). Static arguments are not relevant. Only the dynamic process of technical progress and innovations can maintain and develop new job opportunities. We know barely 20 per cent of the goods that will exist in the 2010s. Once today's products are relocated, advanced countries will have to manufacture tomorrow's. When a country has a comparative advantage in standardized and labour-intensive goods, it seems fairly natural that it should specialize in those products. Developed countries such as France have no

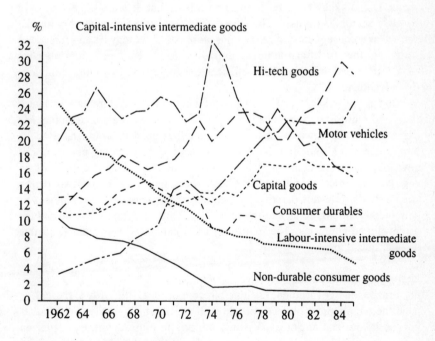

Source: MITI (various years) white paper.

Figure 2.3   Changes in the nature of Japanese exported goods, 1962–85

comparative advantage in such goods. A country that insists on manufacturing all types of goods itself, despite comparative advantages, is bound to fail.

Relocations and unemployment in Europe

It is erroneous to say that Europe has lost jobs and that its industrial production has decreased. Statistical data show the contrary. We may look at employment: it has increased from 126.7 million employed to 133.4 million in the European Community over a period of more than 20 years (1970–92). There has been a net job creation of 6.7 million. In France, employment rose from 21.9 to 22.5 million jobs during the same period. The unemployment upward trend shows only that the increase was not high enough compared to the growth of active population which in Europe put an additional 12.7 millions job seekers on the labour market. In the European Community, industrial production continued to rise. From 1986 to 1991, only nine branches of industry out of 78 had a negative average annual growth rate (Commission Européenne, 1993).

We may also look at external trade: in 1991, the European Community had a favourable extra-EC trade balance for the whole of the manufacturing sector. Deficits may be sizeable in some sectors, but they are largely covered by other sectors' surpluses. Thus there is no empirical evidence of industrial decline as a consequence of relocations, although there may be an accelerated shift from low-qualification declining industries to new innovation-intensive sectors. Relocation is just a side-effect of the evolution of dynamic comparative advantage.

What is the respective importance of international differences in factor costs and innovation dynamics in the evolution of comparative advantage? Is there a tendency towards factor price equalization that would have to be interpreted in a Mundell (1957) type approach? Is the catching-up process of new industrializing economies the result of their low labour cost or of an endogenous process of innovation? All these questions boil down to the choice of the relevant paradigm to explain the accelerated development of new industrializing areas and the correlative shift in comparative advantage of developed countries. The relocation issue cannot be separated from this broader question.

Employment in France

For France, one government institute of economics (DREE, 1994) has calculated the employment impact of trade with developing countries by calculating the labour content of exports and imports in those countries. Using an input–output table for 1991, economists found that, despite a trade surplus between France and developing countries (LDCs) (around 70 billion francs), the import labour content exceeded that of the export. They take into account the price differences between imported goods and substitute ones produced at home: for example, one million imported shoes from LDCs cost 36 million francs and the substitute ones in France cost 87.5 million francs to be produced. So even if France exports 194 billion francs to LDCs in 1991 and imports 126 billions, as the substitute goods in France are 2.6 times more expensive to produce, 126 billion francs of imported goods are equivalent to 264.5 billion of home goods. Using the input–output table, we find that 194 billions of export would create 447 000 jobs and 264.5 billions of substitute imports would create 608 000 jobs. Thus French trade with LDCs generates a deficit of 330 000 jobs. Nevertheless this estimation is considered as a maximum because indirect effects are not taken in account. But even with this estimation, we are very far from the three or four million jobs destroyed by relocation that the Senate report expected.

AN INTERNATIONAL EQUILIBRIUM APPROACH VERSUS A NEO-SCHUMPETERIAN APPROACH TO RELOCATIONS

The recent debate on relocation raises questions which had become, for almost 30 years, more or less irrelevant since international trade and FDI, from the 1960s, were concentrated among developed countries. 'Unfair competition', or social dumping, from low-wage countries was never considered as a serious menace, whereas domination by multinationals (American and, later, Japanese) was rather thought, at one time, to be the real threat to national independence and consequently to long-term welfare.

Recently, trade between developed and developing countries (including industrializing countries) accounts for only 17.5 per cent of total world trade (1990). International trade is dominated by exchanges among developed countries and follows to a very large extent an intra-industry trade pattern incompatible to a large extent with explanations based on the concept of comparative advantage. Yet the expanding phenomenon of relocation into low-wage countries of declining industries of developed countries, and the resulting flows of capital and goods between North and South, give a new impulse to theoretical approaches based on differences of relative endowments of factors, and consequently of relative factor cost, between countries with different levels of development.

However it is still possible to admit the coexistence of even imbrication of two hypotheses of trade and international investment. One, based on rivalry of access to larger market shares, results in concentration of trade and investment flows between countries with high purchasing power. The other is based on the quest for productive efficiency and relies on the exploitation of international differences in costs of production.

Probably world markets with an oligopolistic structure are more and more dominated by this dual logic. The survival and development capacity of the firm in such markets is of course dependent on its ability to maintain or increase its market share as a response to competitors, but profitability is the major condition to investment and therefore to expansion of market share. Relocation, as R&D, improvements in internal organization or alliances, is only one of the ways to reinforce, by lowering costs, the capacity of the firm to resist pressure of competition. It is therefore a paradox that potential profits arising from relocation have not been exploited earlier and to a wider extent by firms that cannot neglect any opportunity to increase profits. As was pointed out above, international differences in wages, at current exchange rates, are still a major characteristic of world economy. They range from one to 50, which poses a threat to the capability of high-wage countries to sustain competition.

The question is, then, to know whether these differences in wages are the result of a disequilibrium (or constrained equilibrium) in resource allocation, as a consequence of insufficient international mobility of goods and factors, or rather reflect only international differences in labour productivity, as a consequence of complex social and technical factors depending more on dynamic forces than on a static problem of optimal allocation. The rather poor export performance of developing countries in manufactured products, including labour-intensive ones, was explained, for the least developed, by the very low total productivity, which was insufficiently compensated for by the very low level of wages in international currency. The level of education and qualification is probably the main reason, but transport and communication infrastructures, sanitary conditions and institutional environment are also responsible in some Asian countries, which are not the least developed and lowest-wage countries, may only be the result of their capacity to improve labour productivity in industry, given the wage cost, compatible with profits.

Still it is possible to maintain that it is essentially market imperfections which limited the exploitation of these differences of wage cost, resulting only from differences of relative scarcity. Among these market imperfections which appear to be fading away and thus favouring relocation, it is possible to name tariff and non-tariff barriers protecting industrialized countries; transport costs; information imperfection resulting from insufficient development and the cost of international communication technologies; informational imperfection resulting from the lack of international experience of firms, which are therefore exposed to opportunism in their international transactions; imperfect diffusion of technologies which remain concentrated in developed countries, among other reasons, because of insufficient protection of intellectual property; and institutional constraints which limit relocations, including union pressure on firms of developed countries. It is clear enough that all these barriers are now disappearing very quickly, which leads to a disequilibrium explaining relocations, with a potential risk of the 'hollowing out' of developed countries. To assess the dynamic effects of this process, and therefore the impact of relocation, it is possible to confront the predictions of two paradigms.

The first is based on the traditional analysis of *international equilibrium*. Each country or block of countries has its own endowment of factors, its technology (set of production functions) and preferences to derive demand as functions of prices and income. The various possible equilibria are the result of the set of constraints that characterize the international economy. These constraints are related to the degree of mobility of goods (from free trade, with perfect information and zero costs of transport, to autarchy) but also to the degree of mobility of factors, especially of capital (from complete immobility, with the traditional HOS model, to mobility under Mundell's assumptions). Constraints upon intersectoral mobility within each county may also be considered (specific factor model).

The other paradigm is based on *Schumpeterian hypotheses*. In this framework, profits are directly related to managerial activity and are not dependent upon the concept of physical productivity of capital. Profits arise from a transitory disequilibrium linked to innovations. The new combination is more productive than routine operation and therefore allows for pure profit until competition wipes out all this profit. Just like technological innovation, product innovation or capture of market power, relocation, as long as it is not imitated, allows for pure profit. Effects of relocation must be analysed in the same way as other Schumpeterian innovations.

This process links economic growth, or rather evolution, to use Schumpeter's concept, to a permanent flow of primary innovations, or innovations induced by primary innovations which modify the structure of relative prices and therefore open the way to new combinations that are more profitable. The process of diffusion, including international diffusion, is intricate and may explain not only irregular growth cycles, but also unequal growth among different countries.

These two paradigms have common characteristics. They both rest on hypotheses of profit maximization under various constraints linked to market imperfections. They both explain the phenomenon of relocation and some of their predictions are compatible with observable reality. Yet on the speed of adjustment, on the transition effects and even more on the long-term consequences of worldwide economic integration, they give different explanations. They consequently deserve careful examination especially as to their adequacy with respect to observable reality.

Relocation: Explanations of the International Equilibrium Models

The standard version of the international equilibrium model, the so-called 'factor model', rests on the dual hypothesis of international mobility of goods and international immobility of factors. In fact the set of hypotheses is not rigid and the model allows the use of the comparative statics method to study the effect of a change of hypothesis or of any exogenous variable on the corresponding equilibrium. The model can be used to study the dynamics of comparative advantage by assuming changes in the relevant factor endowments, that is the increase of capital per head. Comparative statics can be used also to study the effects of technical progress on specialization and even the effects of international differences in the diffusion of techniques (see Kojima, 1973, 1975, 1981, 1982). The danger of the model lies in the observational equivalence of various sets of hypotheses which cannot always be empirically tested. It seems several sets of hypotheses could alternatively be applied to the phenomenon of relocation.

Mundell's approach

Relaxing the international immobility of capital hypothesis, the Mundell model (1957) provides an explanation of the relocation phenomenon and predictions of its impact on factor prices – lowering of wages in developed countries as a consequence of a net outflow of capital and increases in wages in the receiving countries – even though the final equilibrium may bring net welfare gains for countries as a whole. The final outcome of this process is factor price equalization inasmuch as the mobility of goods alone did not realize this equalization (as supposed by the HOS theorem with incomplete specialization). Capital is attracted by higher returns in developing countries and capital mobility will reinforce the tendency to factor price equalization. In this model goods movements and capital movements are *substitutes* to reach factor price equalization in the equilibrium situation.

Of course this is pure deductive logic. Its empirical relevance will depend on how the equilibrium mechanism is interpreted. Should Mundell's model be interpreted as an even stronger demonstration of the HOS conclusion of factor price equalization, it would probably have to be rejected as prima facie contrary to facts. Unless reality is persistently out of equilibrium, it is difficult to account for the persistent difference in wage levels. It is still possible to call upon international differences in labour productivity. Equalization does not apply to hourly wages, but allows for international differences in labour productivity. Even though human capital theory may help, it seems there is a danger of tautology since it is difficult to assess empirically these differences of labour productivity as distinct from total productivity.

However, the model may describe transition instead of long-term equilibrium. So why is it that, after several decades of open international trade and capital movements, deregulation equilibrium has not been reached yet? If external shocks such as technical progress repeatedly prevent equilibrium, is it not preferable to concentrate on the analysis of those shocks rather than on the equilibrium position which is never reached? Besides, welfare theorems can only be established for the equilibrium position. During the transition process, many imperfections may arise. Malleability of capital and labour is limited, which may lead to transitory redundancy of labour and scrapping of capital goods. Mundell's model suggests that relocation as an equilibrium situation brings optimal allocation, but the equilibrium hypothesis is not realistic. In a transition process the situation is much more intricate. The model is not appropriate to describe the short-term effects. One may wonder whether the specific factor model is not a more adequate framework for describing transitory effects of relocations.

The specific factor model

This model, which was implicit in Ricardo's analysis of the effect of the abolition of the Corn Laws, does not strictly speaking take into account international capital movements and therefore relocations. Although the model (see Jones, 1971) rests on the hypothesis of sector-specific factors which cannot be transferred to produce different goods, it can easily be adapted to analyse the consequences of relocation.

Relocation will in fact induce a relative price shock comparable to the lowering of tariff barriers. By transferring the technology to a low-wage country, the relocation process gives a comparative advantage to the host country, whereas it was retained before in the investing country. The result is a lowering of the international price, which reduces production in the investing country. In the traditional model, factors previously used in the industry which is being relocated will shift to other sectors whose comparative advantage has been reinforced by the process. But what happens if some of these factors are specific to the declining industry? The collapse of demand for domestic production lowers the marginal productivity of those specific factors which cannot be put to another use. They may even become redundant, especially if their price is rigid and does not go down together with marginal productivity.

Is the specific factor hypothesis realistic? For describing short-term phenomena it is seductive. Capital goods are scarcely malleable and transfer, if possible, is costly. The effects of relocation will depend on the speed and intensity of the process. Swift and intensive relocation (possibly as a consequence of overcompetition) may result in the scrapping of capital goods, whereas progressive relocation allow for amortization of capital and transfer to expanding sectors. The workforce is subject to similar constraints. Qualifications are sector- (or even firm-) specific and transfer is always a lengthy and difficult process. Only high-speed growth can limit these negative effects. Managerial skills themselves are based on experience and may not be easily transferred to other sectors. To summarize, it seems too optimistic to assume easy transfer of factors between sectors when the comparative advantage is shifting rapidly. The specific factor model seems more realistic and may explain, if not justify, demand for protection, restriction of relocation belonging to the wider category of protectionist measures.

To conclude, the standard model would, in the long-run equilibrium, demonstrate welfare gains, but it is hardly realistic. The specific factor model, on the other hand, will link relocation with industrial decline and unemployment. It will also justify the idea that a lowering of wages is the only way to avoid unemployment by delaying the withdrawal of the declining industry. Still this pessimistic vision is not shared by the pioneer work on relocation of K. Kojima.

Kojima's model

In numerous publications between 1973 and 1985 (see Kojima, 1973, 1975, 1981, 1982), a new model has been developed to assess precisely the impact, in terms of welfare, of relocations of declining industries of developed countries to developing countries. This model is empirically based on the experience of Japanese textile firms relocating to Asian countries in the 1960s and early 1970s. It initiated a famous debate between the universities of Reading and Hitotsubashi (Buckley, 1985).

Kojima's model belongs to the same methodological category as the preceding models, yet one of its hypotheses is in sharp contrast to most models derived from the basic Heckscher–Ohlin model. The set of techniques is not a priori identical between developed countries and developing countries. Consequently, developing countries, with abundant relative endowment of labour, may not be able to develop a comparative advantage in labour-intensive industries because this potential comparative advantage is outclassed by competitive advantages of firms of developed countries. Techniques initiated by those firms do not automatically diffuse to less developed countries and thus allow the maintenance of international division of labour contrary to the potential comparative advantage. (F. List's analysis in the 19th century is not fundamentally different). This is obviously a very realistic hypothesis, although very unusual in its analytical framework. It is also akin to the neo-technological approach which relates diffusion of technologies to developing countries to the last phases of the product cycle.

To study the impact of relocations, Kojima suggests the hypothesis of a technology transfer between the declining firms of developed countries and subsidiaries located in developing countries. This process takes place before the phase of compete standardization of the technique and allows the firms which relocate to maintain monopolistic advantages, which gives an incentive to investment. Such relocations occur in labour-intensive industries handicapped by high wage levels in developed countries and under the pressure of competition of low-wage countries, even though these may not possess the most efficient techniques. This process reveals or deepens the comparative advantage of developing countries which become exporters to developed countries. The technology transfer may be analysed as a relaxation of a constraint in the basic equilibrium model allowing for a more efficient allocation of resources.

Relocation is trade-creating and thus participates in the increase of welfare. There is then a *complementarity* between investment flows and merchandise flows, as opposed to Mundell's approach where goods and capital movements are *substitutes* to reach optimal allocation and factor price equalization. Following the logic of the comparative advantage model, Kojima stresses the point that this new comparative advantage for developing countries goes along with reinforced comparative advantages in capital- (or technology?) intensive goods in developed countries. The rise in exports of developing countries is matched by a rise in exports from developed countries. This given an optimistic vision of harmony. There is no conflict of interest between developed and developing countries and relocations, if accompanied by free trade, are unambiguously beneficial.

This theory has been under heavy attack, first because it could not explain, as it claimed, Japanese firms' behaviour at a time when they precisely turn their back on Asian countries to invest predominantly in North America and Europe. Maybe Kojima was right, but his theory came too early. The current surge of direct investments in Asia, especially from Japan, attenuates this firm criticism. Another criticism levelled against Kojima's model is based on the weakness of its normative conclusions. Trade creation may not be a sufficient criterion to demonstrate positive gains for all countries and does not invalidate the analysis of demand for protection derived from the specific factor model.

Kojima's optimistic approach may be explained by the period and environment in which his theory was developed. In the mid-1970s, Japan was still engaged in the acquisition of new comparative advantages in high-technology industries. An acceleration of its withdrawal from declining industries (textile, heavy and chemical industries) was favourable to the rise of its most advanced industries. Japan was in full employment and growth was still relatively rapid, even though it decelerated after the late 1960s. The decline of some sectors is part of a plan to develop new ones and none of the negative effects of relocations experienced in low-growth developed countries occurred. It is quite different today in most developed countries. With high unemployment, it is more difficult to advocate that the redundant workforce can contribute to the rise of advanced industries. On the contrary, unemployment compensation and related social expenses handicap the profitability of all firms, including the most competitive.

On the whole, Kojima's model fails to provide unequivocal conclusions that would contradict the pessimistic vision of the specific factor model. It is a paradox that the international equilibrium models which are the core of free trade principles fail to provide irrefutable arguments to use against those who see in relocations a major threat of social and economic regression. What could be the conclusions of a quite different approach which never insisted on static optimal allocation of resources, but rather on dynamic analysis and conditions of economic growth?

Relocation: A Neo-Schumpeterian Approach

The influence of Schumpeterian analysis (1934) in international economics is very important. It contributed to the rehabilitation of the Ricardian model which was considered for some time to be outclassed by the factor approach. If technical progress, which is the consequence of innovations, is repeatedly shifting production functions, what could be the contribution of an analytical framework which explains choice of techniques and specialization by a static process of optimal allocation of resources? It is probably better to concentrate on the mechanism of innovation and diffusion of innovations to draw conclusions on international specialization by simply applying the Ricardian comparative advantage concept, in a dynamic framework.

This is probably what most so-called 'neo-technological' approaches did. Product cycle theories described, long ago, the process of relocation of mature standardized industries. They still retain a narrow vision in which hierarchy between countries is established once and for all, relocation being then a natural and minor phenomenon. This approach did not consider relocation as carrying a threat of 'hollowing out' for advanced countries. Yet Akamatsu (1961) showed how a lagging country could gradually catch up and become a leader in technology, but then it was joining the club of advanced countries without necessarily bringing industrial decline in rival countries. Going back to Schumpeter broadens this narrow vision of the product cycle theory.

Schumpeter's model
Schumpeter's theory assumes rational behaviour of entrepreneurs. Economic evolution is the result of a permanent quest for *new* combinations likely to increase profits. Without innovations the economy would very rapidly stabilize in a circular flow (stationary state). Economic growth is not essentially

the result of an Austrian process of capital accumulation hindered by insufficient savings. This does not mean that Schumpeter denies the importance of investment in growth, but he thinks that, without technical progress and innovations, all opportunities for new investments would be exploited very quickly and marginal efficiency of capital would become zero (this point of view was shared by Keynes). With swift technical progress, capital may become scarce if that technical progress is biased towards more capital-intensive techniques, but on the contrary technical progress may contribute to free capital. Capital itself is not a stock that would accumulate monotonously with savings. Credit can mobilize resources for investment, through a 'forced saving' process, although it may be complemented by voluntary savings. But on the other hand new investments destroy existing capital, which becomes obsolete. At a given time capital may be more or less scarce, which will be reflected by the real interest rate, but the notion of a stock of capital is irrelevant inasmuch as it varies permanently with the shocks of innovations.

Relocation is a Schumpeterian innovation
Innovations are of various kinds and do not limit themselves to technical progress. Schumpeter explicitly named 'the conquest of a new source of supply of raw materials or *half-manufactured goods*' (Schumpeter, 1934, p. 66). It is an innovation inasmuch as this new source lowers the cost and allows for a transitory profit. Relocation is a perfect example of this definition. It is a genuine Schumpeterian innovation, it is the result of competition and can only be stopped by interfering with the market mechanism. Like all innovations, it allows only for a temporary profit. It will rapidly be imitated by other relocations and domestic firms in developing countries and the increase in supply lowers the price to the new lower cost of production, wiping out all profit. Consequently, firms that do not relocate lose competitiveness and their specific capital and workforce become redundant.

On the other hand, employment rises in developing countries. The Schumpeterian approach, contrary to the factor model, does not rest on a full employment hypothesis. It fits into the hypothesis of an unlimited supply of labour in developing countries with a classical wage determination mechanism. It is also compatible with wage determination by supply and demand or with a Keynesian regime characterized by a downward rigidity of nominal wages. All this is sufficient for the Schumpeterian model to give the most realistic explanation of the relocation mechanism.

What is the impact of relocation which can be drawn from this model? Being innovations, relocations have impacts which are not fundamentally different from the impact of technical progress or any other kind of Schumpeterian innovation. Technical progress can destroy employment, whether it originates within or outside the national territory. Attempts to control relocations raise essentially the same problems as do attempts to master technical progress.

The debate on the level of wages

The Schumpeterian model also gives answers to the central question of the relocation debate. Would downward pressure on wages limit the negative effects of relocations? If the lowering of wages is limited to the industrial sector concerned by relocations and if it is important enough to compensate the lowering of the competitive price resulting from the rise of production in low-wage countries, it may obviously save employment. But how great should this lowering be? It is likely that it will contradict the market mechanism which would not allow a significant lowering of relative wages for only a section of wage earners. What about a general lowering of labour cost?

One may argue that, prima facie, this will bring effects similar to those obtained automatically by the balance of payments mechanism. Should the trade deficit increase between developed and developing countries out of a loss of competitivity of developed countries, the exchange rate of developing countries with a trade surplus will face an upward pressure, unless capital movements contradict this mechanical effect. It was not necessary to lower wages to sustain the increase of competitive strength of Japan. In 23 years the exchange rate of the yen against the dollar has been multiplied by 3.5. It is very likely that the exchange rates of Asian countries engaged in a process of accelerated growth and technological catch-up will follow a similar trend in the long run. When the catch-up is completed, the shift in exchange rates has fulfilled the so-called 'factor price equalization'. This is not the result of factor reallocation but rather of technological catch-up which equalized labour productivity. But what happens if the exchange rate of a small developed country has downward rigidity and is overvalued? Could wage deflation compensate for a loss of competitiveness? Schumpeter has no answer to this question, but Keynes would probably argue that profits are positively related to effective demand and Kaldor would add that they depend on the rate of growth of the economy. If the economy is in a Keynesian unemployment regime, it is not obvious that wage deflation is the appropriate answer to relocations.

CONCLUSION

The Schumpeterian approach gives general guidelines on the relocations problem. The rate of growth of economies depends in the end on their capacity to generate permanent flows of innovations. Three categories of innovations have to be distinguished: (1) *primary innovations*, flowing essentially out of R&D, of scientific policy and social factors favouring progress; (2) *induced innovations*, resulting from an adaptation of technical choice to changes in relative prices (they suppose an efficient market mechanism); and (3) *catch-up innovations*, which compromise diffusion, through imitation of primary innovations, especially at the international level.

Catch-up innovations are probably the easiest to undertake, while they are not the least efficient in terms of rate of growth of the economy. Industrial policy has some efficiency in promoting such innovations, as demonstrated by most Asian countries. They are an advantage to 'latecomers'. Induced innovations and, even more, primary innovations are not so easy to capture. They depend more on the efficiency of the market mechanism and on the supply of such public goods as education and research. They may also be influenced by the business climate, which can stimulate or inhibit investments which generate economies of scale and external effects.

The true justification for a free trade approach to the relocation problem does not lie in the static theorems of welfare economics, but is to be found in the risks of a slowdown of innovations associated with a policy of defence of declining industries. Relocations are part of the process of creative destruction stimulated by competition and which is the true engine of growth of developed economies.

BIBLIOGRAPHY

Akamatsu, J. (1961), 'A theory of unbalanced growth in the world economy', *Weltwirtschaftliches Archiv*, 2.

Arthuis, J. (rapporteur) (1993), *Délocalisations hors du territoire national des activités industrielles et de services*, Paris: Rapport du Sénat, No. 337.

Banque de France (1995), *Balance des paiements*, annual report.

Buckley, P.J. (1985), 'The economic analysis of the multinational enterprise: Reading versus Japan?', *Hitotsubashi Journal of Economics*, December.

Caves, R. (1960), *Trade and Economic Structures*, Cambridge, Mass.: Harvard University Press.

Chavanes, G. (rapporteur) (1993), *Délocalisations économiques à l'étranger*, Commission d'enquête présidée par F. Borotra, rapport No. 781, Assemblée Nationale.

Combes, E. (1992), 'Alliance en R&D et course technologique', working paper, CESSEFI-Paris I, AFSE congress, September.

Commission Européenne (1993), *Panorama de l'industrie communautaire*, Brussels.

DREE (1994), *Résultats*, 4 pages, February, Bercy.

Detape, Y. et M. Quélennec (1993), *Les implantations industrielles françaises à l'étranger: Réalités et enjeux*, 4 pages, Paris: SESSI.

GATT (1995), *International Trade*, Geneva.

Hawkins, R.G. (1972) 'Job Displacement and the Multinational Firm: A Methodological Review', Occasional Paper No. 3, Washington: Center for Multinational Studies.

Hufbauer, G. and J. Schott (1992), *North American Free Trade, Issues and Recommendations*, Washington, D.C.: Institute for International Economics.

Jacquemin, A. (1989), 'International and Multinational Strategic Behaviour', *Kyklos*, 4.

Jones, R. (1971), 'A three factors model in theory, trade and history', in J. Bhagwati *et al.* (eds), *Trade, Balance of Payments and Growth*, Amsterdam: North-Holland.

Jungnickel, R. (1994), 'Globalization and the International Division of Labour, the Role of Technology and Wage Costs', working paper.

Kojima, K. (1973), 'A macroeconomic approach to foreign direct investment', *Hitotsubashi Journal of Economics*, June.

Kojima, K. (1975), 'International trade and foreign investment: substitutes or complements', *Hitotsubashi Journal of Economics*, June.

Kojima, K. (1981), 'A new capitalism for a new international economic order', *Hitotsubashi Journal of Economics*, June.

Kojima, K. (1982), 'Macroeconomic versus international business approach to direct foreign investment', *Hitotsubashi Journal of Economics*, June.

MITI (various years), *International Trade White Paper*, Tokyo.

Mouhoud, E.M. (1993), 'Changement technique, avantages comparatifs et délocalisation/relocalisation des activitiés industrielles', *Revue d'Economie Politique*, September–October.

Mucchielli, J.-L. (1991), 'Strategic advantages for European firms', in B. Burgenmeier and J.-L. Mucchielli (eds) *Multinationals and Europe 1992, Strategies for the Future*, London, New York: Routledge.

Mucchielli, J.-L. (1993–4), 'Pourquoi les délocalisations sont-elles inévitables?', *L'Expansion*, December–January.

Mundell, R.A. (1957), 'International trade and factor mobility', *American Economic Review*, June.

Mytelka and Delapierre (1988), 'The Alliance Strategies of European Firms in the Information Technology Industry and the Role of Esprit', in J.H. Dunning and P. Robson (eds), *Multinationals and the European Community*, Oxford: Basil Blackwell.

OECD (1993), *Annuaire des statistiques d'investissement direct international*.

Ozawa, T. (1974), *Japan's Technological Challenge to the West, 1950–1974, Motivation and Accomplishment*, Cambridge, Mass.: MIT Press.

Ruttenberg, S. (1971), *Needed! A Constructive Foreign Trade Policy*, Washington, D.C.: AFL-CIO.

Sazanami, Y. (1989), 'Trade and Investment Patterns and Barriers in the United States, Canada and Japan', in R.M. Stern (ed.), *Trade and Investment Relations among the United States, Canada and Japan*, Chicago: University of Chicago Press.

Schumpeter, J. (1934), *The Theory of Economic Development*, Oxford: Oxford University Press.

Shinohara, M. (1979), 'The boomerang effect reconsidered', *Contemporary South-East Asia*, Vol. 1, No. 1.

Stobaugh and associates (1976), *Nine Investments Abroad and their Impact at Home*, Cambridge, Mass.: Harvard University Press.

United States Department of Commerce (1972), *The Multinational Corporation, Studies on US Foreign Investment, 1*, Washington: US Government Printing Office.

United States Tarriff Commission (1973), *Implications of Multinationals for World Trade and Investment and for US Trade and Labor*, Report to the Committee of Finance of the US Senate and its Sub-Committee on International Trade, 93dr Congress, 1st Session, Washington: US Government Printing Office.

UNO (1993), *World Investment Report, Investment, Trade and International Policy Arrangements*, New York.

3. Multinational firm strategies and the impact of their location decisions

Peter J. Buckley

INTRODUCTION

This chapter seeks to examine the strategies of multinational firms and the impact of their location strategies on host countries. It begins by examining the market servicing strategies of multinational firms – broadly the choice which such firms make between exporting, licensing and foreign direct investment. Subsequent sections look directly at the impact of foreign direct investment on host countries and examine the role of government intervention in the investment process and the potential for host governments to use more leverage in this decision making process. A brief conclusion closes the chapter.

FOREIGN MARKET SERVICING STRATEGY: AN OVERVIEW

The foreign market servicing strategy of a firm is the set of decisions on which production plants should be linked to which specific foreign market and the methods or channels through which this should be achieved. The three main generic types of foreign market servicing strategy are exporting, licensed sales abroad and foreign direct investment. The foreign market servicing decision is a complex one both theoretically (Buckley and Casson, 1985) and in practice (Buckley and Pearce, 1979, 1981, 1984).

Elements of a Foreign Market Servicing Strategy

Exporting (X), licensing and other contractual relationships (L) and foreign direct investment (I) all cover a spectrum of types of arrangement in which the channels of distribution and relationship with the buyer vary within the type. Exporting covers the indirect export of goods – through agents,

distributors, merchant houses, trading companies and a variety of other intermediaries – and the direct export of goods and services. Its essential feature is
that production activities are carried out in the home country, although marketing may well be carried out in the host country, separated by a transport
cost barrier.

Exporting is often regarded as merely the first step into a foreign market,
but its persistence as a viable strategy mode even in the largest multinationals
suggests that it still has a role to play. The sequentialist school has made
much of the observed pattern of servicing a foreign market over time which
goes $X \to L \to I$ or $X \to I$. Indeed, exporting itself has been analysed as a
sequential process (for a review of this literature, see Buckley and Ghauri,
1993). Its role in internationalization is well documented but exporting's role
in the market servicing pattern of established multinationals is less well
understood. To be adequately modelled, the relationship between exporting
and other forms of market servicing must be carefully specified, as must the
factors influencing multi-plant operation (Scherer *et al.*, 1975). New thinking
and modelling on strategic trade policy and the new international economics
should reintegrate exporting into realistic models of the multinational firm
(see Krugman, 1986; Dunning and Buckley, 1977).

Licensing is a generic term which covers a variety of non-direct investment
production operations involving arms'-length cooperation with an external
agency (or agencies). Some element of market transfer is included in this
packaged sale of asset services. A spectrum of relationships is possible,
ranging from (the rare) simple sale of embodied knowledge or assets (brand
name, patent) to franchising, turnkey operations, contract manufacturing,
management contracts and so on. A typology of these forms of international
operation is provided in Buckley and Casson (1985) where they are classified
in five dimensions: (1) equity or non equity ventures, (2) time limited or
unlimited, (3) space limited or unlimited, (4) extent of transfer of resources
and rights, and (5) internal or external mode of transfer. (See also Young *et
al.*, 1989, for a survey and Luostarinen, 1979, for an alternative approach.)

Licensing as a mode of market servicing is often regarded as a transitory
mode, perhaps utilized for learning or market testing purposes before a move
is made to a foreign direct investment. A minority of firms are regarded as
specialist licensors and licensing is often seen as a peripheral activity contingent upon (peculiar) extraneous eventualities, such as government restrictions, as a second best choice. It is conceivable that changing world competitive structures make this view outmoded. The 'new forms' of international
operation may be uniquely well suited to the competitive conditions which
prevail in many world markets, including political uncertainty, government
restrictions, idiosyncratic markets and residual technologies. Moreover,
licensing allows international companies to avoid head-to-head competition

by cross-licensing, joint marketing and production agreements and knowledge pooling. These cooperative devices may be genuine or may be methods of reducing competition by collusive behaviour (Buckley and Casson, 1988).

Foreign direct investment, too, covers a range of operations. The normal image of a foreign direct investment is a production facility involving a huge capital outlay. This is not necessarily so. A foreign direct investment can be the creation of a sales subsidiary – one person with stock working from his basement with a car! The key feature of FDI is not scale but control from the parent. This control, exercised most usually through equity ownership, enables direct management of a foreign facility rather than control through a contract. These issues are widely debated in the internalization literature (Buckley and Casson, 1976, 1985; Dunning, 1981; Hennart, 1986, among many others).

Direct investment thus covers marketing operations and production operations: both sales subsidiaries and production subsidiaries ranging from assembly to full production. Moreover, there are other important distinctions: in mode of entry between a greenfield venture and a take-over and in organization form between a joint venture and a wholly owned subsidiary. Direct investment is regarded as the most risky form of entry in terms of capital committed, but is regarded as the most effective in securing market share and strategic competitive advantage. This is confirmed, for instance, in two recent articles on entry into the Japanese Market (Buckley *et al.*, 1987a, 1987b). It also confers prestige as an internationalized company and is seen as the key weapon in a global strategy, as for instance in the 'triad' concept (Ohmae, 1985; Buckley *et al.*, 1987a). It is however, far too easy and incorrect to assume that direct investment is always the correct form of market servicing. External conditions and internal capabilities often suggest otherwise.

Although, theoretically, the same generic options are open to service firms, certain features of services affect foreign market servicing choice and deserve comment. Boddewyn *et al.* (1986) classify types of international services according to their tradeability, based on the extent to which services are embodied in physical goods and the degree of inseparability (that is, the extent to which the provider of the service and the customer need to be present at the point of delivery) in provision of the service:

1. service commodities, which are distinct from their production process, are tradeable across national boundaries and thus exportable;
2. where production cannot be separated from consumption, as in the case of legal advice, a foreign presence is necessary;
3. where services comprise a mix of distinct commodities and location-bound service elements, some location substitution is possible.

Consequently, a different pattern of foreign market servicing options may be expected in this sector. Hirsch (1976), addressing the implications of the inseparability of production and consumption, notes how the 'simultaneity factor' (that is, the fact that certain services are produced and consumed at the same time) serves to retard export trade. The costs associated with satisfying the need for interaction between producer and buyer are compounded by the high price of international travel and communications, and thus the exporting firm is at a cost disadvantage *vis-à-vis* its foreign competitors. When the cost of cultural distance, language, nationalistic and legal barriers are added, the cost disadvantages are further heightened. Edvinsson (1981) notes that foreign service providers, lacking any legitimacy and identity in the foreign market, require some kind of 'platform' and local support environment to operate successfully. Although this is also true for goods manufacturers operating abroad, the intangibility of many services (that is, the fact that there is no physical good which can be judged by the consumer) means that uncertainty about performance is higher and thus greater demands are placed on service firms to win the confidence of the consumer through strong referent promotion and a good local image.

Alternatively, the loss of control over operations which is characteristic of licensing poses problems of quality control. Again, this is true in goods manufacturing, but as many services are produced by people, 'heterogeneity' (variation in the way the service is produced and quality of the service provided) compounds the difficulty of controlling the quality of the delivered service when handled externally. Both arguments therefore suggest that foreign involvement by service firms will show a higher degree of foreign investment options than is the case in the manufacturing sector.

Cross-section Analysis of Foreign Market Servicing

The total foreign sales (TFS) of firms are made up of exports, sales abroad licensed by home country firms (L) and sales arising from FDI. That is,

$$\text{TFS} = X + L + I$$

The amounts of each of these can be measured at a point of time, over time and in particular markets, as we will see below.

At its most simple, X can be differentiated from the other two methods by the location effect, as with exports the bulk of value-adding activity takes place in the home country, whilst the other two methods transfer much of value-adding activity to the host country. Similarly, L can be differentiated from X and I by the externalization effect. L represents a market sale of intermediate goods or corporate assets by the firm. In licensing the firm sells rights and the use of assets to a licensee. In X and I, such activities are internalized (Buckley and Casson, 1976, 1985). This has important implications. Broadly, then, the internalization and location effects separate the three generic forms of market servicing:

$$\text{TFS} = \overset{\displaystyle\text{Internalization}\atop\displaystyle\text{effect}}{\overset{\displaystyle\frown}{X}} + L + \underset{\displaystyle\smile\atop{\displaystyle\text{Location}\atop\displaystyle\text{effect}}}{I}$$

These simple differentiations are in practice highly complex. First, comparative costs are not easily calculable or obvious. In multi product, process and functional firms, the internal division of labour and the costs associated with each activity are difficult to assess accurately. Further, there are many complex interactions between the activities involved. Location abroad of some activities will have 'knock-on' effects on home costs and those of third countries within the firm's international network. Second, the costs and benefits of internalization are nebulous and difficult to measure. Both sets of complications are entirely contingent on circumstances. The difficulties (and intellectual excitement) of these calculations are that the situation is dynamic and the determinants of choice of optimal market servicing strategies are continually shifting.

Cross-section analyses of market servicing are snapshot pictures at a particular moment in time of a continually changing process. The make-up of total foreign sales into X, L, I at the macro level can give us a crude picture (Buckley and Davies, 1981) but this pattern is continually changing as the nature of international competition alters. Further, it is difficult to get meaningful comparative measures of the three modes, although this is usually done by estimating final foreign sales in aggregate (Buckley and Davies, 1981; Luostarinen, 1979).

A major complicating factor in the analysis of foreign market servicing policies is that the forms are often complements, not substitutes. This fact means that a careful analysis of the relationship between modes is essential. For instance, Hood and Young (1979) point to the existence of 'anticipatory exports' (goods exported from the source country in anticipation of building the foreign plant), 'associated exports' (complementary products exported by the parent after establishment of the subsidiary) and 'balancing exports' which result when the first plant built abroad is operating at capacity. Also FDI has a dynamic effect in maintaining the worldwide competitive position of the investing firm (Hood and Young, 1979, pp. 313–15).

This suggests that a dynamic analysis is essential. Assumptions in modelling which do not allow for changes in demand conditions – for instance the existence of a 'presence effect' which results in an increased demand after the establishment of an investment presence (Buckley *et al.*, 1988) – are clearly inappropriate. Similarly, models which ignore the competitive process, in particular the role of 'defensive investment', established to protect a market share, are unlikely to capture the nuances of strategy. Models must be organic rather than static and capable of specifying the relationship between exports, licensing and FDI.

Time Series Analyses of Foreign Market Servicing Strategies

A number of theoretical models of the foreign market servicing strategy of firms are extant. They are almost entirely concerned with the switch from exporting to a foreign market to investing in it. Licensing is a largely neglected phenomenon in modelling (but see Davies, 1977; Buckley and Davies, 1981).

The timing of the switch to FDI

Analyses which are concerned with the dynamics of foreign expansion of the firm should be able to specify those factors which govern the timing of the initial FDI. Aliber (1970) attempts to do this by reference to the capitalization of returns from the firm's alternatives: exporting, licensing and foreign investment. Aliber assumes that the firm possesses a 'patent' or monopolistic advantage. He argues that the costs of doing business abroad prevent investment from being the preferred strategy until a certain market size is attained. Only at a particular size of market will the higher capitalization ratio which applies to source country firms overcome the cost advantage of a local producer (which can be exploited via licensing the 'patent' to a local firm). In Aliber's system, the source country firm will always be a higher cost producer than the host country firm, provided the latter has access to the patent at competitive rates. This limits the analysis by ruling out those situations where the source country firm (through familiarity with the technology, firm-wide economies of scale, and so on) has compensating advantages *vis-à-vis* host country competitors.

The dynamics of the 'switch' from exporting to licensing and then to FDI are thus dependent, according to Aliber, on the host country market size and the differentials in capitalization ratios between assets denominated in different currencies. The latter are determined by the currency premium in the capital market that the compensation investors require so that they will bear uncertainty concerning fluctuations in exchange rates. Tariffs are easily incorporated into this framework: an increase in the host country tariff will bias the foreign patent owner towards use of the patent in the host country; the choice between its use in licensing or internally via FDI remains unchanged, the choice depending on whether host market size allows the capitalization factor to outweigh the cost of doing business abroad.

In a theoretical paper, Buckley and Casson (1985) provide a model which specifies the optimal timing of a 'switch' to direct investment by reference to the costs of servicing the foreign market, demand conditions in that market and host market growth. The market servicing decision is more complex than it appears at first sight, particularly when the initial costs of setting up a foreign investment are time-dependent. A simple model of a firm facing a growing market is illustrated in Figure 3.1. This model specifies two kinds of costs, fixed and variable, and two forms of foreign market servicing: exporting which has low fixed but high variable cost, and FDI which has high fixed but low variable cost; licensing is an intermediate state, which in this example is never the preferred option. Should foreign market size become greater than q, then the firm will switch its mode of market servicing to investment in the market. Removal of tariffs may therefore lead to a switch, not to exports (or to exports only as an intermediate stage), but directly to foreign investment by the multinational firm.

This model enables specification of the optimal timing of a switch in modes by reference to the key variables: (1) mode-related costs, (2) demand

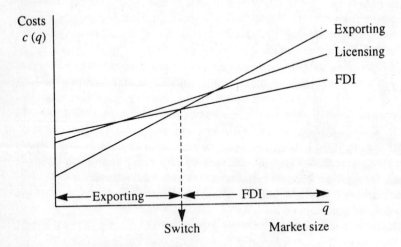

Note: In this example, licensing is never the preferred alternative.

Source: Reproduced from Buckley and Casson (1981, p. 80).

Figure 3.1   The timing of a foreign direct investment

conditions in the host market and (3) target market growth. The introduction of time-dependent set-up costs, in particular, makes the decisions very complex. A similar model has been developed by Giddy and Rugman (1979).

Enderwick (1989) suggests that incremental internationalization is not possible in many service sectors as a result of the inseparability factor. This restricts the scope of firms to learn about the market by following low-investment exporting strategies and utilizing foreign market intermediaries. Although he introduces this issue to demonstrate the greater risks involved for internationalizing service firms than for those in the manufacturing sector, it has important implications for the dynamics of foreign market servicing in the service sector.

For services embodied in tradeable goods, internationalization may follow a similar pattern to that of the manufacturing industry unless firm-specific advantages are best exploited through internal hierarchies or where there are government restrictions on trade. Where production cannot be separated from consumption, however, and FDI and licensing are the only available options, the increased resource commitment involved in adopting these modes may slow down the process of internationalization. As greater returns are required from domestic operations before resource commitment overseas can be considered, and the market from which returns can be made is restricted (exporting is not a viable proposition), the natural progression to foreign direct investment is not so clear-cut. Also retarding the process of internationalization is the fact that many services are highly localized and industries fragmented and thus nationalization of innovative services is the focus of strategic growth, not internationalization. A further restricting factor is the lack of learning opportunities, highlighted in the behavioural models of internationalization, offered by indirect exporting modes of foreign market servicing. As knowledge cannot be acquired cost effectively and at little risk through exporting, the uncertainties involved in licensing or investing resources abroad may deter the consideration of international expansion.

This is not to suggest, however, that all manufacturing firms religiously follow such a process of incremental expansion. In Buckley *et al.*, (1992, Chap. 5) it is noted that an unexpectedly high proportion of British manufacturing firms in the survey moved from little to no market involvement directly to FDI. Although this may be partly explained by their experience of other foreign markets, the nature of the product (being bulky and too expensive to transport) and the need to gain a local identity demonstrate commitment to the market-precluded consideration of export strategies. These factors are not dissimilar to those determining FDI options in the service sector, that is, the nature of the service dictates production in close proximity to customers, and the need to generate a strong image and goodwill determines foreign investment. Thus, whilst it is useful to identify features of many service industries which dictate particular modes of market servicing, the differences between manufacturing and service sectors should not be overstated. It is rather the greater number of instances where factors specific to the nature of services dictate FDI or some form of market presence which characterize the service sector, rather than the fact that services, per se, are implicitly 'different'.

Returning to the issue of acquiring knowledge through incremental international expansion, although exporting is ruled out where the inseparability factor applies, firms may follow a course of learning through contractual arrangements and joint venture options. Thus Buckley and Casson's (1981) assertion that licensing should have a place in the internationalization model appears particularly pertinent. However, whereas their model is based on volume-related fixed and variable costs, for service firms it may be more appropriate to consider the different costings of internal and external markets. The cost of lost sales arising from leakage of competitive advantage in the case of licensing may make equity investment through a joint venture a more risk-averse method of gaining market knowledge. Owing to increased control which a joint venture affords, the risk of leaked advantages is lessened. When the added advantages of pooled resources and the long-term possibility of increasing the equity stake to achieve majority ownership are considered, joint ventures may appear a more favourable option. The international behaviour of location-bound service firms may, therefore, follow a path from low-risk contractual arrangements or joint ventures designed to gather market information and important learning experiences as a precursor to majority-owned or wholly owned FDI activities.

Synthesis

Figure 3.2 is an attempt to encompass the key elements of the market servicing decision. The key functions are shown: production, which may be a multi-stage process, stockholding, distribution control, promotion, generating customers, transport and retailing. The flow of physical product runs through the production stages, distribution control and (possibly) retailing to the customer. These functions are linked therefore by flows of physical product but equally crucial are the flows of information between the functions which also tie in promotion and the generation of customers. These flows are difficult to ensure and secure in an externalized environment. Worries about secrecy, creating competitors and misinformation argue for internalization. However, the local knowledge of agents (and their contacts) performing the role of generating customers and of external promotional agencies may counterbalance these arguments. Moreover, agents and promoters may have specialized skills unavailable to (foreign) entrants. Consequently, the internal/external decision must be taken on a case-by-case basis. It is, however, crucial to recognize the interdependence between the various functions shown in Figure 3.2. It is also the case that imperfect competition (monopoly, monopsony and bilateral monopoly) at one stage of production induces price distortions in this multi-stage process and creates an incentive for backward or forward integration (Buckley and Casson, 1976; 1985).

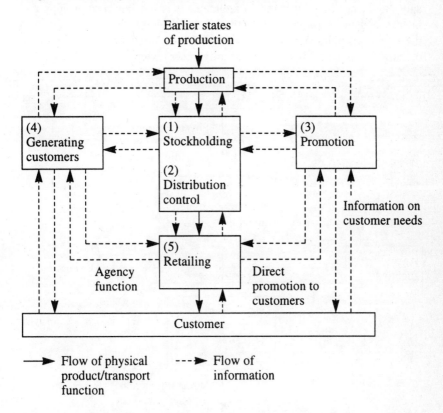

Figure 3.2   Linkages between the activities of the firm

In the service sector, given the greater propensity for firms to interact directly with their customers, there is likely to be less distortion in the flow of information except in cases where external agents mediate between the firm and its customers. In many instances, the physical flow is restricted to paperwork and contracts, and the lack of 'physical product' means that stockholding is absent from the picture. The establishment of business systems is consequently more concerned with providing for supplier–customer interaction than with the movement of the product through the channel. Equally, distribution control is likely to be dominated more by database marketing practices (monitoring the customer base and extending the consumer franchise) than traditional logistics management tasks. (These differences are highlighted in Figure 3.3.) Consequently, any analysis of the foreign market servicing decision must consider all the activities listed and the key elements determining their location and internal versus external performance. The activities cannot and should not be considered in isolation. It is the interrelationships and interdependencies between the activities which make the market servicing decision so complex. Because of the many factors affecting the configuration of activities, policies should be constantly under review.

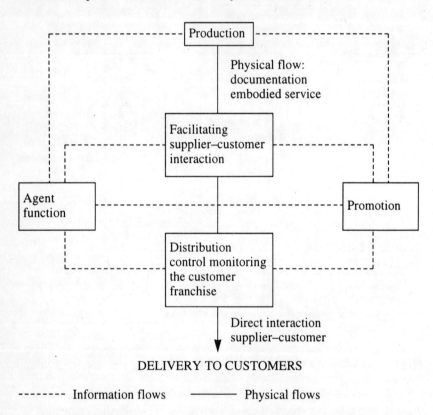

Figure 3.3   A schematic diagram of the interrelationships between functions:services

Flows of information
The flows of information in Figure 3.3 are vital sources of competitive advantage. For instance, the flow of information from the retail/customer interface can be the source of data on consumer tastes, preferences and selection

between closely competing products. The retailer in the manufacturing channel, then, may act as a facilitator or bottleneck for the flow of such information. His willingness to gather and forward relevant data depends, in part, upon the importance of the manufacturer's brand within the product range he offers and the contribution it makes to turnover. The flow back of information from the interface with the customer to distribution control, stockholding and eventually production is a fundamental input into a marketing information system.

In the service sector the more direct interaction between suppliers and customers makes the gathering of market information an easier task. Because of the systems imposed upon them by the nature of the service being provided, service firms, in one form or another (whether through personnel visiting the customer, face-to-face interaction, telecommunication or post) interface directly with their customers. Thus adaptation to individual needs and tailoring promotional efforts are facilitated by more direct information flows. The exception is where firms utilize the services of external agents. Here, as with wholesalers in the manufacturing sector, firms must work to develop good relations with their agents in order to encourage their passing relevant information back to the firm.

Nevertheless, owing to the multirepresentation factor alluded to earlier, the dispersed nature of business activities demands well-developed communication networks in order to maximize the benefits accruing from direct interaction with the market. Furthermore, regional variations in consumer tastes and buying behaviour may make it difficult for firms to standardize their response to market information and autonomy of subsidiaries may prove desirable, the head office merely reinforcing the general direction of the company and its culture.

Summary

The view expressed in this section is that the categorization of foreign market servicing strategies into exporting, licensing and foreign investment is too crude a division because it ignores the crucial role of channel management. Marketing costs cannot simply be aggregated as a lump: costs of distribution, stockholding, transport, promotion, retailing and generating new customers are radically different. The location and internalize/externalize (do or buy) decisions are as crucial for each of these functions as they are for production. An integrated treatment recognizing the interdependencies and cost implications of each function is essential for a complete conceptualization of the foreign market servicing decision. This necessitates an analysis of the crucial role of information flows between and among channel members, be they internal or external, foreign or domestic, and possibilities of information blockage in the channel.

THE IMPACT OF FOREIGN DIRECT INVESTMENT ON HOST COUNTRIES

The Independent Impact of Foreignness or Multinationality

Despite long-standing attention to the question 'what difference does it make if a firm is foreign-owned?', definitive answers are rare. Part of the question depends on the standpoint: difference to the host or source economy, to competing firms, to labour, to the world economy. But all too often all the effects of foreign investment are attributed to foreignness. A related issue is whether it is the fact of foreign ownership or an extra independent effect of multinationality per se.

Take as an example the impact of the entry of an export oriented FDI on the host labour market. The impact of such a plant on the regional labour market is shown in Figure 3.4. The increase in demand for labour bids up wages (to the extent that wage flexibility is present) and increases employment from E to E^*. However, this effect would occur wherever the investment came from. Is there an additional effect arising from multinationality? Is there an effect arising from individual country of ownership (for example, is a Japanese inward investment going to stimulate employment more than one from the United States)?

It is possible that additional effects do exist. Effects arising from vertical integration may mean increased demand for the output arising from economies

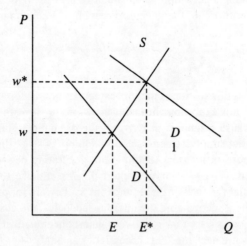

Note: Employment increases from E to E^*; wages increase from w to w^*

Figure 3.4   The labour market effect of an inward foreign direct investment

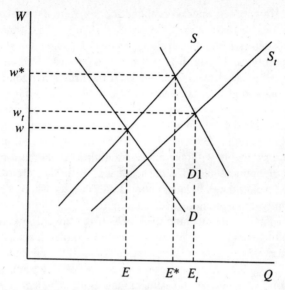

(a) Skilled labour with training: *t*

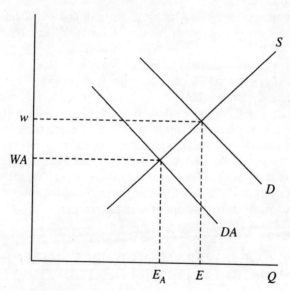

(b) Unskilled labour

Figure 3.5 Foreign direct investment with two classes of labour: skilled labour-intensive investments

of scale. However, it may be possible to substitute external sources of the output from subcontractors if the price so dictates. The conclusion on this effect thus depends on additional hypotheses on technological specificity and substitutability. Moreover, it is still necessary to ask if additional effects in these areas may arise from foreignness. If the firm is horizontally integrated, that is 'competing' internal plants exist elsewhere, how far is it possible to switch production between plants? How high are the cost penalties for such behaviour? This discussion leads into theoretical and empirical questions on multi-plant operation (Scherer *et al.*, 1975). But, again, is it more likely that production switching will take place in a multinational multi-plant operation than in a uninational one? The consequences of the two are of course different at the level of the individual nation-state (the 'for whom' question).

A slightly more complicated version of the model might assume two classes of labour – skilled and unskilled. If the inward investment causes a switch in the techniques of production towards skilled labour then a situation as in Figure 3.5 might arise. In the initial phase of the investment, increase in demand for skilled labour will cause wages to rise to w^* and employment to increase to E^*. The inward investment may result in an increase in training of skilled labour with a further consequent rise in skilled employed to E_t (new training augmented supply curve S_t) and a new equilibrium skilled labour wage rate of w_t. There *may* be a fall in unskilled employment after the investment if the skilled labour substitutes for unskilled labour (Figure 3.5 (b)).

Vertical and horizontal links within the company will be vital in attempting to predict if any special effects arise from foreign ownership. Within integrated regional markets (NAFTA, EU), relative wage rates may determine which location will expand when two similar plants are involved. However, the likely effect of regional integration is that multinationals will reduce horizontal integration (competing plants) and increase vertical integration. Thus subregions could well become specialized in component supply to central 'assembly plants' (Buckley and Artisien, 1986, 1987a, 1987b).

This analysis has wide implications for the potential role of government intervention in the direct investment decision process.

THE ROLE OF GOVERNMENT POLICY INTERVENTION IN MULTINATIONAL FIRMS' LOCATION STRATEGIES

It is important for government policy makers to recognize the strategic decision-making process of multinational firms if they are to be effective in attracting inward investment. Table 3.1 is an attempt to crystallize a large body of theory into a narrow straitjacket. There is a large body of literature

Table 3.1   The process of investment decision making

Phase 1: initial impulse
   Protectionism/threat of protectionism/dumping
   External approach
   From sales office

Phase 2: discussion phase (up to 3 years)
   Internal dialogue: Sales office/international dept, product division/middle
   management
   Definition of project: market size (as defined by sales office), agglomera-
   tion, role models, visibility of country/region

Phase 3: decision phase (1–2 years)
   Project team (3–10 people): detailed examination
   Sometimes target country settled

Source: Literature on international business, especially Aharoni (1966), Buckley *et al.* (1983, 1988), Hood and Truijens (1993).

on the internationalization process (Buckley and Ghauri, 1993) which examines the evolution of direct investment over time. The points made in this
literature translate into a decision process into which governments can intervene – with greater or lesser degrees of success. In terms of Table 3.1,
governments often attempt to attract inward investment almost when the die
is cast (that is, in phase 3). They attempt to get their location onto the short
list of sites to be visited by the project team. This is often too late. The stage
prior to this (phase 2) where the entrant firm, via its sales office, has defined
its market and often its objectives, may be more appropriate. Indeed, there is
no substitute for being in on the first phase – the initial impulse.

   It is thus contended that government promotional efforts would be more
successful if governments better understood the decision processes of multinational firms.

CONCLUSION

The location decisions of multinational firms can only be understood in the
context of their total market servicing strategy. It is essential in order to
comprehend individual location decisions to see the whole picture. The whole
picture is made up of exporting, licensing and FDI to final markets and the
ramifications of this network for intermediate markets. The foreign market

servicing network of a particular firm must be understood in both a cross-section and a time series dimension. The sequencing in time of changes in foreign market servicing decisions is to some degree predictable. This dynamic process must be understood by managers and by government officials who wish to intervene and redirect location decisions.

There is still uncertainty as to whether the effects of inward foreign investment will have different effects on the host country than a comparable domestic investment. This will depend on the vertical and horizontal links which the firm has to the investment in question. Policy will hinge on these issues, but also on the question of whether or not a domestic investment is a feasible alternative.

REFERENCES

Aharoni, Y. (1966) *The Foreign Investment Decision Process*, Graduate School of Business Administration, Harvard University: Boston, MA.

Aliber, R.Z. (1970) 'A theory of direct foreign investment', in C.P. Kindleberger (ed.) *The International Firm*, MIT Press: Cambridge, MA.

Boddewyn, J.J., M.B. Halbrich and A.C. Perry (1986) 'Service multinationals: conceptualisation, measurement and theory', *Journal of International Business Studies*, 16, 3, 41–57.

Buckley, P.J. and P.F.R. Artisien (1986) *Die Multinationalen Unternehmen und der Arbeitsmarkt*, Frankfurt: Campus Verlag GmbH.

Buckley, P.J. and P.F.R. Artisien (1987a) *North-South Direct Investment in the European Communities*, London: Macmillan.

Buckley, P.J. and P.F.R. Artisien (1987b) 'Policy issues of intra-EC Direct Investment', *Journal of Common Market Studies*, XXVI, 2, 207–30.

Buckley, P.J., Z. Berkova and G.D. Newbould (1983) *Direct Investment in the UK by Smaller European Firms*, London: Macmillan.

Buckley, P.J. and M. Casson (1976) *The Future of the Multinational Enterprise*, London: Macmillan.

Buckley, P.J. and M. Casson (1981) 'The optimal timing of a foreign direct investment', *Economic Journal*, 92, 361, 75–81.

Buckley, P.J. and M. Casson (1985) *The Economic Theory of the Multinational Enterprise*, London: Macmillan.

Buckley, P.J. and M. Casson (1988) 'A theory of cooperation in international business', in F.J. Contractor and P. Lorange (eds), *Cooperative Strategies in International Business*, Lexington, MA: Lexington Books.

Buckley, P.J. and H. Davies (1981) 'Foreign licensing in overseas operations: theory and evidence from the UK', in R.G. Hawkins and A.J. Prasad (eds), *Technology Transfer and Economic Development*, Greenwich, Conn.: JAI Press.

Buckley, P.J. and P.N. Ghauri (eds) (1993) *The Internationalisation of the Firm*, London: Dryden Press.

Buckley, P.J., H. Mirza and J.R. Sparkes (1987a), 'Direct foreign investment in Japan as means of foreign market entry: the case of European firms', *Journal of Marketing Management*, 2, 3, 241–58.

Buckley, P.J., H. Mirza and J.R. Sparkes (1987b) 'Planning operations in Japan: the practices of British companies on entry and operation in the Japanese market', *University of Wales Business and Economics Review*, **2**, Winter, 33–40.

Buckley, P.J., G.D. Newbould and J. Thurwell (1988) *Foreign Direct Investment by Smaller UK Firms*, London: Macmillan.

Buckley, P.J., C.L. Pass and K. Prescott (1992) *Servicing International Markets: Competitive Strategies of Firms*, Oxford: Blackwell.

Buckley, P.J. and R.D. Pearce (1979) 'Overseas production and exporting by the world's largest enterprises', *Journal of International Business Studies*, **10**, 1, 9–20.

Buckley, P.J. and R.D. Pearce (1981) 'Market servicing by multinational manufacturing firms: exporting versus foreign production', *Managerial and Decision Economics*, **2**, 4, 229–46.

Buckley, P.J. and R.D. Pearce (1984) 'Exports in the strategy of multinational firms', *Journal of Business Research*, **12**, 2, 209–26.

Davies, H. (1977) 'Technology transfer through commercial transactions', *Journal of Industrial Economics*, **26**, 161–75.

Dunning, J.H. (1981) *International Production and the Multinational Enterprise*, London: George Allen & Unwin.

Dunning, J.H. and P.J. Buckley (1977) 'International production and alternative models of trade', *Manchester School*, **65**, 392–403.

Edvinsson, L. (1981) 'Some aspects on export of services', University of Stockholm, working paper.

Enderwick, P. (1989) *Multinational Service Firms*, London: Routledge.

Giddy, I. and A.M. Rugman (1979) 'A model of foreign direct investment, trade and licensing', New York: Graduate School of Business, Columbia University, mimeo.

Hennart, J.-F. (1986) 'What is internalization?', *Weltwirtschaftliches Archiv*, **122**, 791–8.

Hirsh, S. (1976) 'An international trade and investment theory of the firm', *Oxford Economic Papers*, **28**, 258–70.

Hood, N. and T. Truijens (1993) 'European Locational Decisions of Japanese Manufacturers: Survey Evidence on the Case of the UK', *International Business Review*, **2**, 1, 39–63.

Hood, N. and S. Young (1979) *The Economics of Multinational Enterprise*, London: Longman.

Krugman, P. (ed.) (1986) *Strategic Trade Policy and the New International Economics*, Cambridge, MA: MIT Press.

Luostarinen, R. (1979) *The internationalization of the firm*, Helsinki: Acta Academia Oeconomica Helsingiensis.

Ohmae, K. (1985) *Triad Power: The Coming Shape of Global Competition*, New York: Free Press.

Scherer, F.M. *et al.* (1975) *The Economics of Multi-Plant Operation – An International Comparisons Study*, Cambridge, MA: Harvard University Press.

Young, S. *et al.* (1989) *International Market Entry and Development*, Hemel Hempstead: Harvester Wheatsheaf.

4.   Low-wage countries and trade with the European Union

Pierre-André Buigues and Alexis Jacquemin

Industries exposed to competition from the low-wage countries are not necessarily the same as those benefiting from their net demand for imports. In the short and medium term, this process therefore necessitates structural adjustment and increases the need for reallocation between industries.

This chapter examines the importance of imports from low-wage countries in the European Union's trade, and their nature; it also endeavours to identify the factors likely to encourage or discourage trade flows from these LWCs.

We begin by identifying the countries with low hourly wages in industry, and the proportion of world GDP produced by these countries. Next we determine the importance of imports from LWCs as a proportion of all of the European Union's imports of extra-Community origin; we also relate this proportion to the Union's apparent consumption of industrial products. The third examines the extent to which Community exports to the LWCs follow trends which resemble or differ from the trends for imports.

In the fourth section, the aggregated approach gives way to an examination of sectors at two-digit level, since the overall level may hide substantial disparities between sectors. Again, the proportion of imports of imports from and exports to LWCs are calculated. We then refine this analysis and concentrate in particular on the presence of intra-branch type trade at three-digit level. Finally, we propose an econometric exercise designed to identify certain factors likely to promote or to inhibit from the LWCs to the European Union. These factors are not very mobile and can be influenced by Community policies the aim of which is to encourage the establishment of activities within the European market.

The opinions expressed in this chapter are those of the authors and do not reflect those of the organization to which they belong. The authors wish to thank Montse Berges, Carlos Martinez Mongay, Chantal Mathieu, Jean Pisani-Ferry, André Sapir et Maarten van de Stadt for their comments and assistance.

LOW-WAGE COUNTRIES IN EUROPEAN UNION TRADE

This section considers how wage levels at present compare in different countries and identifies the low-wage countries at the heart of the political debate as a result of the competition they exercise. Figure 4.1 shows the hourly wages of production workers in manufacturing industry for some 30 countries in 1993. There are clearly wide disparities between them, but overall, they can be said to fall into two groups: (1) the high-wage countries (more than $US10 per hour in 1993), which include the United States, Japan, almost all the Community[1] countries and the EFTA countries, and (2) the low-wage countries (less than $US7 per hour in 1993), consisting of virtually all the rest of the world.

A substantial gap therefore exists between the two groups. The gap is huge between the high cost European Union and EFTA countries (more than $US20 per hour in 1993 in Belgium, Germany, Norway and Switzerland) and the very low-wage countries (less than $US1 per hour in 1993 in China, Pakistan and Africa).

Our analysis will divide the countries into two groups: the high-wage countries, consisting of the members of the triad (EU, EFTA, USA, Japan, Canada, New Zealand and Australia) and the low-wage countries, consisting of the rest of the world (black Africa and the Arab world, Latin America, Asian NICs, other Asian countries and Eastern Europe). This snapshot of the situation is clearly destined to change in the course of time. As the low-wage countries develop and increase their productivity, earnings gradually rise. Japan is a case in point. In 1980, the hourly earnings of production workers in manufacturing industry were $US5.5 in Japan and $US9.9 in the United States, but by 1993 the figure for Japan was higher than for the United States. Nevertheless, Japan is something of an exception, since over the period 1980–93 the relative position of wages between major world areas remained more or less the same. Admittedly, in 1980, the hourly industrial costs of the fast-growing economies of Southeast Asia were one-tenth those of the United States, but the ratio was still 4:5 in 1993. Over the decade, the definition of the low-wage country area is therefore fairly stable, since Japan was already one of the high-wage countries in 1982 and the fast-growing economies of Southeast Asia were still among the low-wage countries in 1993.

In order to assess the respective overall importance of these high- and low-wage countries, Table 4.1 shows their share of world gross domestic product in 1995. In 1995, low-wage countries accounted for some 48 per cent of world GDP, but this share should increase appreciably in the future.

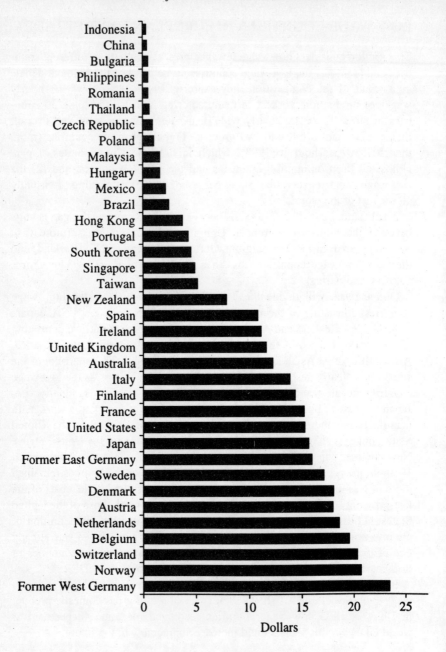

Notes: Conversion on the basis of current exchange rates.
Source: Morgan Stanley, Bureau of Labor Statistics, Washington, DC.

Figure 4.1   Hourly wage costs for industrial workers in 1993

Table 4.1   Geographical distribution of world GDP

	Share in world GDP (%) 1960	Share in world GDP (%) 1995
High-wage countries		
Western European	26.0	22.0
North America	27.0	21.0
Japan, Australia, New Zealand	6.0	9.0
TOTAL	59.0	52.0
Low-wage countries		
Black Africa and Middle East	6.0	7.0
Latin America	8.0	9.0
Asia	12.0	25.0
Eastern Europe	15.0	7.0
TOTAL	41.0	48.0
World Total	**100.0**	**100.0**

Source: Groupings into HWCs and LWCs based on CEPII data, Mimosa.

IMPORTS FROM LOW-WAGE COUNTRIES

An initial indication of the importance of the LWCs with regard to the European Union is given by the following figures. In 1995, and excluding the European Union, the LWCs account for 61.5 per cent of world GDP. But only 44 per cent of the Union's total imports of manufactured products came from the LWCs, so that their supplies to the European Union are relatively small compared with their economic importance in the world. Nevertheless, these supplies do increase over time, rising from 32.1 per cent in 1982 to 43.9 per cent in 1994. The 11.8 points increase observed between 1982 and 1994 is mainly attributed to the Asian LWCs (China, ASEAN and NICs). The Asian LWCs accounted for 13.3 per cent of imports from outside the Community in 1982 and 21.6 per cent in 1994, an increase of 8.3 points, while the share of the non-Asian LWCs fell by 3.2 points during the same period.

Among the large Community countries we see appreciable differences in level, even if the general trend is the same. Figure 4.2 presents the low-wage countries' share of five countries' total imports from outside the Community. Given that this index is based on the difference in labour costs, it may be

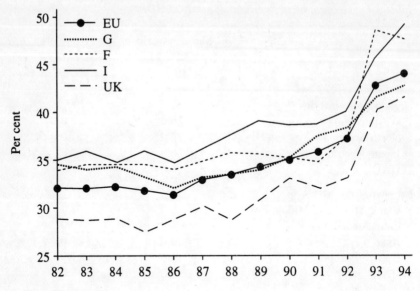

Source: Eurostat data.

*Figure 4.2   Low-wage countries' share in total imports from outside the
             Community*

regarded as an indicator of comparative advantage. This shows that in 1994
the LWCs' share is lowest in the United Kingdom, at 41.4 per cent, followed
by Germany (43.0 per cent), France (47.6 per cent) and Italy (49.2 per cent).
However, since 1992, LWC penetration has increased considerably for all the
countries considered.

   It may be useful to supplement these findings by calculating imports from
LWCs as a proportion of demand for manufactured products (Figure 4.3).
The demand for manufactured products in the European Union is identified
by apparent consumption (output + imports – exports). The trends are on the
whole comparable since it can also be seen that imports from LWCs increase
as a proportion of demand for manufactured products. But in 1994 only 7.3
per cent of the demand for manufactured products in the European Union was
satisfied by the LWCs: 5.7 per cent in France, 6.3 per cent in Italy, 8.2 per
cent in the United Kingdom and 7.2 per cent in Germany. Overall, this import
penetration from the LWCs remains remarkably low, irrespective of which of
the member states of the European Union are considered. It can therefore be
seen that the globalization process is, at this stage, extremely slight in relation to the LWCs and that there is virtually no European dependence on these
countries.

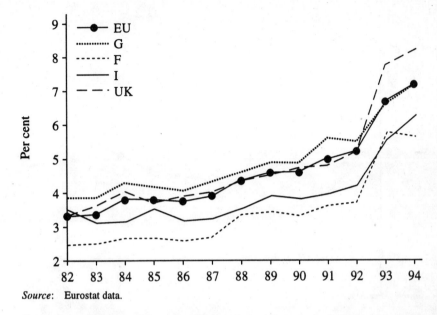

Source: Eurostat data.

Figure 4.3   Imports from low-wage countries as a proportion of demand for manufactured products

EXPORTS TO LOW-WAGE COUNTRIES

In 1982, the low-wage countries accounted for 54.7 per cent of the European Union's total exports of manufactured products outside the Community, compared with 51.6 per cent in 1994, that is, a decline of 3.1 points in ten years. If we again isolate the Asian LWCs, we see that this fall is explained mainly by the decline in the markets of these countries, rather than in those of the non-Asian LWCs. The change in the proportion of our exports of manufactured products going to low-wage countries is, however, uneven over the period since after an appreciable fall in the relative proportion up to 1987 (only 42.3 per cent that year), we see a sharp increase which accelerates between 1990 and 1994 (Figure 4.4).

The break in trend observed in 1987 for both imports and exports can be explained by macroeconomic and microeconomic factors. We see that it is after the middle of the period 1985–90 that the low-wage developing countries begin to record economic growth rates higher than those observed in the industrialized countries. This 'growth effect' was automatically reflected in a greater share of the European Union's trade with low-wage countries, whose

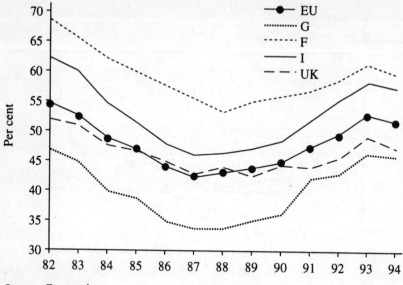

Source: Eurostat data.

Figure 4.4   Low-wage countries' share of total extra-Community exports

economic dynamism increased relative to the high-wage countries. At the microeconomic level, it must also be stressed that structural reforms – greater openness to international trade, privatization and deregulation – were established in low-wage countries at around the same time. However, the European Union does not derive as much benefit as Japan and the United States from the economic dynamism of Southeast Asia. Thus Japan, the newly industrialized countries of Southeast Asia and China account for only 12.5 per cent of extra-Community exports, the comparable figures being 22.3 per cent for the United States and 24.8 per cent for Japan (European Economy, 1994). The situation is similar for direct investment between 1979 and 1992. As an illustration, the European Union accounted for some 6 per cent of all capital invested in China compared with 10 per cent in the case of the United States and 13 per cent in the case of Japan.

The trends relating to extra-Community exports are again fairly similar for the four large countries of the European Union, although there are wide differences in level. In 1994, of France's total exports outside the Community, 59.1 per cent went to the low-wage countries; the comparable figures are 57.2 per cent for Italy, 47.1 per cent for the United Kingdom and only 45.6 per cent for Germany. These percentages point to a situation in which the LWCs are more important in terms of exports than of imports in the foreign trade of the

European Union. This is particularly true of France, where 59.1 per cent of exports went to the LWCs but only 47.6 per cent of imports came from them.

If we take the indicator of the share of output exported to the LWCs (Figure 4.5), the trends observed are similar, but the break observed in 1987 is more marked. The levels for this indicator are relatively low, as they are for the share of consumption of manufactured products coming from the LWCs. Only 9.4 per cent of the European Union's manufacturing output was exported to the LWCs in 1994. The differences between member states were very small, the figures being 8.2 per cent for the United Kingdom, 9.1 per cent for Germany, 8.8 per cent for France and 10.1 per cent for Italy.

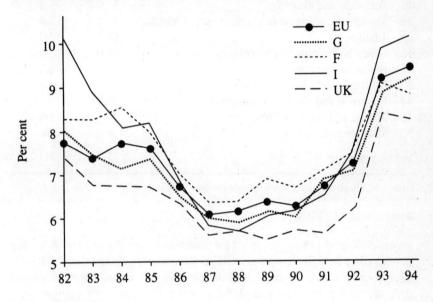

Source: Eurostat data.

Figure 4.5   Share of manufacturing output exported to low-wage countries

THE SECTORAL DIMENSION OF EUROPEAN TRADE WITH THE LOW-WAGE COUNTRIES

Imports from Low-Wage Countries

While imports from the LWCs admittedly account for a very limited proportion of the European Union's demand for industrial products, wide differences may well exist between sectors of activity. Table 4.2 shows the sectors

Table 4.2   Low-wage countries' share in demand for manufactured products, by sector (%)

		Largest sectors	
		1994	1994/1982
49	Other manufacturing industries (toys, jewellery, musical instruments)	80.7*	47.6*
44	Leather	38.4	20.7
45	Footwear and clothing	31.0	15.4
36	Transport equipment (excluding motor vehicles)	19.3	17.4
43	Textiles	18.7	10.4
33	Office and computing machinery	17.0	15.3
37	Precision and optical instruments	11.2	6.8
22	Iron and steel, processing of metals	10.7	4.7
34	Electrical and electronic equipment	8.6	6.2
46	Timber and wooden furniture	8.3	1.6
26	Man-made fibres	8.0	NA
Industry average		7.2	3.9

Note: *   Situation in 1992 and difference between 1992 and 1982.

Source: COMEXT, VISA.

at two-digit level (18 sectors in all for manufacturing industry) for which the LWCs' share is higher than the average for industry. We see that the LWCs already cover a large proportion of demand (15 per cent or more) in sectors such as textiles, footwear and clothing, and leather, and they dominate the manufacture of toys and musical instruments. In addition, observation of the trend over the period 1982–92 reveals that these sectors are also those in which the LWCs' relative importance has increased the most. There is therefore apparently a relative specialization which has grown more marked in these sectors.

However, the LWCs also satisfy an appreciable share of demand for industrial products in the sectors with higher technological content, such as office and computing machinery (17.0 per cent of demand in 1994), precision and optical instruments and apparatus (11.2 per cent) and electrical and electronic equipment (8.6 per cent). There too the increase over the period 1982–94 is higher than for the industry average.

Exports to Low-Wage Countries

As Table 4.3 shows, the LWCs also absorb an appreciable proportion of exported Community production in a number of sectors, including machinery and mechanical equipment (21.5 per cent), transport equipment (excluding motor vehicles) (26.6 per cent), leather (23.4 per cent) and precision and optical instruments (20.1 per cent). Thus, with regard to both imports and exports, we see that trade between low-wage and high-wage countries is not exclusively of the inter-industry type, in which the LWCs export traditional products to the high-wage countries and the latter's export capital equipment and high technology goods to the LWCs.

At the level of aggregation at which this analysis is carried out (NACE two digits), the results show that for very many sectors the LWC share in European Union exports is higher than the industry average and that for these same sectors the proportion of LWC imports in demand for manufactured products is also higher than the industry average.

Figure 4.6 presents a simplified classification by sector which illustrates this. It shows that in seven sectors trade is high in both directions: iron and steel, electrical and electronic equipment, transport equipment (excluding motor vehicles), precision and optical instruments, textiles, leather, and other manufacturing industries (jewellery, musical instruments, toys). Conversely,

Table 4.3   Low-wage countries' share in European production of manufactured products, by sector

		Largest sectors	
		1994	1994/1982
36	Transport equipment (excluding motor vehicles)	26.6	14.7
44	Leather	23.4	17.1
32	Machinery and mechanical equipment	21.5	1.1
37	Precision and optical instruments	20.1	5.3
43	Textiles	12.8	7.0
34	Electrical and electronic equipment	12.0	1.9
25	Chemical products	10.8	NA
26	Man-made fibres	10.0	1.4
22	Iron and steel, processing of metals	9.5	−0.1
	Industry average	9.4	1.6

Source: COMEXT, VISA.

Low-wage countries' share in European production of manufactured products by sector		Low-wage countries' share in demand for manufactured goods: **Low**	Low-wage countries' share in demand for manufactured goods: **High**
	Low	24 Non-metallic mineral products 31 Metal articles 35 Motor vehicles 41 Food, drink and tobacco 47 Paper and printing 48 Rubber and plastics	33 Office and computing machinery 45 Footwear and clothing 46 Timber and wooden furniture
	High	26 Chemical products 32 Machinery and mechanical equipment	22 Iron and steel, processing of metals 34 Electrical and electronic equipment 36 Transport equipment (excluding motor vehicles) 37 Precision and optical instruments 43 Textiles 44 Leather 49 Other manufacturing industries (jewellery, musical instruments, toys)

Note: The intersecting vertical and horizontal lines separate the situations which are low or high by comparison with the industry average.

Source: COMEXT, VISA, authors' calculations.

Figure 4.6 Flow of trade between European Union and low-wage countries, 1994

in six sectors trade is limited in both directions: non-metallic mineral products, metal articles, motor vehicles, food, drink and tobacco, paper, and rubber and plastics.

Only five sectors out of 18 do not correspond to this classification. These are, first, office and computing machinery, footwear and clothing, and the timber industries, where the LWCs account for a large share of imports of manufactured products while European Union exports are low. On the other hand, for machinery and chemical products, the situation is reversed: these sectors represent a large proportion of European Union exports but a small proportion of imports from the LWCs.

Of course, this analysis is carried out at a high level of sectoral aggregation, and the analysis of trade between the European Union and low-wage countries may be entirely biased for purely statistical reasons. Certain studies (see in particular Lassuderie-Duchêne and Mucchielli, 1979) have shown that, even with high intra-branch trade, specializations exist for products or groups of products. Take for example the sector of transport equipment (excluding motor vehicles): the European Union represents a large market for low-wage country exports of cycles and baby carriages, whereas the European Union exports aeronautical equipment to the low-wage countries. Similarly, in the electrical and electronic equipment sector, the low-wage countries represent a large market for European Union exports of wires and cables, telecommunications equipment and electrical capital equipment, while the European Union is a large market for LWC exports of electric household appliances, electric lamps and other forms of electric lighting equipment. Lastly, in the case of textiles or leather, the low-wage countries represent a large market for European Union exports of high unit cost, high-quality products whereas the low-wage countries export low unit cost, low-quality textile and leather products to the European Union.

It is therefore necessary to analyse trade flows between the low-wage countries and the European Union in greater detail, although we do not claim to be able to eliminate the statistical bias. The next section is devoted to a disaggregated approach to data at three-digit level.

INTRA- AND INTER-INDUSTRY TRADE

Trade between the OECD countries, which roughly covers the high-wage country area, is trade between countries with comparable factor endowments, trading similar products with one another. Moreover, attempts to test the Heckscher–Ohlin model of the basis of trade between OECD industrialized countries have generally been unsuccessful. One of the conclusions of the analysis of trade between industrialized countries is that the more comparable the per capita incomes and the more similar the production structures in these countries, the higher will intra-industry type trade be.

The types of trade, first between high-wage countries, and second between high-wage and low-wage countries, should consequently be very different. In order to illustrate the question, intra-industry trade intensity was calculated on the basis of 110 three-digit sectors for manufacturing industry. Several indicators have been proposed for analysing the share of intra-industry trade in a country's total trade. The one most used is that of Grubel and Lloyd (1975):

$$B_i = \left(1 - \sum_{i=1}^{n} \frac{|X_i - M_i|}{(X_i - M_i)}\right) \times 100$$

Nevertheless, this indicator can also be formulated to take into consideration the overall balance on the trade account:

$$C_i = \left\{ \frac{\sum_{i=1}^{n}(X_i - M_i) - \sum_{i=1}^{n}|X_i - M_i|}{\sum_{i=1}^{n}(X_i - M_i) - \left|\sum_{i=1}^{n} X_i - \sum_{i=1}^{n} M_i\right|} \right\} \times 100$$

The adjustment indicator C_i has the advantage of facilitating comparisons over time, allowing for the trade balance, and over space, allowing for the volume of trade (Neme, 1982). In this way it measures the share of intra-branch trade, with the trade account in equilibrium.

An initial comparison between the information provided by B_i and C_i may be made for trade between the European Union and high-wage third countries. Figure 4.7 shows that the two measurements produce almost identical results, roughly 70 per cent, in 1982. The increases in level over the period 1982–92 are similar but, in a situation of balanced trade, intra-branch trade is probably above 80 per cent in 1992, whereas with accounts in disequilibrium, it is under 75 per cent. In 1994, the figure is around 76 per cent for both indicators. With the prospect of more balanced trade, the proportion of intra-branch trade is therefore bound to increase.

What is the situation with regard to trade with the low-wage countries? As shown by Figure 4.8, the share of intra-branch trade using the non-adjusted formula, namely about 35 per cent in 1982, is far smaller than the share of such trade between high-wage countries, namely 70 per cent for the same year. This result is in line with the theories of international trade. Nevertheless, two pieces of information lead us to qualify this result. First, the adjustment for the account disequilibria has, in the case of the LWCs, a major effect on the percentage of intra-branch trade: in 1982, it goes up from almost

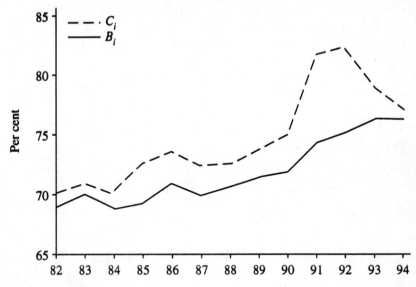

Source: Eurostat data.

Figure 4.7 European Union's share of intra-branch trade with high-wage countries

35 per cent to almost 60 per cent. Second, the non-adjusted index indicates substantial growth in such trade.

In fact, at the beginning of the 1980s, the difference observed between the non-adjusted share of intra-branch trade and the share which is adjusted by the trade account corresponds to a situation of severe imbalances in trade between the two areas. As and when the trade account moves into equilibrium, unadjusted intra-branch trade tends towards the values observed with the indicator adjusted by the trade balance.

From the European Union standpoint, an increase in intra-branch type trade with the low-wage countries tends to reduce adjustment costs, whereas inter-branch trade, based on comparative advantage, exerts strong competitive pressure on the European Union's sectors of activity in which the low-wage countries are in a favourable position. By contrast, intra-branch type trade takes place in a situation of imperfect competition and relates to cross-flows of goods belonging to the same sectors of activity. Since these goods can be partly substituted for one another within the same sector, and firms can more easily achieve differentiation for similar products, the competitive shock will be smaller in the sectors of activity in which intra-branch trade is predominant.

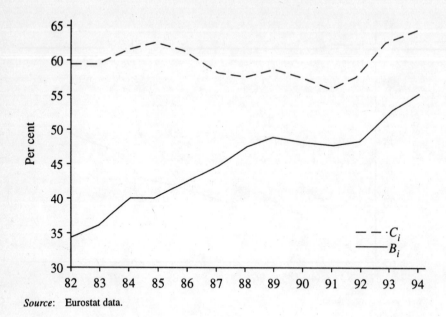

Source: Eurostat data.

*Figure 4.8   Share of European Union's intra-branch trade with low-wage
countries*

Comparable figures are obtained for the share of the large European countries' intra-branch trade in their trade with the low-wage countries (see Table
4.4). Some of the differences are nevertheless interesting. The lowest figures
are observed for Germany, which corresponds to that country's type of industrial specialization in capital goods and chemicals, for which trade with the
low-wage countries is of the inter-industry type. The argument of Drèze
(1988) and Linder (1961) applies, namely that the greater the similarity of
per capita incomes between countries, the higher will be their reciprocal
trade in manufactured goods. Germany is the country whose per capita incomes differ most from those of the low-wage countries.

COMPARATIVE ADVANTAGES AND TRADE WITH LOW WAGE COUNTRIES

This section proposes an econometric exercise designed to identify certain
factors likely to promote or to inhibit imports from the low-wage countries to
the European Union and, as a result, to determine the sectors most exposed to

Table 4.4   Intra-branch trade with low-wage countries

	B_i	C_i
1982		
Germany	26.0	43.7
France	26.4	57.8
Italy	30.1	61.6
UK	32.9	51.5
1992		
Germany	43.7	52.2
France	52.9	69.0
Italy	47.2	65.7
UK	53.3	54.3
Difference		
Germany	17.7	8.5
France	26.5	11.2
Italy	17.1	3.1
UK	20.4	2.8

Source: Eurostat data.

competitive pressure from the LWCs and those which best withstand or even benefit from the markets of these countries.

The preceding sections have shown that, overall, imports from the LWCs represent a small proportion of imports in the European Union and an even smaller part of its apparent consumption. But, in some specific sectors, the scale of these imports is considerable. These sectors relate both to traditional activities and to sophisticated production activities, and the corresponding trade is of both the inter-industry and intra-industry type. It is therefore unlikely that import flows from the LWCs are determined by a single type of factor. Simultaneous use of the variables identified by the Heckscher–Ohlin principle and those emanating from the 'new theory of trade' is appropriate.

The dependent variable is the relationship between imports from the LWCs and total imports of extra-Community origin, in 1992. The explanatory factors are the following. Two variables correspond to determinants of intersectoral trade. The first is the relationship between physical capital and labour (K/L). The index of capital intensiveness is measured by gross fixed capital formation, per employee, over the period 1985–90. The second is an index of labour skills (*Qual*), measured by non-manual workers as a proportion of total wage and salary earners. With regard to the trade in similar products, that is, intra-branch trade which takes place in a situation of more or less imperfect competition, the variable used is a measurement of economies of scale *(Ech)* linked to monopolistic competition. It is defined by the average size of enterprises, measured by the number of employees per enterprise. Lastly, the buoyancy of demand as a factor of attraction *(Dem)* is measured by the annual growth rate of domestic demand in the European Union between 1982 and 1992.

Our analysis relates to all the observations available to three figures (n=74) and the multiple regressions are calculated on the basis of a double logarithmic relationship:

$$\log \frac{I_{PBS}}{I_{TOT}} = a + b_1 \log \frac{K}{L} + b_2 \log Qual + b_3 \log Dem + b_4 \log Ech$$

The results shown in Table 4.5 confirm the simultaneous role of variables belonging to the two types of theory. According to the coefficients of elasticity, penetration of the European Union by low-wage countries is lowest in the sectors with highly skilled labour and large economies of scale. If we consider the result for the four large countries with which a disaggregation of our data is possible, it would appear that capital intensiveness is an explanatory factor in the case of Germany, the United Kingdom and France. For these countries the greater a sector's capital intensiveness, the lower the penetration of low-wage countries. But a contrast emerges between Germany, where

Table 4.5   *Result of regressions: effect of sectoral characteristics on the relationship between imports from LWCs and total imports of extra-Community origin*

	a	K/L Capital intensiveness	Qual Levels of skills	Dem Demand growth	Ech Economies of scale	R^2 F
European Union	3.70	0.03	−1.24	−0.02	−0.20	0.37
	(5.76)	(0.23)	(3.68)	(0.07)	(1.89)	F=7.54
Germany	2.90	−0.57	−0.90	0.07	−0.15	0.29
	(3.59)	(2.83)	(2.12)	(0.20)	(1.14)	F=6.9
France	0.69	−0.75	−0.20	0.68	−0.50	0.26
	(0.70)	(3.05)	(0.40)	(1.56)	(2.50)	F=6.0
Italy	3.47	−0.33	−1.41	0.11	−0.25	0.23
	(3.30)	(1.26)	(−2.56)	(0.24)	(−1.40)	F=5.2
United Kingdom	1.27	−0.57	−0.25	0.52	−0.51	0.24
	(1.17)	(2.11)	(0.44)	(1.08)	(2.93)	F=5.3

Note: The t value is given in brackets.

the level of skills produces a significant effect, whereas economies of scale do not, and France and the United Kingdom, where the type of skills does not at present seem to be an asset, whereas the role of economies of scale remains considerable.

The results of this econometric exercise may be set alongside two other pieces of research. A study by Jacquemin and Sapir (1988) identified a set of variables, namely human capital and economies of scale, which reduce the importance of imports of extra-Community origin relative to intra-Community imports. More recently, a study by Oliveira-Martins (1993), applied to the OECD countries, concludes that the impact of penetration of LWCs, generally outside the OECD area, on average wages in the OECD area, tends to be negative in industries with small economies of scale and low product differentiation.

CONCLUSION

To sum up, the pressure of competition from low-wage countries differs in intensity and nature depending on the sectors. Some industries suffer keen competition, whereas others benefit from the development of markets in the low-wage countries, as a result of greater export demand. The political response to the challenges of structural adjustment facing the countries of the European Union can therefore be expressed at several levels:

1. encouragement of higher cumulative investment per worker;
2. increased expenditure on training, with the aim of gradually improving skills;
3. strengthening the European single market which constitutes the industrial base, making it possible to benefit from economies of size.

NOTE

1. Apart from Greece and Portugal.

BIBLIOGRAPHY

Arthuis, J. (1993), 'Rapport d'information sur l'incidence économique et fiscale des délocalisations hors du teritoire des activités et des services', séance du 4 juin, rapport d'information No. 337, Paris: Sénat.
Baldwin, Robert E. (1994), 'Trade, Foreign Direct Investment, and Employment', OECD Economics Department Working paper.

Dreze, J. (1988), 'The Standard Goods Hypothesis', in Jacquemin and Sapir (1989).

European Economy (1994), 'Annual Economic Report – Analytical Studies No. 4', Brussels.

Grubel, H.G. and P.J. Lloyd (1975), *Intra-industry Trade, the Theory and Measurement of International Trade in Differentiated Products*, London: Macmillan.

Jacquemin, A. and A. Sapir (1988), 'International Trade and Integration of the European Community: an Econometric Analysis', *European Economic Review*, **32**, reprinted in Jacquemin and Sapir (1989).

Jacquemin, A. and A. Sapir (1989), *The European Internal Market*, London: Oxford University Press.

Lassuderie-Duchêne, B. and J.L. Mucchielli (1979), 'Les échanges intra-branche et la hiérarchisation des avantages comparés dans le commerce international', *Revue Economique*, May.

Linder, S.B. (1961), 'An essay on trade and transformation', Wiley.

Oliveira-Martins, J. (1993), 'Market Structure, International Trade and Relative Wages', OECD Working Paper No. 134.

Saucier, Ph. (1987), *'Spécialisation Internationale et Compétitivité de l'économie Japonaise'*, Paris: Economica.

Turcq, D. (1995), 'The Global Impact of Non-Japan Asia', *Long Range Planning*, **28**, (1).

Van Mouik, M. (1994), 'Wages and European Integration', Maastricht: BIV Publication.

Wood, A. (1994), *'North–South Trade, Employment and Inequality'*, London: Oxford University Press.

5. International relocation strategies of Italian firms

Giovanni Balcet[1]

INTRODUCTION

This chapter discusses some aspects of the impact of foreign direct investments (FDIs) and of internationalization processes on the home country economy in the Italian case, with special reference to cost-saving industrial redeployment and relocations. It is crucial that the different typologies of FDIs and international operations be distinguished according to their prime motivations. The implications of a market-oriented and tariff-jumping acquisition abroad, for instance, will be very different from those of a cost-saving, export-oriented affiliate or joint venture in a low-wage area.

We can, as a first approximation, refer to the following prevailing motivations (Balcet, 1981) in order to define a taxonomy of multinational productive strategies:

1. access to raw material and energy sources, through vertical upstream integration;
2. market-oriented strategies, with high complementarity between productive and commercial affiliates, consistent with the product life cycle model, a special case being that of FDIs as a reaction to protectionism, and to import-substitution policies in developing countries;
3. cost-saving export-oriented manufacturing relocations, aiming to take advantage of favourable cost conditions abroad, due to wage differentials, scale economies, energy prices, local incentives or other factors;
4. technology-oriented affiliates or minority participations oriented towards the acquisition of technology and know-how abroad, mainly in highly innovative activities and in technological districts;
5. 'global' strategies, oriented towards rationalizing R&D, production and distribution within the Triad, in a context of oligopolistic interaction.[2]

In the current debate concerning international relocations of industrial activities, the emphasis is often put on type (3) strategies. However, the impact of such strategies should be evaluated in the context of all the dynamic aspects and consequences of the internationalization processes.[3]

In the case of Italian firms, the second type of motivation has largely prevailed, although other strategies have been emerging in recent years. From an historical point of view, Italy is a late international investor and a multinational follower, even if a few firms have been operating abroad since the first half of the century.[4] The remarkable export competitiveness of Italian industrial firms in the post-war period has contrasted with their poor performance in terms of multinational growth. A long-term catching-up process ended in 1992, when the number of employees in Italian affiliates abroad balanced that in foreign affiliates in Italy (Figure 5.1). At the same time, the traditional gap between export shares and FDI shares was substantially reduced.

If we focus on the evolution of the internationalization processes in the last two decades, we can distinguish three stages (see Table 5.1), that will be discussed in the following sections. In the first stage, a traditional pattern of internationalization was characterized by the divergence between very good export performance of Italian firms and their weak and delayed multinational growth. Moreover, the pattern of trade specialization diverged greatly from the pattern of FDI, and market-oriented motivations were dominant. Large industrial groups operated mainly in scale-intensive sectors, while minor multinationals were active in traditional sectors.

In the second stage, the restricted 'oligopolistic heart' of Italian industry expanded abroad through acquisitions, mainly in Europe, in order to enlarge its market shares and to improve the economies of scale. In more recent years, a third stage has been characterized by the emergence of a new wave of medium-sized investing firms, whose motivations are more diversified. New geographical areas, such as Central and Eastern Europe and the Far East, emerged as the destination of foreign operations, as well as new sectors, especially among traditional industries, where most comparative advantages of Italian firms are concentrated.

The evolution in one of these sectors, the textile and clothing industry, will then be discussed in more detail. It sheds light on some crucial aspects of the new pattern of international growth, and offers possible elements of interpretation. Finally, some concluding remarks will be made on the impact of relocations on the Italian economy.

THE TRADITIONAL PATTERN: UNTIL THE 1970s

The fast industrial growth in post-war Italy was mainly export-led. However, the international position of the country until the second oil shock reveals a double asymmetry. The first was between a remarkable export performance and FDI outflows: in the 1970–1980 period, the Italian share of OECD manufacturing exports was 7.3 per cent on average, while (according to Bank of Italy data) its share of estimated FDI flows was 1.3 per cent. The second asymmetry appeared between inward and outward flows of direct investments. Sales and employment in foreign-controlled firms in Italy were more than double those of foreign affiliates of Italian firms. Italy was increasingly

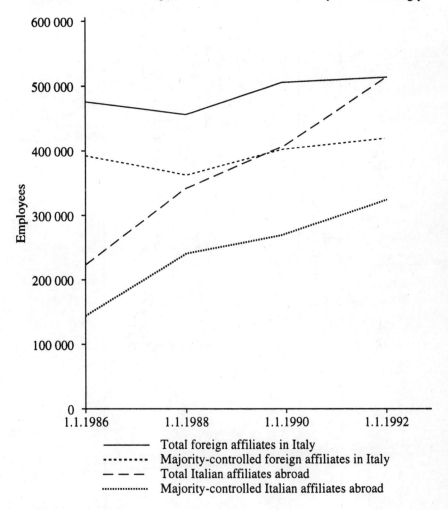

Source: Database reprint.

Figure 5.1 Employment in foreign affiliates in Italy and in Italian affiliates abroad

Table 5.1 Stages of multinational growth of Italian firms

	Main actors	Areas of destination	Sectors involved	Main motivations	Forms	Exchange rate
Stage I (until the 1970s)	Big groups Minor multinationals	Latin America EC	Scale-intensive	Market-oriented (tariff-jumping)	Greenfield FDIs Joint-ventures Cooperative agreements	Devaluing
Stage II (1980–88)	Big groups	EC	Scale-intensive	Market-oriented Economies of scale	Acquisitions Joint-ventures Cooperative agreements	Stable
Stage III (1988–93)	New multinationals	EU Eastern Europe Far East	Scale-intensive Traditional	Market-oriented Cost-saving	Acquisitions Joint-ventures Cooperative agreements	Strong until September 1992 Devaluing since September 1992

attractive for foreign multinationals, as a market and as a production location, while domestic firms had a very limited propensity to expand abroad. One consideration, crucial to understanding these asymmetries, is the deep divergence between the pattern of specialization in foreign trade, on the one hand, and the pattern of productive internationalization on the other.

If we refer to the taxonomy of industrial sectors proposed by Pavitt (1984), we observe in the Italian case a strong export specialization and positive trade balances both in 'traditional industries' (textile, clothing, footwear, ceramics, leather, furniture and so on) and in 'specialized supplier industries' (mechanical engineering and specialized equipment). In both groups of industries the average size of firms is small, labour skills are an important factor of competitiveness, and innovation often takes the form of imitation and adaptation of imported process technologies, or the form of differentiation and new product design (Onida and Viesti, 1988). The same sectors are characterized by the presence of typical Marshallian industrial districts: specialized areas in central and northern Italy, where strong concentrations of small and medium-sized firms, competing and cooperating with each other simultaneously, create crucial synergies and externalities.

Areas of competitive disadvantage are concentrated in 'scale-intensive' sectors (with some exceptions, such as household appliances) and in 'science-intensive' sectors, including electronics, information and telecommunication equipment, precision engineering and pharmaceuticals. In each of these sectors large firms and groups predominate. This structural weakness is due to the problems and deficiencies of the big firms, as well as the backwardness of the technological base and infrastructure, and to government policy.

The distribution of foreign affiliates of Italian firms did not follow this pattern during the 1970s. Participations abroad were mainly concentrated in scale-intensive sectors; that is, mainly in areas of competitive disadvantage where the big firms are concentrated, while international operations in sectors of strong competitiveness were episodic and often took the form of joint ventures or non-equity operations. From a geographical point of view, Italian FDIs were distributed in three main areas of destination, each accounting for about one-third of total FDIs:

1. the EC, where their presence was explained by proximity factors and by the growing integration of the markets;
2. Latin America (mainly Argentina and Brazil), as a result of the cultural links created by massive migrations in the past, and where Fiat, Olivetti and other firms had invested for a long time;
3. Mediterranean countries, especially Spain before its entry into the Community, in order to penetrate markets and bypass protectionism.

Market-oriented motivations dominated the FDI decisions, while limited operations in mining were carried on in developing countries (mainly by the state-owned ENI group in oil) and redeployment to low-wage countries in labour-intensive activities was rare.[5] Therefore FDIs and the other international operations were mainly complements of commercial export strategies, seeking to achieve better access to foreign markets.

The main explanation given in the literature for the low propensity of Italian firms to develop low-cost international operations, especially in traditional sectors, was the persistent dualism between northern and southern regions and the massive financial incentives given in the latter. Such cost differentials stimulated relocations within the country rather than foreign investments, for instance in North Africa (Onida and Viesti, 1988). We must note, however, that most networks of domestic subcontracting developed in the northern or the central regions of the country, exploiting more the great flexibility of small and very small firms, and often their ability to escape labour and fiscal regulations, than the state incentives.

Beginning in this period of early multinational development, we can observe another kind of dualism, between a few large multinational groups, on the one hand (Fiat–IFI, Pirelli, Olivetti–CIR, Montedison, and state-owned ENI and IRI groups), which accounted for the bulk of foreign affiliates' sales, and on the other a number of 'minor multinationals'. The former, which represented the 'oligopolistic heart' of Italian industry, operated mainly in scale-intensive and to a lesser extent in science-intensive or specialized sectors. However, during the 1970s they faced serious financial and organizational difficulties, as well as social conflict. At the same time, family-controlled, specialized medium-sized firms expanded abroad for the first time, thanks to niche advantages in specific products and technologies, mainly in traditional industries, such as food, beverages and textile and clothing (TC).[6] However, the great majority of small and medium-sized firms did not internationalize, as their financial resources were insufficient and their competitive advantage was strictly connected to the local environment (especially in the case of industrial districts).

Another specific feature of the Italian experience was the high propensity to engage in cooperative strategies of international growth, through joint ventures and various non-equity agreements (Balcet, 1988). In 1985, 36 per cent of total employment abroad was in minority participations or in 50–50 joint ventures. This propensity was correlated with the weight of developing countries as destinations of FDIs, but also with the size, the organizational characteristics and the specific strategies of minor multinationals (Balcet, 1990).

Thus it is evident that the delayed and weak internationalization until the end of the 1970s was due both to the organizational and technological backwardness of the few big industrial groups and to the characteristics of the competitive advantages of the small and medium-sized firms. Finally, public policies and the exchange rate were unfavourable to FDIs during the 1970s owing to administrative regulations on capital flows and international payments, and the continuing deterioration of the lira. But we can conclude that the modest internationalization during this period was mainly due to the structural factors we have referred to, such as industrial and regional dualisms.

THE EXPANSION OF THE 'OLIGOPOLOSTIC HEART', 1980–88

In the early 1980s, large firms and groups overcame most of the difficulties they had faced during the 1970s, due to oil shocks, recession and social conflict. They benefited from a process of financial recovery, industrial restructuring and technological innovation, which deeply affected the internationalization process, in terms of both its rate of growth and its reorientation.

The expansion through productive FDIs was very rapid in this period: from 1985 to 1988, sales by Italian affiliates abroad increased by 60 per cent (against an increase of 27 per cent registered for foreign affiliates in Italy).[7] Thanks to this expansion, the inward–outward ratio for affiliates' sales declined from 2.06 in 1985 to 1.74 in 1988, and the convergence of the Italian pattern with that of the other large European countries accelerated.

Multinational growth was highly concentrated in this period: in 1987, the top ten multinational firms (MNFs) accounted for 86.6 per cent of total employment abroad, and for 88.4 per cent of foreign affiliates' sales (Cominotti and Mariotti, 1992). In fact the four major private groups (IFI–Fiat, Pirelli, CIR–Olivetti and Ferruzzi–Montedison) alone controlled about 59 per cent of total employment in foreign affiliates, and about 52 per cent of total sales. If we take into account the two state-owned holdings (ENI and IRI), these percentages increase to 67 and 73 per cent, respectively. This narrow club of investors was deeply involved in the wave of international mergers, acquisitions and alliances of this period, mainly in Europe. Industrial strategies aiming at diversification (Fiat, Montedison), scale economies (Pirelli, Olivetti) and technological upgrading (Olivetti) coexisted with portfolio diversification strategies (IFI, CIR, Ferruzzi Finanziaria). As a consequence, the weight of minor, family-controlled multinationals decreased in relative terms. Many authors, emphasizing the role of large groups as the protagonists of this period, suggest an overall picture where the previous dualism between major and minor multinational was fading out (Cominotti and Mariotti, 1990). However, the role of minor multinationals continued to be an interesting aspect of the overall picture; among them, we see success stories of rapid growth (like Benetton, Ferrero and Merloni), as well as stories of crisis followed by acquisition by foreign multinationals (like Buitoni, Zanussi and Cinzano).

Scale-intensive sectors (vehicles, tyres, chemicals) and, to a lesser extent, science-intensive industries (information technologies, cables) continued to represent the bulk of Italian multinational investments. However, geographic destinations changed markedly during the 1980s, following important divestments in Latin American countries, affected by the debt crisis (as in Argentina) and new operations in the EC. At the end of this period, the share of Latin America decreased to 21 per cent while the EC's increased to 60 per cent in terms of employment in foreign affiliates.

Most of the studies on this period concur that market-oriented strategies continued as in the previous period to prevail over cost-saving export-oriented strategies. However, many acquisitions or alliances, especially in Europe, were also motivated by the need to reach better scale economies, comparable to those of the main competitors (for instance, in the case of Pirelli, Fiat and Olivetti). Moreover, a number of technology-oriented ventures were created, mainly in the United States.

This diversification of the motivations of Italian operations abroad holds important implications for our discussion. In general terms, FDIs and other international operations continued to be complementary rather than alternative to commercial strategies. Stimulus to exports from Italy came through the supply of intermediate goods to foreign affiliates and especially through the commercial role of foreign affiliates in the distribution of the final goods of the multinational firm. Therefore a positive impact on growth and employment at home was observed (Onida and Viesti, 1988). Moreover, the propensity to operate through joint ventures and minority participations, although still relevant, was declining, partly as an effect of geographic reorientation and of the decreasing importance of developing countries as recipients of FDIs. The share of non-majority-owned participations in total employment abroad decreased from 36 per cent in 1985 to 29 per cent in 1987. The nature itself of joint ventures and cooperative agreements changed, as they were more frequently employed in OECD countries and in scale- or technology-intensive activities (Balcet, 1990). At the same time, foreign acquisitions increasingly exceeded greenfield FDIs.

Finally, we should note that the multinational expansion of the restricted 'oligopolistic heart' of Italian industry was favoured by a stable exchange rate of the lira during the 1980s, after Italy joined the European Monetary System (EMS), and by the deregulation of capital flows. Another consequence of the strong exchange rate was that it reduced price competitiveness in many traditional industries, thus stimulating new organizational patterns and new strategies in industrial districts. In particular, mergers and acquisitions between medium- and small-sized firms engendered the emergence of new leading firms and groups, which became the protagonists of the internationalization processes in the following period.

NEW PATTERNS AND NEW ACTORS IN RECENT DEVELOPMENTS, 1988–93

As a consequence of the tendencies that we have described, 1992 marks a turning point as well as the conclusion of a long process of catching up. For the first time, employment in foreign affiliates of Italian firms exceeded that in foreign-controlled affiliates in Italy (see Figure 5.1). In 1992 and 1993, the outward flows continued to grow. Existing data (R&P, 1994) shows 343 new industrial participations created abroad (against a stock of 1156 participations at year-end, 1991), with about 135 000 employees (in addition to the 511 000 estimated in 1991).[8] In the same biennium 152 new FDIs were made in Italy, in addition to the 1438 existing in 1991. These data confirm the speed of the outward internationalization process compared with the inward flows. The greatest expansion took place in 1992, while the pace decreased in 1993, owing to recession in Europe and, to a lesser extent, to the devaluation of the lira (Table 5.2).

Table 5.2   Employment in new foreign affiliates by Italian firms, 1986–93

1986	64 001
1987	54 647
1988	45 336
1989	55 516
1990	54 417
1991	79 650
1992	83 292
1993	52 299

Source: Database reprint.

One of the most interesting features of this process is a significant increase in the number of international direct investors: by 10 per cent in 1990–91, and by 50 per cent in 1990–93 (Cominotti and Mariotti, 1992; R&P, 1994). About 80 new firms went multinational in the 1992–3 period, adding to the 263 firms or groups operating abroad in 1991. The emergence of new actors, the medium-sized multinational groups, compensated for the slowing down of international growth of big oligopolistic groups at the end of the 1980s and the early 1990s. This trend may be interpreted as a new stage of growth of the firms we have called the 'minor multinationals': those which have been active since the previous periods, mainly in those sectors ('traditional' or 'specialized suppliers') where Italian competitive advantages in international trade are concentrated.

An in-depth inquiry carried out through interviews of 20 highly internationalized medium-sized groups (Onida, 1994) sheds light on the crucial features of these 'new Italian multinationals'. While their growth patterns are differentiated, they are primarily the result of growth of highly specialized and flexible firms, which have strong capacities to adapt imported technology and to develop design, brand and marketing policies. These firms achieved greater economies of scale in the 1980s. As a result, they were able to take advantage of new opportunities offered by the unification of the European market, industrial growth in the Far East (including China) and the opening of Central and Eastern European economies. The expectations of the '1992 effect' seem to have accelerated the choice of internationalization by many small and medium-sized firms, while the opening of the Eastern European bloc created additional incentives for redeployments in low-wage areas.

As a consequence, new sectors became involved in multinational growth. Among traditional industries, the most interesting case is probably the textile and clothing, followed by the food industry.[9] Capital-intensive activities (cement production), scale-intensive ones (transport equipment and household appliances) and mechanical engineering were also involved in relevant international operations, as well as the steel industry, where some of the typical Italian minimills became multinationals.[10] In contrast, a fall in new initiatives can be seen in science-intensive industries, where foreign acquisitions in Italy accelerated (for example, in the pharmaceutical sector), providing additional evidence that they constitute a persistent area of structural weakness in the Italian industrial system.

Parallel changes took place in the geographical distribution of international operations. The predominant feature is the sharp increase in the share of Central and Eastern European countries as destinations of new ventures. Before 1992, this area accounted for less than 2 per cent of total employment abroad, while in the two years considered it represented 28 per cent of the new affiliates and 43 per cent of new employment abroad, according to recent estimations (R&P, 1994). Notwithstanding some new operations in Brazil, the share of Latin America continued to decline, while China attracted new joint ventures. Some 38 per cent of new participations (35 per cent of employees) were located in the European Union.

One of the most interesting consequences of these trends is the increased diversification of motivations of Italian investors abroad. First, a number of technology-oriented operations (usually venture capital or cooperative agreements) were concluded in Europe and the United States in science-intensive sectors. Second, some multinationals tried to develop integrated global strategies (for example Olivetti with its network of alliances, and Benetton with its innovative worldwide product and marketing strategies). Finally, a new wave of cost-saving, export-oriented relocations to low-wage areas affected sectors such as clothing, footwear, household appliances and motor vehicles. Acquisitions were in most cases preferred to internal growth because they allow fast access to distribution networks and brands, and in some cases to subcontracting networks. Alliances, joint ventures and cooperative agreements continued to play a significant complementary role to acquisition.[11]

Finally, we must note that, from a macroeconomic perspective, a primary feature of this period, which positively affected the internationalization process, was a strong real exchange rate of the lira, which appreciated constantly from January 1987 to September 1992, in a context of financial deregulation. The devaluation of the lira weakened the multinational expansion in 1993, but it did not stop the trend.

NEW TRENDS IN THE TEXTILE AND CLOTHING INDUSTRY

The case of the TC industry, usually considered a 'traditional' sector, in which the issue of redeployment is highly sensitive, allows us to better appraise the new patterns of internationalization and their implications.

Until the mid-1980s, the Italian TC industry was only marginally multinationalized, although it was able to keep a large international market share, thanks to highly competitive exports.[12] This situation, consistent with the traditional pattern described earlier, was a kind of Italian paradox: how could an excellent trade performance such as this be maintained in a mature sector, notwithstanding the growing competitive pressure from Asian and other low-wage countries? Why were international relocations so rare, in comparison with other industrial countries? The explanations proposed for this paradox partly coincide with the factors of strength of Italian firms in traditional sectors in general:

1. intensity of labour skills;
2. product differentiation (fashion), design and marketing intensity;
3. process innovation and automation;
4. externalities and domestic subcontracting within industrial districts;
5. low average firm size: the sector was composed of a very large number of small and very small firms.

In particular, the continuous upgrading of production, in order to concentrate on less price-elastic market segments, is one of the most frequently proposed explanations for such export performances. Empirical evidence is not conclusive here, but it is interesting to note the high income-elasticity of Italian exports of clothing to European markets, while their price-elasticity is low (IRS, 1993).

The non-price competitiveness of Italian firms, essentially due to design, product quality, flexibility and marketing, was built on a dual strategy, based on process innovations and technological modernization, on the one hand, and on domestic subcontracting, on the other (Mytelka, 1991). Some authors (for example, Viesti, 1993) argue that process innovations have been so strong that the notion of 'maturity' becomes misleading in this sector. The massive introduction of electronics, in particular, generated gains in productivity and improved the quality of production. Protectionism, through MFA (Multi-Fibre Agreement), against Asian producers was another condition for the effectiveness of this pattern during the first half of the 1980s.

The Benetton case became the successful model within the clothing industry, showing the competitiveness gains deriving from organizational changes (domestic subcontracting, flexible production, franchising network) and from the introduction of information technologies in production, logistics and distribution.

In order to explain the low level of internationalization of Italian firms before the mid-1980s, their small size may be considered a main obstacle to multinational expansion, while the organization of industrial districts and domestic subcontracting networks created competitive advantages dependent on the local economic environment. In the second half of the 1980s, this picture changed rapidly. FDIs from Italian TC firms boomed, reaching a peak in 1991 (see Figure 5.2). The trend is confirmed by data on acquisitions, joint ventures and non-equity cooperative agreements provided by Osservatorio Acquisizioni e Alleanze (Figure 5.3). This acceleration of the international growth of firms was due to a large extent to the clothing industry, where most relocation took place: 60 per cent of the firms operating abroad in 1992 belong to this sector.

How can we explain this important change? Several factors created the favourable conditions for the new trend:

1. In the second half of the 1980s a process of concentration took place, with the growth of medium-sized and large firms and groups, also within industrial districts (Onida *et al.*, 1992); this allowed firms to overcome previous financial and organizational constraints to multinational growth.
2. The real exchange rate appreciated, reducing price competitiveness and weakening Italian firms; their market shares in the largest European countries consequently decreased between 1985 and 1988.[13]

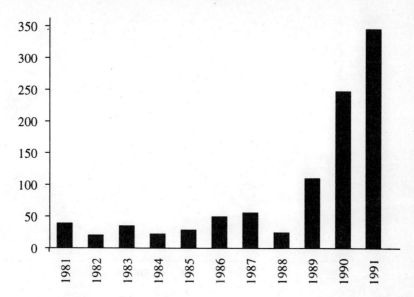

Source: Bank of Italy.

Figure 5.2   Foreign direct investments by Italian textile and clothing firms,
1981–91 (billion lire)

3. Competition increased from both developing-country exporters (mainly
    Asian) and OECD country firms that produced in low-wage areas, through
    affiliates and subcontracting networks (for example, German firms).
4. The prospects and the expectations of relaxed trade barriers (that is, the
    gradual dismantling of the MFA) emphasized this competitive threat.
5. New opportunities were offered by the unification of the European mar-
    ket (for market-oriented, scale-oriented or global operations) and by the
    opening of Central and Eastern European countries (for cost-saving
    operations).

In particular, the opening of Central and Eastern Europe to foreign investments represented a great opportunity to benefit from labour cost advantages
in an area closer to the main final markets compared to most of the developing countries offering similar advantages. This allowed the delocalization not
only of standard products, but also of fashion-intensive product, sensitive to
frequent changes in market trends and constituting the core production for
most Italian firms.

Furthermore, the different impact of process innovation and automation on
total costs in the textile and clothing industries helps to explain why cost-

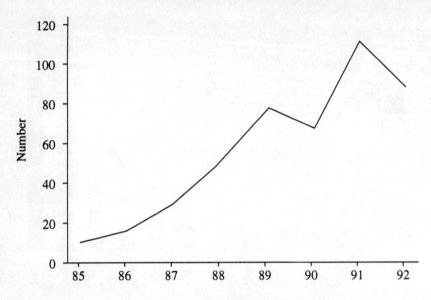

Note: Operations: acquisitions, joint ventures, non-equity agreements.

Source: Osservatorio Acquisizioni e Alleanze (1993).

Figure 5.3   International operations by Italian textile and clothing firms

saving multinational operations have been much less important in the former than in the latter. The higher complexity of technologies, the process innovations and the intensity of know-how incorporated in textile manufacturing explain the tendency to keep production at home in this industry, while redeployment and relocation are increasingly adopted by clothing firms.

The strategic answer to these new conditions has developed along two main axes: (1) acquisitions in OECD countries, especially in Europe,[14] aiming to better penetrate local markets through access to successful brands and distribution networks, and (2) industrial relocations and international subcontracting in low-wage areas (East Asia and China, Central and Eastern Europe, North Africa). The development of international subcontracting networks increasingly complements domestic suppliers in a selective way, as in the case of Benetton and of other groups.

Moreover, we must stress the strategic complementarity of acquisitions and international subcontracting: in some cases one of the main reasons for acquiring a firm, especially in Germany, has been the access to a well-established subcontracting network in Eastern Europe.[15] Employment in subcontracting firms may exceed by eight to ten times the employment within

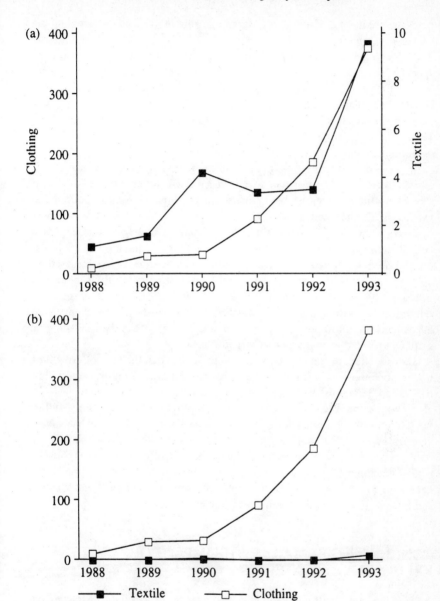

Source: Federtessile (Textile Industry Association).

*Figure 5.4   Italian textile and clothing imports under OPT regulations
              (billion lire)*

the principal itself.[16] This element should be kept in mind when assessing the impact of redeployment.

Cost-saving relocation and international subcontracting also explain the spectacular growth of clothing imports consequent to outward processing trade (OPT) flows (see Figure 5.4), even if OPT regulations are less favourable in Italy than in other OECD countries, such as Germany. Textile OPT imports are much less relevant, but they too have increased sharply since 1992 (Figure 5.4(a)). The number of clothing firms involved in the OPT operations increased from 36 in 1988 to 160 in 1992.

In 1992, however, the total number of international operations decreased, especially in the Far East and in North America, reflecting the impact of recession. But they were stable in the European Union, and they continued to expand in Central and Eastern Europe, where a growing number of new investors implemented cost-saving, export-oriented strategies (Osservatorio Acquisizioni e Alleanze, 1993). Following the sharp devaluation of the lira at the end of 1992, Italian TC imports from EU countries in 1993 decreased by 6.3 per cent. However, in the same period, imports from non-OECD countries increased by 11.4 per cent, reflecting the persisting trend of cost-saving relocation and international subcontracting (IRS, 1993). The exchange rate once again was an important macroeconomic factor, but not the prevailing or sufficient reason for multinational expansion.[17]

One key effect of the recent relocation process is that the path of growth of international competitiveness of the firms and that of the employment within the Italian TC industry diverge. The improvements in the first, in fact, go along with a trend towards a reduction in employment levels in Italy within the TC industry, as provisional analysis shows (IRS, 1993). Such a divergence, however, does not necessarily imply a globally negative balance of relocations. If we take into account their indirect effects on the exports of textile machinery, technology and services, and more generally the flows generated by the growth of host country markets (the Far East and Central and Eastern Europe), the overall evaluation can be reversed.

CONCLUDING REMARKS: THE IMPACT OF RELOCATION STRATEGIES

A diversified pattern of internationalization is under way in Italy, characterized by the internationalization of new sectors, where Italian firms traditionally have competitive advantages but limited their internationalization to exports, while the 'oligopolistic heart' concentrated in scale-intensive sectors.

This evolution, well illustrated by the case of the textile and clothing industry, does not necessarily imply a sharp reduction of the specific locational advantages of Italy, or a crisis of the model of industrial districts. Rather, it is the consequence of a set of changes in the macroeconomic context, in light of expectations of reduced protectionism and of competitive threats and opportunities created by the growing integration of the world economy. It is also due to a process of concentration from which new enterprises and groups have emerged, as well as new organizational patterns and corporate strategies.

As we pointed out in the introduction, different types of foreign involvement of firms have different impacts on the home economy. The fact that multinational strategies of Italian firms have been primarily market-oriented implies that they have been complementary to, rather than substitutes for, exports. This feature has deeply and positively affected their impact on growth, employment and trade balance. Only in recent years have different types of motivations emerged. During the 1980s, some of the major groups invested in technology-oriented ventures. In the early 1990s, the opening of Central and Eastern European countries offered to numerous emerging MNFs the opportunity for cost-saving relocations, mainly in the very sectors, traditional or mechanical, in which Italian firms held competitive advantages.

In this respect, new relocation strategies in Central and Eastern Europe could differently affect income, employment and trade flows *vis-à-vis* market-oriented strategies, as we have illustrated in the case of the textile and clothing industry. A negative impact on the trade balance and employment in Italy is possible. However, it should be noted that (1) mixed forms and motivations are frequent in the real world, and (2) they can *evolve*, for instance from cost-saving to increasingly market-oriented or global strategies. This is still the case of many affiliates in the Far East, which were initially oriented to re-export to the home country, and subsequently have been increasingly oriented to the expanding local markets. The same evolution can be expected in the future in Central and Eastern Europe.

As we have pointed out, a feature peculiar to Italian multinational growth is the high propensity to promote joint ventures and cooperative agreements. Their impact seems largely positive in terms of technological and organizational learning by Italian firms; a mechanism of 'learning by cooperating' has been illustrated in the case of the penetration of Italian firms in developing areas (Balcet, 1988). Moreover, alliances promoted by big groups often create production and R&D capabilities in Italy, with positive spillovers to the smaller firms, especially in the north-western part of the country.[18] An interesting point is that alliances often create two-way flows of resources, knowledge and skills.

The impact of the internationalization process on the development of technological capabilities in Italy may be considered positive, thanks to the creation of scale economies in innovative activities and to the (still limited) cases of international operations oriented to the acquisition of technology abroad. On the other hand, a negative impact on technological capabilities has been observed in the case of some recent foreign acquisitions in Italy, especially in the pharmaceutical industry, where a strategy of acquisitions of market shares was coupled with the objective of stopping competition from Italian research laboratories (Mariotti, 1993).

Recent tendencies of international growth thus illustrate once more the central issue of the structural weakness of the Italian industrial system, especially in technology-intensive sectors. Such areas of competitive weakness are also a consequence of the lack of industrial policy, and especially of R&D and technology policies capable of narrowing the gap with other industrial countries. In the Italian case, the indirect impact of such policies on the multinational growth of industrial firms could be much more important than direct incentives or regulations.

NOTES

1. The author wishes to thank Michel Delapierre, of FORUM-CEREM, Université de Paris X, for his useful comments and suggestions, as well as the participants of the conference held on 9–10 June 1994 at the Sorbonne. Financial support by the Italian Ministry of University and Research is acknowledged.
2. See Michalet (1993) for a discussion of this notion.
3. See J.L. Mucchielli and P. Saucier, 'European Industrial Relocations in Low-Wage Countries: Policy and Theory Debates', in this volume.
4. Pirelli opened its first foreign plant in Spain in 1902. Other early Italian multinationals include Fiat, Olivetti, Martini and Buitoni.
5. A relevant exception is given by the Miroglio textile group, which in the 1970s invested in Mediterranean countries such as Greece, Turkey and Tunisia. In the same period SGS (STET-IRI group, state-owned) created export-oriented affiliates in Singapore and Malaysia for the production of electronic components.
6. Examples include Ferrero, Buitoni, Martini & Rossi, Cinzano, Merloni, Miroglio, GFT and Benetton. Also the highly diversified Ferruzzi group went multinational during the 1970s.
7. According to REPRINT database. Information on the total number of affiliates, their sales and employees is not available for the period before 1985, while data of FDI flows are incomplete and misleading.
8. The number of divestments in 1992–3 has not been estimated.
9. Noteworthy cases are represented by the Ferrero, Barilla and Parmalat groups.
10. The most important case is represented by the Lucchini group.
11. In 1991, about 37 per cent of total employment abroad was in non-majority-controlled affiliates (Cominotti and Mariotti, 1992).
12. Italy is the world's second largest exporter both of textiles and of clothing; its shares in world exports accounted for 8 per cent in the first and for 9.6 per cent in the second in 1991.
13. During this period, the Italian share of total imports decreased from 32 per cent to 21 per cent in France, from 21 per cent to 17 per cent in Germany, and from 11 per cent to 9 per cent in the UK (Viesti, 1993).
14. Germany accounted for about 20 per cent of the employment created abroad by the Italian TC firms in 1992 (REPRINT database).

15. The most relevant example is the acquisition of Hugo Boss by Marzotto in 1991.
16. In the case of Benetton, 45 000 to 50 000 jobs are estimated in domestic and international subcontracting, as opposed to only 3500 within the group itself.
17. This tends to confirm the observations developed by Rainelli (1990) with reference to the FDIs in the United States.
18. Examples are the joint ventures created by Olivetti and Fiat with Japanese partners.

BIBLIOGRAPHY

Balcet, G. (1981), *Industrializzazione, multinazionali e dipendenza tecnologica*, Turin: Loescher.
Balcet, G. (1988), 'Italian Non-equity Ventures Abroad', in F. Onida and G. Viesti (eds), *The Italian Multinationals*, London: Croom Helm.
Balcet, G. (1990), *Joint venture multinazionali. Alleanze tra imprese, competizione e potere di mercato nell'economia mondiale*, Milan: Etas Libri.
Cominotti, R. and S. Mariotti (1990), *Italia multinazionale 1990*, Milan: Etas Libri.
Cominotti, R. and S. Mariotti (1992), *Italia multinazionale 1992*, Milan: Etas Libri.
Forte, A. and G. Viesti (1992), 'Il settore tessile-abbigliamento', in Centro Studi Confindustria, *L'impresa motore dello sviluppo* (Vol II: 'La dimensione internazionale dello sviluppo'), Rome: SIPI.
IRS (1993), *Struttura produttiva e distributiva nell'internazionalizzazione dei settori maturi*, report to CNR, Progetto Finalizzato 'Servizi e strutture per l'internazionalizzazione delle imprese', Milan.
Mariotti, S. (1993), 'Internazionalizzazione e fattori tecnologici nell'industria italiana', *Economia e politica industriale*, 79.
Michalet, C.A. (1993), *Globalisation, attractivité et politiques industrielles*, Paris: LAREA-CEREM.
Mytelka, L. (1991), 'Technological Change and the Global Relocation of Production in Textile and Clothing', *Studies in Political Economy*, 36.
Onida, F. (1994), *La crescita multinazionale dei gruppi italiani di medio-grande dimensione. Rapporto di sintesi*, CESPRI Working Papers, Milan: Università Bocconi.
Onida, F. and G. Viesti (eds) (1988), *The Italian Multinationals*, London: Croom Helm.
Onida, F. and G. Viesti and A.M. Falzoni (1992), *I distretti industriali: crisi o evoluzione?*, Milan: EGEA.
Osservatorio Acquisizioni e Alleanze (1993), *Acquisizioni, accordi e joint venture nell'industria tessile/abbigliamento, 1985–92*, Modena.
Pavitt, K. (1984), 'Sectoral Patterns of Technical Change: Towards a Taxonomy and a Theory', *Research Policy*, 13.
Rainelli, M. (1990), *Les investissements étrangers aux Etats-Unis*, Paris: Economica.
R&P Ricerche e Progetti (1994), *Italia multinazionale 1994. Gli investimenti diretti italiani all'estero ed esteri in Italia nel biennio 1992–1993*, Rapporto preliminare al CNEL, Rome.
Viesti, G. (1993), 'Multinational Strategies in a Mature Business: the International Expansion of the Italian Textile–Clothing Industry', EIBA Conference, Lisbon, December.

6. US direct investment abroad and US exports in the manufacturing sector: some empirical results based on cross-sectional analysis[1]

Edward M. Graham

INTRODUCTION

The effects of foreign direct investment (FDI) on the home nation is a topic that has long been of interest to policy makers and to certain constituencies. Nonetheless, no comprehensive theory of these effects has emerged, at least certainly not in the form of a body of theory or empirical evidence that would enable evaluation of these effects on overall national welfare. Rather, much of the policy debate has centred around the concerns and claims of individual constituencies. In the United States, for example, the organized labour movement has since the 1950s held that outward FDI is tantamount to export of employment.[2] This belief was one premise behind organized labour's opposition to the NAFTA during the last half of 1993: it was felt by the major US labour unions that NAFTA would facilitate large-scale relocation of productive capacity from the United States to Mexico. This, in the eyes of the unions, would have resulted in transfer of employment opportunities to Mexico from the United States, with adverse welfare implications for the US worker.

The position of organized labour has as an unstated premise that outward FDI and exports are substitutes rather than complements. We shall in what follows abbreviate the hypothesis that outward FDI and exports are substitutes as 'hypothesis S' and that they are complements 'hypothesis C'. Let us note that in equilibrium a net increase or decrease in exports should have no long-term effect on overall levels of employment. (Transitional effects can, of course, occur if a decrease in exports reduces aggregate demand below full employment levels.) But when spokespersons for the labour movement (including, during the NAFTA debate, H. Ross Perot) claim that outward FDI will lead to job loss, these claims might be taken as shorthand for a more defensible and less simplistic position, such as that outward FDI reduces the demand for exports, and thus causes export-generating industries to shrink relative to the rest of the economy. Workers thusly displaced from these industries must relocate to industries which are import-competing or are in the non-traded goods sectors. In the United States and other advanced countries, these latter industries exhibit a lower marginal productivity of labour than export industries, and hence lower hourly wages. Thus the hourly incomes of relocated workers are reduced by the relocation and the interests of the workers represented by us – the labour unions – are adversely affected by outward FDI.[3] This restatement of the labour claim is not offered in defence of labour's position on outward FDI; rather, the point is simply that whether or not the claim is true largely rests on whether one accepts hypothesis C or hypothesis S.

This issue has long concerned empiricists. In both the United States and in the United Kingdom during the late 1960s, for example, there was a period of official concern over the effects of outward FDI on the overall balance of payments on a current account basis. Central to this issue was the question of the impact of outward FDI on trade flows, but the effects of financial flows were of concern as well. Two major studies of the issue were prepared at that time, and these studies as well as more contemporary ones are reviewed in the section that follows.

The remainder of this chapter is divided into three sections. The first of these is, as just noted, a review of the major empirical studies published to date on the issue of whether FDI and exports are substitutes or complements. The second presents new findings on this issue based on recent research conducted at the Institute for International Economics. The final section is a brief discussion of the implications of all these findings.

EMPIRICAL STUDIES ON THE RELATIONSHIPS BETWEEN EXPORTS AND FDI

In this section we examine empirical evidence as to whether FDI and exports are substitutes or complements. We shall see that most studies of this relationship tend to indicate that the relationship is positive, that is, that more FDI is associated with more, rather than less, exports.

In both the United States and in the United Kingdom during the late 1960s, for example, there was official concern over the effects of outward FDI on the overall balance of payments on a current account basis. Central to this concern was the question of the impact of outward FDI on trade flows. (But the effects of financial flows were of concern as well.) In response to the concern, two of the most careful studies of these effects (Reddaway *et al.*; Hufbauer and Alder, 1968) were carried out under official auspices. These remain among the best empirical studies of the effects of FDI.

Using somewhat different methodologies and coverage, the studies arrived at roughly similar conclusions: if future cash flows are not discounted, the overall long-term effects of outward FDI on the balance of payments are positive. That the effects of financial flows alone are positive should not be a surprise to anyone. This is because a firm assumes an investment undertaking of any sort on the expectation that the investment will yield a positive return for the firm's shareholders, and ultimately that return must be reflected in dividend payments by the parent organization to those shareholders. Thus, to the extent that the shareholders of the firm are nationals of the home country, the returns accruing to the foreign affiliates of a firm must ultimately accrue to home country nationals funded through the parent organization.

However, both studies also indicated that outward FDI tended to stimulate exports (mostly of capital goods and intermediate goods) without a stimulating effect on imports of equal magnitude. In spite of this, both studies found that new outward FDI projects tend to generate net cash outflows during their early years, so that on a balance of payments basis, a new FDI undertaking creates negative net cash flows for the home economy during the years immediately following the initial investment. However, with time, cash flows turn positive as the investment matures. The calculated 'crossover' point for the average foreign direct investment undertaking – that is, the elapsed time for which the cumulative effect on the balance of payments was zero – was estimated to be about 14 years by Reddaway *et al.* for the United Kingdom and about nine years for the United States by Hufbauer and Adler.

Later studies yielded results generally consistent with the Reddaway *et al.* and the Hufbauer and Adler findings. Bergsten *et al.* (1978), for example, found that the growth of US affiliates abroad had a significantly positive effect on the growth of exports of the US parent firms. Lipsey and Weiss (1981) also found that US outward FDI was associated with increased US exports, even after controlling for other effects (firm size, expenditures on R&D and marketing, and so on) but that the production of US affiliates abroad substituted for exports to the host country of third countries. A later study by Lipsey and Weiss (1984) employed unpublished US Commerce Department data at the level of the individual firm to examine foreign production and US exports in 14 industries in the manufacturing sector. The authors reported positive and significant relationships in 11 of these industries.

A study of the effects of offshore production of Swedish-owned firms upon the exports of manufactured goods of the home country (Sweden) was published by Blomström *et al.* (1988). Sweden is an advanced industrial economy located in close proximity to other advanced economies, and most of Sweden's direct investment is located either elsewhere in Western Europe or in North America. Blomström *et al.* found that increases in the production of affiliates of Swedish firms are positively related to increases in exports for the seven industrial categories studied. Also they showed that there was no propensity for this positive relationship to change as the foreign production grew.

Pearce (1990) followed an approach similar to that of Blomström *et al.* noted above. Pearce examined the exports and foreign production of 458 of the world's largest industrial multinational enterprises (MNEs) for the year 1982. His findings are that increases in foreign production are generally positively related to increases in exports. This was found to be especially true for intra-firm (as opposed to inter-firm) exports, which tends to underscore the importance of vertical relationships among the various international affiliates of this sample of MNEs.

Buigues and Jacquemin (1994) examine the issue of complementarity versus substitution between FDI and exports with respect to both US and Japanese direct investment in the European Union. The basic assumption is that, if share of the total exports from each of these countries going to the EU is positively related to the share of FDI going to the EU after controlling for three additional variables, the relationship is complementary. The three additional variables are intra-EC non-tariff trade barriers, rate of growth of final demand and the EC's sectoral specialization, all of which are assumed to be positively related to FDI. Buigues and Jacquemin's sample is pooled cross-sectionally across seven industries (six for the United States) and ten years. They find the relationship between FDI and exports to be complementary for both the United States and Japan.

Industry Canada (1994) finds that FDI from Canada is associated with increases of both Canada's exports and imports. The same finding is reported with respect to foreign direct investment in Canada. The findings are aggregate and (apparently) based on time series analysis. Estimates are made of the elasticities of exports and imports with respect to Canada's outward investment and the latter are higher than the former. These estimated elasticities of trade with respect to investment stocks (see Industry Canada, 1994, Table 7) are not, however, controlled for the influence of factors such as economic activity, comparative costs or other variables that could affect the outcomes.

Thus all of the studies cited conclude that the relationship between FDI and exports is positive. As is described in the next section, the Institute for International Economics (IIE) results point to a consistent result, but with some twists.

THE IIE STUDY OF RELATIONSHIPS BETWEEN FDI AND EXPORTS

Most of the studies cited above could be criticized for ignoring the possible effects of simultaneous determination of FDI and exports, which could be causing a spurious correlation between these two and hence lead to an erroneous interpretation of complementarity. This would be the case if both FDI and exports were responding to a common, unspecified causal element. For example, suppose that size of market alone determined both US direct investment abroad and exports – that is, both US exporters and direct investors put their energies into developing large markets and ignored small ones. Then simply to show that a large share of US exports was associated with markets where the share of US direct investment was also large would not be sufficient to show that US exports and US direct investment abroad were complementary. They could still be substitutes once the effects of market size were taken into account.[4] Likewise, elements of simultaneous determination could distort results of studies based on differences across industries.

Thus the effort was made in the results reported in this section to remove factors that might simultaneously determine US exports and US FDI and then to examine the relationship between these two latter variables with the source of the simultaneity bias removed. Specifically, a gravity model was used first to estimate the effects of three variables deemed to be very important determinants of both FDI and exports. The three variables chosen were (1) per capita income in each national market (for which GDP per capita was used), (2) total size of market (for which total population was used), and (3) distance from the market to the United States (for which the great circle distance from the economic center of the United States – located close to Indianapolis – to the relevant national capital was used).[5] The gravity specification was multiplicative; that is, the assumed relationship was

$$\log y = \log(C x_1^\alpha x_2^\beta x_3^\delta \varepsilon)$$

where y is the dependent variable (FDI or exports), the xs are the three independent variables, and ε is an error term (assumed, as usual, to be log normally distributed with mean 1). The expected signs of α and β are positive (both US exports and US FDI would be expected to be positive functions of per capita income and market size); the expected sign of δ is negative for US exports (the further the market is from the United States, the higher the transport costs, and hence the less likely that firms would export from the United States) but indeterminate for direct investment (for example, if direct investment were to be a substitute for US exports, then arguably the substitution would be most likely in those markets for which transactions costs associated with exports were high, and the expected sign of δ would be positive; but one can envisage circumstances where direct investment would occur in geographically proximate markets: see, for example, Graham, 1996).

The residuals from each of the two estimations (exports and FDI as a function of the three variables) were then regressed upon one another. The presumption was that, if the gravity models have succeeded in removing simultaneity bias, then any correlation of the residuals would reflect some other causal relationship between FDI and exports, such as that due to sourcing substitution or to complementarities in production or distribution and marketing. A positive correlation coefficient would suggest complementarity and a negative coefficient substitutability.

Also performed were similar two-stage analysis between US imports and US direct investment abroad. The gravity analyses were performed using aggregate manufacturing sector data (that is, total US exports of manufactured goods and the total stock of US direct investment abroad in manufacturing; this latter was meant to act as a surrogate for total activity of US-controlled firms in the relevant market) pertaining to 40 individual countries that were destinations of both US exports and US direct investment. These 40 countries accounted in 1991 for over 96 per cent of the stock of US direct investment abroad and over 95 per cent of US manufactured goods exports. The analyses were run for three different years (1991, 1988 and 1983) and the results were roughly consistent for each year. Only the results for 1991 are reported here. Separate analyses were performed using (1) the data for all 40 countries (reported in the tables below as 'World'), (2) only those countries located in Europe, (3) only those countries located in the western hemisphere, and (4) only those countries located in East Asia. It should be noted that some countries in the sample are not in any of Europe, the western hemisphere or East Asia; thus the 'World' sample contains more observations than the sum of those in each of the three identified regions.

Summary results of the gravity analyses are given in Table 6.1 below. As can be seen, the specification led to overall good fits for the whole sample ('World') and for the sub-samples subsuming Europe and the western hemisphere: for all of these, the F-tests were significant at the 99+ per cent confidence level, and the R^2s are all in excess of 50 per cent. Thus it would appear that the three independent variables – income per capita, population and distance – 'explain' fairly robustly cross-country patterns of US exports, imports and outward direct investment in the manufacturing sector. The overall fit for the East Asian sub-sample is substantially less good than for the other two sub-samples, with the fit being particularly poor for US imports, where the F-test is significant at only the 90 per cent level and the R^2 statistic suggests that only 31 per cent of the total variance of the dependent variable is 'explained' by the three independent variables. For US exports and US direct investment to Asia, the overall

Table 6.1　Gravity model results, 1991

Dependent variable	F-test	Coefficients of independent variables (standard error in parentheses)			R^2
		Income/cap	Population	Distance	
US exports					
World	***	0.66 (0.11)	0.11 (0.10)	−0.38 (0.22)	0.54
Europe	***	0.29 (0.88)	0.60 (0.64)	−1.56 (2.3)	0.63
W. hemisphere	***	0.46 (0.61)	0.41 (0.42)	−0.98 (0.31)	0.93
East Asia	**	0.89 (0.50)	−0.23 (0.46)	−0.77 (2.4)	0.40
US imports					
World	***	0.94 (0.08)	−0.00 (0.07)	0.27 (0.16)	0.80
Europe	***	0.82 (0.15)	0.27 (0.13)	−1.33 (1.2)	0.87
W. hemisphere	***	1.15 (0.20)	−0.24 (0.19)	−0.14 (0.26)	0.93
East Asia	*	0.53 (0.26)	−0.07 (0.14)	−0.61 (2.1)	0.31
US direct investment abroad					
World	***	0.92 (0.14)	0.17 (0.13)	−0.77 (0.29)	0.60
Europe	***	0.86 (0.47)	0.80 (0.39)	−9.57 (3.6)	0.66
W. hemisphere	***	1.31 (0.22)	0.10 (0.20)	−0.31 (0.28)	0.96
East Asia	**	0.93 (0.30)	−0.15 (0.16)	1.09 (2.5)	0.49

Note:　*** significant at 99+%; ** significant at 95%; * significant at 90%.

fit is better, but the F-test is still only significant at the 95 per cent level and the R^2 statistics indicate that the relationships 'explain' less than 50 per cent of the total variance of the dependent variables.

The coefficients on the independent variables are mostly of the expected sign (recalling that the expected sign of the coefficient of the distance variable is indeterminate in the investment equation), but in many cases are not statistically significant. There are a few anomalies. The biggest of these is that the coefficient of the size of market variable (as measured by population) is often not of the expected sign but also is not significant (except for US direct investment in Europe, where the sign is as expected; see below). A second anomaly is that none of the coefficients of the independent variables for the US exports to Europe are significant, even though the overall relationship is. This suggests the possibility of multicollinearity among the independent variables and hence that additional tests for joint significance of the three variables would be appropriate (for example, calculation of joint confidence intervals for the variables taken two at a time).

It is perhaps noteworthy that the coefficient on the income per capita variable is highly significant for US imports with the expected (positive) sign for the 'World' sample and for all three of the sub-samples. Thus, *inter alia*, the 'pauper labour' argument so often heard these days in the United States is not supported by this result. This is because US imports are associated with high-income – hence high-wage – source countries, not low-wage countries.

Likewise, the coefficient for income per capita is highly significant for US direct investment abroad with the exception of Europe, suggesting that the 'runaway plant' argument is not supported by the analysis. That Europe is an exception – that for Europe the income per capita coefficient is not significant – may be due to the fact that US firms have concentrated a disproportionate amount of direct investment in the United Kingdom, a country whose per capita income is not high relative to the rest of Europe. However, the UK per capita income is high by world standards and, hence, this concentration probably does not distort the results for the 'World' sample. The variance in per capita incomes in Europe is in fact not as great as in the other regions and perhaps this is the reason why, for Europe alone, market size appears to be a more important determinant of direct investment than does per capita income: most European nations are in the 'advanced industrial' category and, given this, it would seem reasonable to expect that those nations with large populations would receive more US direct investment abroad in the manufacturing sector than nations with smaller populations.

It is worth noting that the first stage results were the most robust for the western hemisphere. For this sub-sample, the R^2 statistic was in excess of 0.9 for all three dependent variables, suggesting that over 90 per cent of the variance in the dependent variables was 'explained' by the independent variables.

Table 6.2   *Regressions of residuals on residuals of gravity equations, 1991*

	Coefficient	Std error	Significance
US FDI and US exports			
World	0.486	0.207	**
Europe	0.479	0.126	***
W. hemisphere	−0.866	0.253	**
East Asia	0.524	0.228	**
US FDI and US imports			
World	0.282	0.138	**
Europe	0.174	0.080	*
W. hemisphere	−0.392	0.303	n.s.
East Asia	0.208	0.261	n.s.

Notes: *** significant at 99+ %; ** significant at 95%; * significant at 90%; n.s. not significant.

Table 6.2 gives the results of the second-stage regressions. As can be seen, the relationship between the remaining unexplained variation in US outward direct investment in the manufacturing sector and the remaining unexplained variation in US exports of manufactured goods for the 'World' sample was positive and significant at the 95 per cent level. The relationship between these variables was also positive and significant for both the Europe and the East Asia sub-samples, but it was negative and significant for the western hemisphere sub-sample. These results suggest that US outward direct investment and exports are complements globally and in the European and East Asian regions, but that they are substitutes in the western hemisphere. We return to the western hemisphere result shortly.

The results of second-stage regressions of the relationship between US outward direct investment in the manufacturing sector and US imports of manufactured goods are also indicated in Table 6.2. The coefficient is positive but only significant at a 95 per cent level for the 'World' sample. The coefficients are not significant with respect to either the East Asian sub-sample or the western hemisphere sub-sample, albeit that the signs of the coefficients are consistent with those reported above for outward direct investment and exports. For the European sub-sample the coefficient is positive and marginally significant. Thus the residual relationship between FDI and imports is weak, if there is one at all.

Why are the signs of the coefficient for the western hemisphere different from those of the remainder of the sample? The author's guess is that these results are a fall-out from the import substitution policies that were pursued throughout much of Latin America during the 1970s and early 1980s, whereby multinational corporations were often induced to establish local production facilities that would then operate behind protectionist walls and enjoy quasi-monopolistic status in the relevant market. Because such operations were frequently inefficient, most governments that pursued such policies have in recent years begun a process of policy reform. Nonetheless, the legacy of import substitution seems to have survived into the early 1990s.

This possibility – that the negative relationship between US direct investment and US exports in the western hemisphere is the legacy of import substitution programmes – is reinforced by the results of running the gravity model for the hemisphere with Canada removed from the sub-sample of countries. When this is done, the coefficient on the second-stage regression for the direct investment abroad and US exports variables becomes greater in magnitude (but remains negative: it goes from –0.866 to –0.955) and becomes more significant (it is now significant at the 99+% level of confidence).

Having noted this, however, it is important to note the fact that the coefficient for the relationship between US outward direct investment and US imports for the western hemisphere sub-sample is negative and not significant. This result runs contrary to the often made claim that multinational firms are transferring production to low-wage areas south of the (US) border in order to service the domestic US market. If this claim were true, one would expect that this coefficient would be positive and significant. Much the same statement can be made about East Asia. For this sub-sample the sign of the coefficient is positive (which, *ceteris paribus*, would support the transfer of production story) but it is not statistically significant.

What the results do seem to support is the following: that there is, overall, a positive relationship between US outward direct investment and US exports in the manufacturing sector. There is also weak evidence for a positive relationship between US outward direct investment and US imports in this sector. Thus direct investment seems to be trade-enhancing, but the story is much more one linking direct investment to exports than to imports.

Given the last statement, an effort was made to calculate directly what was the elasticity of US exports to US outward direct investment and likewise the elasticity of US imports to outward direct investment in the year 1991. The specification for this calculation was

$$\frac{X_{US \to i}}{Y_i} = A \frac{DI_{US \to i}^{\alpha}}{Y_i} \frac{MM_i^{\beta}}{Y_i}$$

The idea of this specification was that the US share of imports of national income of country i (the dependent variable) is a function of the ratio of the US stock of direct investment in the same country (used as a proxy for activity of US-controlled firms in the economy of country i) as a share of the national income and of the average propensity of the country to import merchandise (MM_i/Y_i). (Shares of national income were used primarily to remove heteroscedasticity from the specification.) The results are reported on Table 6.3 where, again, the sample was broken down into the world, Europe, western hemisphere and East Asia. The results are generally consistent with the gravity model results. For example, the results are, for both sets of specifications, stronger for US exports and US outward direct investment than for US imports and outward direct investment. Also the elasticity of US exports with respect to direct investment is calculated to be positive and significant for the world sample and for the European and East Asian sub-samples, consistent with the gravity results (although for the elasticity calculations, the coefficient for direct investment for Europe is only significant at a 90 per cent level of confidence). The results for the western hemisphere elasticity calculation are not consistent with the gravity specification, however. Consistency would demand that the calculated elasticity of US exports with respect to outward direct investment for the western hemisphere be negative, whereas the result is a positive (but statistically insignificant) elas-

Table 6.3   Elasticity of US exports and imports with respect to outward direct investment (manufacturing sector, 1991)

	α	significance	β	significance
US exports				
World	0.416	***	0.344	***
Europe	0.238	*	0.697	**
W. hemisphere	0.066	n.s.	1.083	**
East Asia	0.320	**	0.693	***
US imports				
World	0.316	**	0.888	***
Europe	0.180	n.s.	0.235	***
W. hemisphere	0.414	n.s.	1.306	n.s.
East Asia	−0.08	n.s.	1.742	***

Notes:
F-test indicates that overall relationship is significant at 99% confidence level for all specifications.
*** significant at 99+ %; ** significant at 95%; * significant at 90%; n.s. not significant.

ticity. A Chow test reveals that the combined significance of the regional sub-samples exceeds that of the 'World' sample, and hence that the elasticities do differ from region to region.

CONCLUSIONS

The empirical evidence presented in this chapter is generally consistent with that of earlier studies which we have reviewed. The evidence tends to support US outward direct investment and US exports in manufacturing being complements and not substitutes. An exception may be the western hemisphere nations, which in this sample are predominantly developing or newly indus-trializing ones (with the exception of Canada). For the western hemisphere nations, the results of the IIE study were inconclusive. The sign of the relevant coefficient from the gravity model specification was negative, con-sistent with a substitutive relationship, and was statistically significant at a 95 per cent level of confidence but not at a 99 per cent level. The estimated elasticity of US exports with respect to direct investment in the western hemisphere was, however, positive, consistent with a complementary rela-tionship, but was statistically not significant.

The analyses presented in this chapter are not supportive of the claim that US direct investment abroad is associated with loss of US jobs or deindustrialization of the United States. In particular, the analyses do not support contemporary variants of the 'pauper labour' hypothesis (for example, that US workers are facing competition from nations where workers are highly productive but are paid low wages). Indeed, US outward direct investment in the manufacturing sector, US imports of manufactured goods and US exports of manufactured goods all seem to be positively related to the per capita income of the recipient (or source) nations.

NOTES

1. The author is grateful to Professor J. David Richardson for numerous helpful suggestions regarding methodology and to Ms. Ming Wah Lam for research assistance.
2. The best statement of the position of the US AFL–CIO on outward direct investment remains that of Goldfinger (1971), according to whom, 'The mushrooming growth of US-based multinational companies – with plants, offices, sales agencies, laboratories, licensing, patent, and other joint venture arrangements in as many as forty or more countries – is a new factor of accelerating importance in the deterioration of the US position in world economic relationships.'
3. Somewhat surprisingly perhaps, nowhere does there appear (to this author's knowledge) such a statement by the organized labour movement, even though the nuances contained therein would greatly enhance the credibility of the labour position.
4. That is, in any market, an increase in FDI could at the margin reduce US exports.
5. One problem arises with this last variable with respect to Canada and Mexico, because much commerce between the United States and each of these nations originates very close to the border and hence the distance measure might overstate the effective distance; however, as reported later in the text, the variable did not appear significant with respect to the estimations for the North American nations.

REFERENCES

Bergsten, C. Fred, Thomas Horst and Theodore H. Moran (1978), *American Multinationals and American Interests*, Washington, D.C.: Brookings Institution.

Blomström, M., R.E. Lipsey and K. Kulchyck (1988), 'US and Swedish Direct Investment and Exports', in Robert E. Baldwin (ed.), *Trade Policy Issues and Empirical Analysis*, Chicago: University of Chicago Press, for the National Bureau of Economic Research.

Buigues, Pierre and Alexis Jacquemin (1994), 'Foreign Direct Investment and Exports to the European Community', in Mark Mason and Dennis Encarnation (eds), *Does Ownership Matter? Japanese Multinationals in Europe*, Oxford and New York: Oxford University Press.

Goldfinger, Nat (1971), 'A Labour View of Foreign Investment and Trade Issues', Commission on International Trade and Investment Policy, *United States International Economic Policy in an Interdependent World*, Washington, D.C.: US Government Printing Office.

Graham, Edward M. (1996), *Global Corporations and National Governments: Are Changes Needed in the International Economic and Political Order in Light of the*

Globalization of Business?, Washington, D.C.: The Institute for International Economics.

Hufbauer, Gary C. and F.M. Adler (1968), *Overseas Manufacturing Investment and the Balance of Payments*, US Treasury Department Tax Policy Research Study No. 1, Washington, D.C.: US Government Printing Office.

Industry Canada (Micro-Economic Policy Branch) (1994), 'Canadian-Based Multinational Enterprises: An Analysis of Activities and Performance', in Steven Globerman (ed.), *Canadian Direct Investment Abroad*, Calgary: The University of Calgary Press.

Lipsey, R.E. and M.Y. Weiss (1981), 'Foreign Production and Exports in Manufacturing Industries', *Review of Economics and Statistics*, 63, pp. 488–94.

Lipsey, R.E. and M.Y. Weiss (1984), 'Foreign Production and Exports of Individual Firms', *Review of Economics and Statistics*, 66, pp. 304–8.

Pearce, R.D. (1990), 'Overseas Production and Exporting Performance: Some Further Investigations', University of Reading Discussion Papers in International Investment and Business Studies, No. 135.

Reddaway, W.B., J.O.N. Perkins, S.J. Potter and C.T. Potter (1967), *Effects of U.K. Direct Investment Overseas*, London: HMSO.

7. Strategies of Japanese multinationals: changes in the locational importance of Asia, the EC and North America

Yoko Sazanami and Wong Yu Ching

INTRODUCTION

Japanese foreign direct investment (FDI) abroad experienced an upsurge after 1985, the major factor being the rapid appreciation of the yen, which accelerated Japanese firms' move towards international production. A strong yen lowered the cost competitiveness of Japanese exports, and Japanese manufacturing firms responded by relocating their production to countries with lower wage costs. At the same time, the strength of its currency also reduced the cost of foreign venture for Japanese firms.

The growth in Japanese FDI outflows reached its peak in 1989, and the annual outflow declined for three consecutive years in the period 1990–92. In general, the decline in outflow could be attributed to the poor performance of firms in the growth recession largely caused by the 'bursting of the bubble economy' in Japan. However, while the share of Japanese FDI flows to North America and the EC had declined, the share of Japanese FDI received by Asia[1] had recorded a positive growth in the same period. The question is, why has Japanese FDI outflow to Asia been least affected by the downturn in the Japanese economy?

This chapter aims to provide some explanations for the observed differences in the development of Japanese FDI in Asia, the EC and North America, through an econometric analysis on the determinants of Japanese FDI in the three regions. We focus on the developments in the second half of the 1980s and the changes in the 'post-bubble period'. Instead of the usual country-based analysis, we compare Japanese firms' direct investments in the above three regions, because of the greater interdependent economic relationships of host countries in their respective regions, and the growing importance of the above three regions in the globalization strategies of Japanese firms.[2] The second section below reviews the pattern of Japanese FDI in Asia, the EC and North America in the 1980s, and changes that have occurred since 1990. The third section provides a brief literature review on the determinants of FDI. The specification and results of our econometric analysis are presented in the fourth section. The fifth section discusses the findings and implications obtained from our model and in the last section we provide concluding remarks.

TRENDS OF JAPANESE FDI SINCE THE 1980s

Japanese FDI flows abroad had gained unprecedented growth in the second half of the 1980s. As a result of the sharp appreciation of the yen since September 1985, with the yen appreciating by 41.5 per cent between 1985 and 1986, Japanese FDI outflows increased rapidly, from $US12 billion in 1985 to $US22 billion in 1986.[3] Thereafter, Japanese FDI outflows to the world were maintained at a high average growth rate of 45 per cent per annum in the period 1987–9, as compared with the average yearly growth rate of 21.3 per cent in the first half of the 1980s (1980–84). Annual outflows reached their peak at $US67.5 billion in 1989.

However, FDI outflows declined for three consecutive years over the period 1990–92, owing mainly to the poor performance of parent firms in the slowdown of the domestic economy after the bursting of the 'bubble' economy and the economic uncertainty in the industrial markets (Table 7.1 and Figures 7.1–7.3). The yearly changes in total Japanese FDI outflows were −15.7 per cent in 1990, −26.9 per cent in 1991 and −17.9 per cent in 1992.

The emergence and the 'bursting' of the so-called 'bubble economy' in Japan coincided with the boom and recession of the recent business cycle, whose expansion phase started in the fourth quarter of 1986, with its contraction phase beginning some time in 1990. A characteristic feature of the boom period is the high rate of capital investments in Japan, which grew from an annual average of 4.5 per cent in the period 1975–86 to 12.7 per cent in the period 1987–90. This boom in capital investment could be attributed to factors such as low interest rates and the rapid rise in assets prices (land and stock prices).[4] The above-mentioned domestic factors could have contributed to the rapid rise in Japanese FDI abroad in the second half of the 1980s. On the other hand, with the end of the bubble economy, firms' balance sheets were adversely affected because of the increased burden of interest-bearing debts, the lowering of assets efficiency (measured in terms of ordinary profit per unit of tangible fixed asset) and the increase in assets requiring redemption.[5] This may again explain at least some of the decline in firms' direct investments abroad after 1990.

In terms of geographical distribution, Japanese FDI became more concentrated in Asia, the EC and North America towards the second half of the 1980s. About 80 per cent of total Japanese FDI outflows went into the above

Table 7.1 Japanese foreign direct investment in all sectors (thousand of US dollars)

FY	World	North America	%	EC	%	Asia	%
1977	2 806 000	735 000	26.2	214 000	7.6	858 000	30.6
1978	4 598 000	1 364 000	29.7	312 000	6.8	1 337 000	29.1
1979	4 995 000	1 438 000	28.8	386 000	7.7	968 000	19.4
1980	4 693 000	1 596 000	34.0	542 000	11.5	1 176 000	25.1
1981	8 932 000	2 521 697	28.2	719 000	8.0	3 316 645	37.1
1982	7 703 000	2 905 050	37.7	787 000	10.2	1 378 070	17.9
1983	8 145 000	2 700 925	33.2	945 303	11.6	7 769 423	21.7
1984	10 155 000	3 544 128	34.9	1 691 276	16.7	1 602 366	15.8
1985	12 217 000	5 495 297	45.0	1 850 475	15.1	1 414 393	11.6
1986	22 320 000	10 440 849	46.8	3 322 378	14.9	2 309 025	10.3
1987	33 364 000	15 356 879	46.0	6 280 882	18.8	4 838 754	14.5
1988	47 022 000	22 327 806	47.5	8 328 847	17.7	5 526 397	11.8
1989	67 540 000	33 902 160	50.2	14 030 820	20.8	8 120 471	12.0
1990	56 911 000	27 191 941	47.8	13 303 460	23.4	6 946 259	12.2
1991	41 584 000	18 823 156	45.3	8 786 635	21.1	5 864 635	14.1
1992	34 138 000	14 572 247	42.7	6 643 792	19.5	6 187 196	18.1
1951–92	386 530 000	169 580 403	43.9	70 671 000	18.3	58 924 000	15.2
1977–92	367 123 000	164 915 135	44.9	68 143 868	18.6	53 612 634	14.6
1986–92	302 897 000	142 615 038	47.1	60 696 814	20.0	39 792 737	13.1

Notes:
1. Asia includes Hong Kong, Singapore, South Korea, Taiwan, Indonesia, Malaysia, the Philippines, Thailand and China.
2. Percentage share indicated the share of the region in the world, total.

Source: Ministry of Finance.

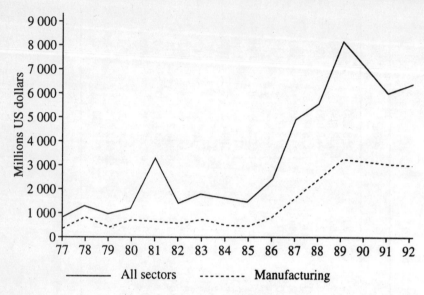

Figure 7.1   Japanese FDI in Asia (notification base)

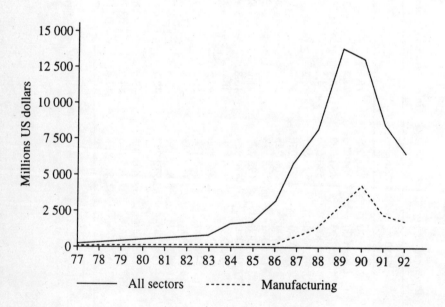

Figure 7.2   Japanese FDI in the EC (notification base)

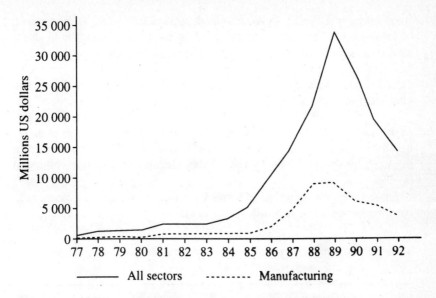

Figure 7.3   Japanese FDI in North America (notification base)

three regions. However, regional differences emerged as Japanese FDI outflows decreased after 1989. While the share of Japanese FDI flows to North
America decreased from 47.8 per cent in 1990 to 42.7 per cent in 1992, and
the share of outflows to the EC also fell from 23.4 per cent in 1990 to 19.5
per cent in 1992, the share received by Asia grew, from 12.2 per cent to 18.1
per cent over the same period. Japanese FDI flows to Asia in fact recorded a
small growth of 5.5 per cent in 1992, in contrast to the 18 per cent decline in
its total direct investment to the world (Table 7.1). This suggests that Japanese firms were relocating their activities more to the Asian region in the
period 1990–92.

One characteristic feature of the upsurge in Japanese FDI in the 1986–9
period was that it comprised FDI in the tertiary sectors and such investments
were larger in North America and the EC. For instance, in 1989, the ratios of
non-manufacturing FDI to manufacturing FDI in the EC, North America, and
Asia[6] were approximately 3.6:1, 2.5:1 and 1.6:1, respectively. Non-manufacturing FDI comprised largely real estate (26 per cent of total Japanese FDI in
the United States in the period 1986–92), finance (45 per cent of total
Japanese FDI in the United Kingdom in the period 1986–92), commerce and
services. Coincidentally, when Japanese FDI outflows declined after 1989,
the reduction was also larger in non-manufacturing FDI than in manufacturing FDI in all three regions. This characteristic is depicted in Figures 7.1 to
7.3.

As shown in Table 7.2, by the first three years of the 1990s, 40–50 per cent of Japanese FDI in Asia was in the manufacturing sectors. This is in sharp contrast to direct investment in North America and the EC, in which manufacturing FDI constituted 25–35 per cent of the total. More importantly, Japanese manufacturing FDI in Asia only declined by a minute 7 per cent after the peak in the 1989, as compared to the case of North America and the EC, where manufacturing FDI is only half of the amounts recorded in the peak years of 1989 and 1990, respectively. Hence Asia's reception of Japanese FDI is largely maintained by the continual shift of Japanese manufacturing activities abroad, a trend that began after the rapid appreciation of the yen in 1985.

Three issues regarding the pattern of Japanese FDI need to be resolved. First, an important point worth noting is that 88 per cent of the cumulative

Table 7.2   Japanese foreign direct investment in manufacturing sectors (thousands of US dollars)

FY	North America	Mfg/all	EC	Mfg/all	Asia	Mfg/all
1977	217 000	29.5	58 000*	27.1	334 000**	38.9
1978	329 000	24.1	162 000*	51.9	858 000**	64.2
1979	447 000	31.1	162 000*	42.0	437 000**	45.1
1980	398 000	24.9	161 000*	29.7	724 000**	61.6
1981	1 005 117	39.9	198 000*	27.5	681 097	20.5
1982	817 320	28.1	139 000*	17.7	538 191	39.1
1983	990 738	36.7	242 446	25.6	719 994	40.7
1984	1 241 781	35.0	321 894	19.0	497 052	31.0
1985	1 223 355	22.3	314 964	17.0	441 040	31.2
1986	2 198 744	21.1	328 172	9.9	788 967	34.2
1987	4 847 582	31.6	817 876	13.0	1 652 671	34.2
1988	9 190 825	41.2	1 464 201	17.6	2 337 074	42.3
1989	9 585 713	28.3	3 061 782	21.8	3 106 005	38.2
1990	6 792 995	25.0	4 524 459	34.0	2 994 232	43.1
1991	5 867 716	31.2	2 449 584	27.9	2 893 685	49.3
1992	4 177 223	28.7	2 055 389	30.9	2 896 901	46.8
1951–92	50 366 939	29.7	16 761 767	23.7	24 116 909	40.9
1977–92	49 330 154	29.9	16 460 767	24.2	21 899 909	40.8
1986–92	42 660 798	29.9	14 701 463	24.2	16 669 535	41.9

Notes:
1. Asia includes Hong Kong, Singapore, South Korea, Taiwan, Indonesia, Malaysia, the Philippines, Thailand and China.
2. * total data of Europe; ** total data of Asia.
3. Mfg/all indicates the share of FDI in the manufacturing sectors in that of all sectors.

Source: Ministry of Finance.

Table 7.3 Japanese foreign direct investment in the manufacturing sectors in North America, the EC and Asia (thousands of US dollars)

	North America		EC		Asia	
	1951–92	1986–92	1951–92	1986–92	1951–92	1986–92
Food	2 586 835	2 079 204	573 409	509 620	1 377 871	1 133 130
Textiles	1 057 503	813 837	1 086 666	905 138	2 207 048	1 030 326
Wood & Pulp	2 507 868	1 901 745	62 306	62 217	603 892	416 762
Chemicals	5 922 556	5 253 360	1 983 836	1 773 782	4 119 197	2 832 968
Iron & non-ferrous	5 027 024	3 989 315	689 902	434 102	3 279 022	1 606 794
General machinery	4 722 579	3 947 884	2 828 341	2 619 555	2 107 239	1 530 360
Electric/electronic	12 707 312	10 552 282	5 202 560	4 803 997	5 527 811	4 704 892
Transport machinery	6 311 945	5 095 481	2 815 233	2 415 145	1 910 848	1 256 171
Others	9 523 702	9 027 637	1 491 103	1 178 820	2 921 269	2 157 713
Total	50 367 324	42 660 745	16 733 356	14 702 376	24 054 197	16 668 816

Notes:
1. Asia includes Hong Kong, Singapore, South Korea, Taiwan, Indonesia, Malaysia, the Philippines, Thailand and China.
2. Fiscal years.

Source: Ministry of Finance.

stock of Japanese manufacturing FDI in the EC was made in the period 1986–92. Corresponding figures are, for North America, 85 per cent and, for Asia, a lower 70 per cent. Table 7.2 shows the breakdown of Japanese manufacturing FDI in the three regions in greater detail. There is no doubt that the rapid appreciation of the yen after 1985 pushed Japanese manufacturers to seek lower production locations abroad. However, the currency factor and cost factor do not seem to be able to account fully for the above differences, in view of the fact that both the surge and the slowdown of FDI in the EC and North America were more acute than they were in Asia. Other possible factors which may account for the above differences are the rise in trade friction between Japan and the other industrialized countries since the late 1970s and the threats and opportunities of greater economic integration in the EC.

Second, in terms of the distribution within the manufacturing industry for the EC in the period 1986–92, the electric and electronics industry came top with 33 per cent of the total manufacturing FDI, followed by general machinery (18 per cent), transport machinery (16 per cent) and chemicals (12 per cent). Direct investment in the electric and electronics industry also came top in North America, with 25 per cent, followed by chemicals (12 per cent) and transport machinery (12 per cent). Similarly, Japanese manufacturing FDI in Asia was led by investments in electric and electronics (28 per cent) and chemicals (17 per cent) over the period 1986–92 (Table 7.3). Therefore it can be seen that Japanese direct investment abroad was concentrated in manufacturing industries in which Japanese exports were also particularly high.[7] While there is much debate on the relationship between Japan's exports and FDI, empirical evidence so far has not provided definitive conclusions.[8] We will examine this second issue in greater detail later in the chapter.

The third issue worth examining is how the pattern of Japanese FDI to the above three regions will emerge in the 1990s. If Japanese manufacturing FDI to Asia, the EC and North America is motivated by different factors, then the pattern of flows to the three regions should also emerge differently. In the next section we review briefly the empirical literature on the determinants of FDI.

DETERMINANTS OF FDI: A REVIEW OF THE LITERATURE

There is an extensive empirical literature on the determinants of FDI (see Agarwal, 1980). Economic factors most often considered include, for instance, firm size, capital and labour intensity, firm-specific knowledge, profitability, relative labour cost and economic growth in the host countries.

However, a large portion of the literature is related to the studies of US foreign direct investment patterns or investment behaviours of US MNCs (for instance, Horst, 1972; Dunning, 1980; Grubaugh, 1987).[9]

There are fewer studies on the determinants of Japanese FDI, and most of them appeared only in the late 1980s. For instance, Heitger and Stehn (1990), Urata (1991) and Sleuwaegen and Yamawaki (1991) focused on determinants at the industry level, whereas Kimura (1989), Horaguchi (1992) and Yamawaki (1993) worked on firm level analysis.

Urata (1991) works on the determinants of Japanese FDI in Asia for the period 1977–86. The mean size of establishment, export–output ratio and import–domestic absorption ratio are found to be positive and statistically significant. Advertisement expenditure to sales and R&D expenditure to sales are, on the other hand, found to be insignificant. Horaguchi's (1992) analysis of Japanese manufacturing firms which have invested in Asia, using 1987 data, found that the greater the size of sales and the higher the ratio of net worth to total capital, the higher the level of FDI.

Sleuwaegen and Yamawaki's (1991) analysis showed that, for the 43 manufacturing industries where Japanese MNCs control 50 per cent or more of their distribution subsidies in the United States, growing market size, high transport costs, tariffs, non-tariff barriers and quantity restrictions lead to a substitution of exports in favour of local production.

Heitger and Stehn (1990) found that European effective protection and firm-specific non-tangible assets of Japanese firms determined the structure of Japanese FDI in Europe in 1985. Yamawaki (1993), on the other hand, tested the locational decisions of Japanese multinationals within the EC using the data of 236 Japanese manufacturing subsidiaries in 15 European countries in 1988. The regression analysis showed that Japanese FDI is attracted to countries in the EC where labour costs are low, where R&D is considerable and where market size is large.

THE MODEL

Dunning's (1981, 1988) widely accepted eclectic approach deduces the determinants of FDI by comparing the efficiency of serving foreign markets in exports, licensing or international production. International production or FDI will be taken when the OLI conditions are satisfied.[10] Our model focused on the locational advantages of the host regions in attracting Japanese FDI.[11]

We evaluate the significance of locational specific variables in explaining the geographical distribution of Japanese manufacturing firms in Asia (NIEs, ASEAN-4 and China), the EC and North America over the period 1977–92.

The model estimated is as follows:

$$LFDIi = f(LEXPi, RGDPi, IDWJi, IDERJi)$$

where i = Asia, North America, EC; *LFDIi* is the annual flow of Japanese FDI to region i (in logarithm form); *LEXPi* is Japan's total exports to region i expressed in logarithm form (to measure trade intensity): this variable could also be interpreted as a proxy for the demand for Japanese exports; *RGDPi* is the relative growth rate of region i with respect to Japan where growth rate is calculated on the basis of GDP at current prices (as a proxy for an increase in sales or market growth); *IDWJi* is the ratio of the index of the hourly manufacturing wage rate of Japan to the corresponding average index of region i; *IDERJi* is the ratio of the index of yen/$US to the average index of national currency/$US in region i. An index less than 1 indicates that the yen is appreciating with respect to region i average national currencies. *IDWJi* and *IDERJi* are included to measure production costs. Definitions and data sources of the above variables are summarized in the appendix.

The expected sign on the export variable is less certain. To the extent that FDI and exports are not substitutive, the coefficient of the export variable should be positive. This is because, even if production in foreign markets may have reduced the flow of final goods exports from Japan, Japan's exports of intermediate goods and capital goods are expected to increase with international production. At the same time, exports of final goods with higher value added are also likely to offset the original decline. Moreover, it is also hypothesized that growth in exports from Japan may also exert pressure forcing Japanese firms to engage in local production to reduce the likelihood of future trade frictions.

If Japanese firms tend to invest in foreign countries to take advantage of a growing foreign market relative to the Japanese domestic market, the coefficient on *RGDPi* should have a positive value. As a higher wage cost in Japan should encourage firms to shift their production to locations where production cost minimization is possible, the coefficient for relative wage rate should also have a positive sign. The exchange rate variable is to capture the effects of Japanese firms' adjustment behaviours following the sharp appreciation of the yen after 1985. As the appreciation of the yen accelerated Japanese firms' moves towards international production, the sign for the exchange rate variable should be negative.

EMPIRICAL RESULTS AND IMPLICATIONS

Regression results are summarized in Table 7.4.[12] For Japanese FDI in Asia, *LEXPi* and *IDWJi* are positive and significant at the 1 per cent level. The sign of the coefficients for *RGDPi* and *IDERJi* are uncertain but these two locational-specific variables are not statistically significant. Hence the empirical findings confirm that Japanese FDI in Asia is very much governed by fundamental factors such as the availability of relatively low-cost labour and the high demand for Japanese goods.

For Japanese FDI in North America, exports have a positive influence on the level of FDI. *LEXPi* is positive and statistically significant. The strength of the yen is found to influence FDI positively, as expected; the coefficient for the exchange rate variable is negative and significant at the 5 per cent or 10 per cent level.

As for Japanese FDI in the EC, the export variable, *LEXPi*, is found to be positive and significant at the 1 per cent level in all the equations. The *RGDPi* variable is significant at the 5 per cent or 10 per cent level, but, contrary to expectation, the sign of the coefficient is negative. This implies that Japanese firms invest more in the EC in years in which the relative growth rate of the EC *vis-à-vis* Japan is low, which is inconsistent with the hypothesized behaviour.

To summarize, our model suggests that Japanese manufacturing firms invest in Asia to minimize labour costs, and such investments are positively related to Japanese exports to Asia. Japanese firms' investments in North America, on the other hand, are better explained by the need to regain cost competitiveness owing to the negative effect caused by appreciation of the yen. As for Japanese FDI in the EC, our model could only show that it is influenced positively by Japan's exports to the EC.

One concern which may arise out of the empirical results in this chapter involves the relationship between FDI and exports. Our findings suggest that there is a positive relationship between Japanese exports and FDI in all the three regions. Some possible explanations for the positive relationship between local production and exports will be that first, direct investments or local production increase the home country exports of intermediate goods and capital equipment. Second, local production may also enhance the familiarity of the parent company's brand names or goods, which increases the demand for the exports of other products manufactured by the parent company.[13] Finally, Saucier (1991) has also suggested that the fight for market share among Japanese firms and at the level of world oligopolies led Japanese firms to supplement their export drive with FDI in the most important markets.[14] Hence it is not contradictory to find a complementary relationship between FDI and exports from Japan.

In general, our determinant model underestimated Japanese outward FDI flows in the period 1987–90. Hence Japanese FDI in the late 1980s is less motivated by fundamental locational factors singled out in the model. Other factors, such as the effect of the 'bubble' economy, may have influenced firms' decisions about location to a certain extent. Further, although our

Table 7.4 Results of regression

		Independent variables					
	Constant	LEXPASIA	RGDPASIA	IDWJAS	IDERJAS	R-squared	F
LFDIASIA	−21.9	2.54 (6.5)***	−0.03 (−0.4)	2.67 (3.3)***		0.91	39.39
	−8.5	1.42 (2.33)***	0.01 (0.12)		0.13 (0.11)	0.83	18.96
	−17.55	2.17 (4.86)***		3.01 (3.64)***	−1.07 (−1.22)	0.92	44.25
	−17.85	2.19 (4.46)***	−0.02 (−0.18)	3.03 (3.49)***	−1.04 (−1.13)	0.92	30.52
	Constant	LEXPNA	RGDPNA	IDWJNA	IDERJNA	R-squared	F
LFDINA	−16.60	2.19 (5.83)***	−0.11 (−0.41)	0.15 (0.06)		0.9	37.05
	−7.11	1.47 (3.38)***	−0.14 (−0.60)		−2.33 (−1.78)*	0.92	47.83
	2.00	0.9 (1.26)		−2.74 (−1.04)	−3.26 (−2.06)	0.93	50.84
	8.50	0.5 (0.64)	−0.29 (−1.20)	−4.23 (1.47)	−3.88 (2.37)**	0.94	39.93

114

LFDIEC	Constant	LEXPEC	RGDPEC	IDWJEC	IDERJEC	R-squared	F
	−12.6	1.93 (3.6)***	−0.47 (−1.99)*	−0.09 (−0.06)		0.93	56.4
	−11.17	1.81 (4.27)***	−0.49 (−2.29)**		−0.43 (−0.39)	0.93	57.14
	−19.24	2.42 (4.47)***		2.06 (1.05)	−0.82 (−0.50)	0.91	42.41
	−12.16	1.89 (3.35)***	−0.46 (−1.89)*	0.44 (0.22)	−0.64 (−0.42)	0.93	39.47

Notes:
1. Two-Tail test.
2. * significant at the 10% level; ** significant at the 5% level; *** significant at the 1% level.
3. Numbers in parentheses are t-ratios

determinant model on Japanese FDI in Asia, the EC and North America is by no means complete, our results supported the hypothesis that the factors determining Japanese FDI in the three regions are quite different. The model explains the motivations of Japanese FDI in Asia better than Japanese FDI in North America and the EC. This could also be justified by looking at the performance of Japanese multinationals in the above three regions. Table 7.5 shows that the profit rate of Japanese manufacturing affiliates is highest in Asia. This supports our view that Japanese multinational companies (MNCs)' activities in Asia are governed mainly by cost factors and they have performed well. The performance of Japanese affiliates in Europe ranked second, with the rate of profit turned negative in 1991. The rate of profit in North America was the lowest, with a worsening trend since 1988.

Table 7.5   *Profit rate of Japanese manufacturing affiliates (per cent)*

FY	World	N. America	Europe	Asia
1985	1.3	−0.5	1.7	2.9
1986	1.4	0.7	1.2	2.3
1987	2.2	0.4	2.0	4.0
1988	2.9	0.7	2.3	4.4
1989	1.8	0.2	2.3	3.8
1990	1.8	−0.9	3.2	5.0
1991	0.9	−1.9	−0.6	4.8

Notes:
1. Profit rate = ordinary profit/sales.
2. Fiscal years.

Source: MITI, *Kaigai chokusetsu toshi tokeisofan*, no. 4; MITI, *Wagakuni kigyo kaigaikatusdo chosa*, no. 22.

We have not included variables to capture the effects of tariff and non-tariff barriers on FDI in our model, owing to the lack of data on suitable proxies. This is expected to reduce the explanatory power of our equations for Japanese FDI in the EC and North America, as empirical evidence showed that much of the investment in these two regions is made to overcome the barriers on direct exports. For instance, Belderbos (1991) has shown that there is a high correlation between the timing of trade policy measures by product and the timing of the establishment of Japanese assembly plants in the EC. Belderbos showed that most of Japanese manufacturing investment in the EC has been a response to trade frictions, as Japanese firms usually started the productions of VTR, PC printers, PPC and CD players after anti-dumping actions or other protectionist measures in the EC became known. On the other hand, the results of a survey by the Export and Import Bank of Japan revealed that the numbers of firms investing in North America and the EC to counter trade restrictions such as voluntary export restraints and anti-dumping duties have been on the decline since 1990.[15] This external factor may account for part of the stagnation in Japanese manufacturing FDI in the industrialized countries after 1990.

Another major factor that has not been taken into account in our model will be the effect of economic integration in the EC. Japanese FDI in the EC recorded an upsurge in the period 1986–90 and this could be interpreted as largely due to the corporate strategy of Japanese firms in response to EC integration in 1992. Table 7.6 shows the profit rate of Japanese manufacturing affiliates in 1991, classified in terms of the period of establishment. In general, affiliates established in the later period are expected to have poorer performance. However, it is worth noting that in the case of Japanese affiliates in the EC established in the period 1986–8 recorded a profit of –4.3 per cent in 1991, as compared to –0.2 per cent for affiliates established after 1989. This may suggest that, for Japanese FDI in the EC in the period 1986–8, it is made in expectation of the greater difficulties in exporting to the EC after 1992 and/or the greater market opportunities that are expected to follow from the greater integration of the EC.

Table 7.6   Profit rate of Japanese manufacturing affiliates, FY1991, in terms of period of establishment (per cent)

	World	N. America	Europe	Asia
Pre-FY1979	3.2	1.2	–0.3	5.6
FY1980–82	1.8	–1.4	2.6	4.9
FY1983–85	0.4	–1.7	–1.1	6.2
FY1986–88	–1.8	–4.2	–4.3	3.5
FY1989–	–2.7	–6.9	–0.2	0.3

Notes: As for Table 7.5.

Source: As for Table 7.5

Finally, an issue which may attract much attention is the pattern of Japanese manufacturing FDI in Asia, the EC and North America which will emerge in the rest of the 1990s. One concern is the consistent upward pressure on the value of the yen since the beginning of the 1990s. The strength of the yen reached a new high of 103.71 yen/$US in August 1993 and approaching 100 yen/$US again in May 1994. The yen appreciated by 12.2 percentage point against the US dollar in 1993. A survey conducted by the Economic Planning Agency revealed that exporting firms found that they will only break even at an exchange rate of 117.50 yen/$US and half of the firms in the manufacturing sector are expected to have production activities overseas by 1998 in order to regain their price competitiveness.[16] Another survey by the Export and Import Bank of Japan showed that 62 per cent of the 372 firms surveyed plan to invest in Asia (26.9 per cent in China, 21.2 per cent in ASEAN and 13.7 per cent in the NIEs), as against 12.1 per cent in North America and 11.3 per cent in the EC.[17] The fact that Japanese firms are attracted to Asia, and China in particular, is not surprising if we take into account the market potential of the region and rapid economic growth in China.

Hence, with other things remaining constant, we expect that Japanese FDI in Asia may pick up faster than direct investment in North America or the EC, as the growing strength of the yen will increase the economic rationales for Japanese firms to shift more of their production to Asia, where Japanese firms could recover their cost competitiveness. Further, in view of the fact that the economic prospects of Asia are much brighter than those of the industrialized countries, the locational attractiveness of Asia will surpass that of North America and the EC in the 1990s.

CONCLUSIONS

In previous studies on the determinants of Japanese FDI, various factors accounting for inter-industry or inter-country differences have been tested. In this chapter we have examined the differences in the locational factors governing Japanese manufacturing investment in Asia, the EC and North America. Our results indicate that the share of Japanese exports has a positive influence on Japanese FDI. We also found support for the hypothesis that Japanese firms invested in Asia because of the attractiveness of lower wage rates, whereas the appreciation of the yen is the main factor that encouraged Japanese firms to invest in North America. As our model only tested on variables in which proxies or data are available for the three regions, the above results are by no means exclusive. Japanese manufacturing FDI in the EC and North America may be better explained by other locational pull factors specific to the respective regions, such as trade restrictions and market integration. In view of the continual upward pressure on the strength of the yen and the growing market potential following economic liberalization in Asia, the Asian region will be a more attractive location for Japanese manufacturing firms in the 1990s.

NOTES

1. Asia in this chapter includes the NIEs (Hong Kong, Singapore, South Korea and Taiwan), ASEAN-4 (Indonesia, Malaysia, the Philippines and Thailand) and China.
2. See Sazanami (1992a and b).
3. Foreign direct investment figures in this chapter are notification-based data from the Ministry of Finance, Japan. These data are in fiscal years (from 1 April to 31 March).
4. The term 'bubble' refers to the rapid rise in assets prices and/or the deviation of assets prices away from their fundamental values. See Yoshikawa (1993) and Asako (1993).
5. Economic Planning Agency (1993, pp. 169–86).
6. There is a greater amount of Japanese FDI in the primary sector in Asia than in North America or the EC. Non-manufacturing FDI in North America and the EC are predominantly direct investment in the tertiary sectors.
7. In 1992, Japan's total exports consisted mainly of electrical machinery (22.8 per cent), general machinery (22.5 percent), motor cars (17.8 per cent) and chemicals (5.6 per cent).
8. For instance, Urata (1991).
9. Grubaugh (1987), using a random sample of 300 US firms in 1982, found that, using the linear probability model, only firm size is significant in determining FDI when inter-industry differences are held constant. His results are similar to the results obtained by Horst (1972). However, Grubaugh found that R&D and product diversity are also significant when a light model was used. Dunning's (1980) empirical analysis of US affiliates in 14 manufacturing industries in seven countries in 1970 showed that the main advantages of US firms are revealed in one locational variable – relative market size – and one ownership-specific variable – the skilled employment ratio.
10. The OLI conditions are as follows:
    (a) ownership advantages (O) largely rest on the possession of firm-specific intangible assets;
    (b) internalization advantages (I) to avoid the difficulty in pricing intangible assets and the costs having to enforce property rights in the case of contractual resource transfers; and
    (c) locational advantages (L) when factors endowments or institutional settings of the host country are superior to those of the home country.
11. As our time series analysis focused on the determinants at the industry level, we are not able to differentiate the ownership-specific advantages of firms investing in the respective three regions owing to data constraints. Theoretically, other than the small and medium-size firms investing is Asia, the competitive advantages of Japanese firms investing abroad should not be too different.
12. The statistical method used is ordinary least squares. Initially, single variable regressions with each of the dependent variables are carried out so that only variables with explanatory power are included in the final set of equations.
13. Blomstrom, Lipsey and Kulchycky (1988) found empirically that the higher the level of Swedish production in a country, the higher the level of Swedish exports to that country. A complementary relationship is also found to exist between US exports and production by minority-owned US affiliates.
14. Saucier (1991, p. 123).
15. Export and Import Bank of Japan (1994, p. 23).
16. The survey was conducted in January 1994. Quoted from *Nihon Keizai Shimbun*, 14 April 1994.
17. Export and Import Bank of Japan (1994, p. 18).

REFERENCES

Agarwal, J.P. (1980), 'Determinants of Foreign Direct Investment: A Survey', *Weltwirtschaftliches Archiv*, pp. 739–73.

Asako, K. (1993), 'Baburu no Jittai Keizai e no Eikyō (The Effects of the 'Bubble' on the Real Economy), *Keizai Seminaru*, August.

Belderbos, R.A. (1991), 'On the Advance of Japanese Electronics Multinationals in the EC: Companies, Trends and Trade Policy', paper presented at the eighth conference of the Euro-Asia Management Studies Association, 17–19 October.

Blomström, M., R.E. Lipsey and K. Kulchycky (1988), 'US and Swedish Direct Investment and Exports', in R.E. Baldwin (ed.), *Trade Policy Issues and Empirical Analysis*, Chicago: NBER, University of Chicago Press, for the National Bureau of Economic Research.

Dunning, J. (1980), 'Toward an Eclectic Theory of International Production: Some Empirical Tests', *Journal of Business Studies*, Vol. II, pp. 9–31.

Dunning, J. (1988), 'The Eclectic Paradigm of International Production: a Restatement and Some Possible Extensions', *Journal of International Business Studies*, Vol. 19, No. 1, pp. 1–30.

Economic Planning Agency (1993), *Keizai Hakusho* (The White Paper on the Economy), Japan.

Export and Import Bank of Japan (1994), '1993 Nendo Kaigai Chokusetsu Tōshi Ankēto Chōsakekka Hokoku' (Results of the 1993 Survey on Overseas Direct Investments), *Kaigai Tōshi Kenkyūjo*, January.

Grubaugh, S. (1987), 'Determinants of Direct Foreign Investment', *Review of Economics and Statistics*, Vol. 69, pp. 149–52.

Heitger, B. and J. Stehn (1990), 'Japanese Direct Investments in the EC – Response to the Internal Market 1993?', *Journal of Common Market Studies*, pp. 1–15.

Horaguchi, H. (1992), *Nihon Kigyō no Kaigai Chokusetsu Tōshi: Asia e no Shinshutsu to Tettai* (Foreign Direct Investment of Japanese Firms: Investment and Disinvestment in Asia), Tokyo Daigaku Shuppankai.

Horst, T. (1972), 'Firm and Industry Determinants of the Decision to Invest Abroad: An Empirical Study', *Review of Economics and Statistics*, Vol. 54, pp. 258–66.

Kimura, Y. (1989), 'Firm-Specific Strategic Advantages and Foreign Direct Investment Behaviour of Firms: The Case of Japanese Semiconductor Firms', *Journal of International Business Studies*, pp. 296–314.

Saucier, P. (1991), 'New Conditions for Competition between Japanese and European Firms', in B. Burgenmeier and J.L. Mucchielli (eds), *Multinationals and Europe 1992*, London and New York: Routledge.

Sazanami, Y. (1992a), 'Determinants of Japanese Foreign Direct Investment: Locational Attractiveness of European Countries to Japanese Multinationals', *Revue Economique*, Vol. 43, No. 4, pp. 661–70.

Sazanami, Y. (1992b), 'Globalization Strategy of Japanese Manufacturing Firms and its Impact on Trade Flows between Europe, Asia and North America', paper presented at Europe–Japon: concurrents ou partenaires, Université de Paris I, Panthéon-Sorbonne, February.

Sleuwaegen, L. and H. Yamawaki (1991), 'Foreign Direct Investment and Intra-firm Trade: Evidence from Japan', in J. Koekkoek and L.G.M. Mennes (eds), *International Trade and Global Development: Essays in Honour of Jagdish Bhagwati*, London: Routledge.

Urata, S. (1991), 'The Increase of Direct Investment Abroad and Change in Japan', in

E.R. Ramstetter (ed.), *Direct Foreign Investment in Asia's Developing Economies and Structural Change in the Asia–Pacific Region*, Boulder, Col.: Westview Press.

Yamawaki, H. (1993), 'Locational Decisions of Japanese Multinational Firms in European Manufacturing Industries', in K.S. Hughes (ed.), *European Competitiveness*, Cambridge: Cambridge University Press.

Yoshikawa, H. (1993), 'Heisei no Keiki Junkan to Baburu no Kankei o Tadasu' (An Inquiry into the Relationship between the Heisei Business Cycle and the 'Bubble'), *Ekonomisuto*, 27 July.

APPENDIX: DATA DEFINITIONS AND SOURCES

Variable Name	Description
LFDIASIA	Japanese manufacturing direct investment in Asia (NIEs, ASEAN-4 and China)
LFDINA	Japanese manufacturing direct investment in North America
LFDIEC	Japanese manufacturing direct investment in the EC – all three variables are in logarithm forms *Source*: Ministry of Finance.
LEXPi	Japanese total exports to the respective region (Mil $US) (in log form) *Source*: MITI, *boeki doko* (Direction of Trade).
RGDPi	Relative growth rate of the respective region (with respect to Japan) (e.g. rate of GDP growth (at current prices) of Asia/rate of GDP growth of Japan) *Source*: IMF, *International Financial Statistics*.
IDWJi	Index of hourly wage rate of Japan/index of average hourly wage rate of i (1977=100). Wages in manufacturing expressed as earnings per hour in national currency are used; such data are available directly for EC-12, the USA and Canada. Estimations from earnings per month to earnings per hour are made for the rest of the Asian countries. However, for Indonesia and Malaysia, only labour cost data are available. *Source*: ILO, *Yearbook of Labour Statistics*.
IDERJi	Index of yen/$US/index of average national currency/$US (1977=100, Index < 100: appreciating with respect to $US) *Source*: IMF, *International Financial Statistics*.

8. The impact of foreign investment on domestic manufacturing industry of OECD countries

Thomas Hatzichronoglou

INTRODUCTION

During the second half of the 1980s, foreign investment was the most dynamic element in industrial restructuring worldwide. Behind this rapid growth, which mainly concerned the OECD area, was the proliferation of policies to liberalize foreign investment and capital movements against a particularly favourable background of economic growth. It was after 1990 that foreign investment slowed appreciably and began, more than in the past, to concentrate on developing countries which were enjoying strong growth, especially in Asia and South America.

The growth of direct investment over the last decade revived the debate and, in some cases, the controversy concerning the influence it actually has on domestic economies. In view of the fact that all OECD countries are both investors and host countries for foreign investment, the actual principle of this development is no longer in doubt. What is at present in doubt is, rather, what policies and strategies should be adopted in order to make these investments more profitable for all partner countries. For these questions to be answered, it is above all important to know in what geographical areas and in what sectors the investment is concentrated, and what influence it has on the different industrial activities (production, employment, investment, R&D and trade) of the host country's domestic economy.[1]

There are many reasons why firms should prefer foreign direct investment to exporting and it is not easy to see exactly what determines their choice. Since a direct investment is a long-term investment, it could be said that it is primarily a *strategic element*. Firms have to decide beforehand whether their strategic objectives require a direct investment abroad in order to circumvent, for example, open or hidden protectionism in the form of technical or regulatory barriers to trade, or to avoid anti-dumping regulations, to penetrate a distribution network and thereby increase export flows, or to take over a firm with products of a strategic kind (in terms of technology, for example). Also a vertical integration strategy at world level may require a local foothold in a major market, especially when competitors also have one. Once a direct investment is integrated in a firm's global strategy, the final decision will depend on any obstacles confronting the firm in the implementation phase and the ways of getting over them. Lastly, direct investment may be motivated by factors on the *demand* or *supply* sides.

Factors on the demand side include the need to adapt more efficiently to the local characteristics of markets, the need to expand outlets and increase market shares, or the necessity of internationalizing a brand. On the supply side, the factors include the reduction in labour costs achieved by relocation and re-exports, lower transport costs, protection from exchange rate risks, guaranteed access to certain products or raw materials, economies of scale or the acquisition of new or complementary technologies.

In his 'eclectic' paradigm, Dunning[2] proposes a framework and methodology to explain the decision to produce abroad. According to this paradigm, such a decision is based on three determinants: (1) a firm's competitive advantages, (2) the advantages provided by foreign countries and (3) the possible advantages which can be obtained if the firm internalizes certain activities. A firm which invests abroad must have a competitive advantage allowing it to have access to the foreign market, withstand competition and get over entrance barriers. This advantage may be given by a firm's products, technology and know-how in a particular field. For example, the competitive advantage held by multinationals may be due to their ability to organize and manage production at world level. The second determinant in the decision to produce abroad concerns the advantages provided by the host countries. These advantages may be due to the existence of natural resources, low labour costs, abundant skilled labour, the quality of infrastructure and other externalities. The third determinant concerns the advantages of internalization where markets are imperfect and transaction costs high.[3] It may be more advantageous for a firm to have information processed or to trade intermediate products, services and knowledge via its own subsidiaries rather than via the market. From this viewpoint, cooperative agreements with or without a financial stake may be seen as cases of partial internalization that would be more advantageous for the firms involved than full internalization (for example, via an acquisition), especially when the aim is to pool intangible assets such as know-how.

A distinction can be drawn between the determinants in the choice of a particular transaction method and the motives for setting up an establishment abroad. The latter are based on a comparison of a firm's strategy and its resources, hence the importance of a sectoral analysis to assess the different competitive positions; the determinants in the choice of a transaction method

are based on a comparison of the motives of the firm and the various constraints and opportunities it will encounter.[4]

While the large majority of firms invest abroad mainly in order to increase
their market shares or to circumvent protectionist barriers, the involvement of
other firms is related to sector-specific issues as well as the long-term strategies. At the macroeconomic level, the main benefits to be derived from
'inward' foreign direct investment are the conventional gains associated with
integration,[5] that is, everything that facilitates trade in goods and services. To
these benefits must be added those stemming from 'external economies'. The
effects of integration are reflected first of all in industrial restructuring at
international level via the purchase, sale or creation of subsidiaries which, for
all the reasons referred to above, will be able to ensure sustained growth,
create new jobs and improve productivity and competition.

At the microeconomic level, another of the objectives of restructuring is to
improve firms' *return on investment* and exploit each country's comparative
advantages at world level. The new way in which firms are organized will
reduce transaction costs thanks mainly to intra-firm trade and facilities with
regard to technology transfers and the circulation of information. Weighing
against these advantages are a number of potential costs. These have mainly to
do with risks relating to sovereignty or national security when activities considered to be 'strategic' come under foreign control. Other, more economic, costs
include possible workforce reductions and increases in the trade deficit. Some
authors advance more subtle theories, arguing that foreign investment could in
some cases shift production and employment in the host country into unsuitable activities, with the result that the externalities generated, such as R&D,
could move abroad. There is not for the time being a consensus on the majority
of these considerations, but they do probably warrant further investigation.

The effects arising from 'external economies' are more difficult to measure
than the effects of integration. They involve various categories of externality
and spillover. When, for example, foreign subsidiaries introduce new technologies or new management methods, these can spread extensively through
the industrial fabric of the host country, which will derive numerous benefits,
but of a differing nature, in particular as regards learning and skills. Although
difficult to measure, these advantages must be taken into account when
drawing up an overall balance sheet of the costs and benefits of foreign
investment to national economies.

It is not the purpose of this chapter to assess all the above-mentioned
effects of integration or 'external economies', or to carry out a full cost/
benefit analysis of foreign investment. More modestly, its aim is to essay a
quantitative assessment of the direct impact of 'inward' foreign investment
on host country economies in two areas of special importance: employment
and trade.

EMPLOYMENT IN FOREIGN SUBSIDIARIES

Measurement Problems

Arguments about the impact of foreign investment usually focus on employment, especially when economic activity is at a low ebb and unemployment is high. Evaluating the net job creation attributable to direct investment raises many methodological problems. As stated in the introduction, this section will do no more than seek to quantify the way employment in foreign subsidiaries in host country manufacturing industries evolves (inward investment), if possible by sector of activity and by geographic origin. No account is taken of the indirect influence of such investment on national economies (such as local subcontractors) or of the impact of outward direct investment on employment, in particular the transfer abroad of manufacturing units.[6]

Similar difficulties arise in measuring the impact of inward investment on employment in the receiving countries. Though intersectoral effects can be assessed, it is by no means easy to measure the indirect effect of replacing imports with on-the-spot production. These difficulties are compounded by the fact that net job creation in one region of a given country may be achieved at the expense of other regions less attractive to foreign investors; the latter may lose jobs as competition gets tougher or as a result of overcapacity. The effects of foreign investment on employment depend on *the type of investment* concerned. Three investment categories may be distinguished: (1) new investment, (2) disinvestment, and (3) a combination of new investment and disinvestment in one and the same operation (see Figure 8.1).

In the first of the three sub-categories of new investment, obviously new jobs are created, though it still has to be seen whether this may not entail the closing of other existing establishments. In the second, jobs are transferred from a domestically owned company to one which now becomes a foreign affiliate. Evaluating the effects on employment of mergers and buy-outs raises further problems, in that the jobs concerned are considered to be new jobs. Of course, if there had been no buy-out some of those jobs would probably have gone, but it is impossible to say exactly how many would simply have been transferred under the new ownership.

In the case of disinvestment, the first category also involves methodological difficulties when it comes to evaluation, because the sale of a business, unlike its winding up (the second category) does not automatically bring job losses. The buyer (not necessarily a foreign firm) may retain some jobs, or may create others, or may make some workers redundant. Reductions of existing capacity (third category) usually bring job losses. Assessing the results of a combination of new investment and wind-ups or sale at one and

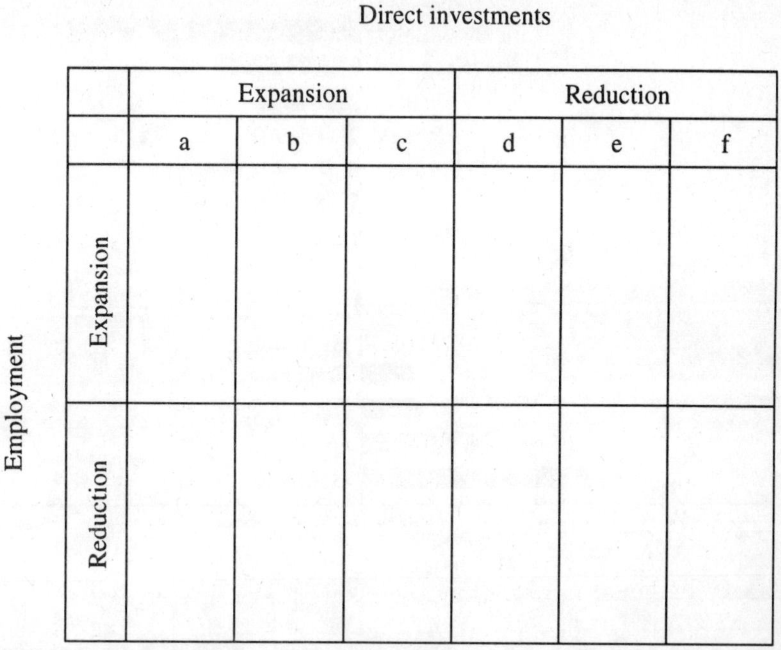

Direct investments

	Expansion			Reduction		
	a	b	c	d	e	f
Employment — Expansion						
Employment — Reduction						

Notes:
1. New investments – expansion: (a) creation of new establishments, (b) acquisition of existing establishments, (c) extension of existing capacities.
2. Disinvestments – reduction: (d) sale of establishments, (e) liquidations, (f) reduction of existing capacities.

Figure 8.1   Links between direct investment flows and employment

the same time is tricky when the effect on employment is counted as an end result, without any notice being taken of the number of jobs created or lost at each stage of the operation.[7]

Trend in Employment

In manufacturing industry as a whole
Bearing in mind the limitations enumerated above, the main trend that can be deduced from the available figures is that during the 1980s there was a more rapid increase in jobs in foreign affiliates than in domestically owned companies. In these countries (the United States, Austria, the United Kingdom, Sweden, Turkey, Portugal, Ireland, Finland and Norway) an increase in the number of jobs in foreign affiliates was recorded, against a fall for domestic firms, except in Turkey (see Figures 8.2 to 8.5).

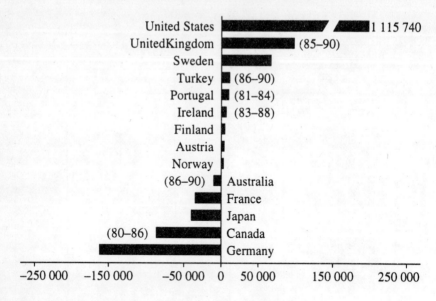

Source: OECD, EAS Division, Industrial Activity of Foreign Affiliates data bank.

Figure 8.2   Numbers employed by foreign-owned affiliates in the manufacturing industry (changes between 1980 and 1990 or nearest years)

In Australia, Japan, France, Canada and Germany, growth in the number of jobs in foreign-owned subsidiaries slowed down. In France and Australia, unlike the other three countries, it was slower than employment growth in domestic firms. In two countries (Japan and Germany) domestic firms did continue to recruit. In Canada the number of jobs in foreign-owned subsidiaries fell more rapidly than in domestically owned firms.

Before going on to look at certain employment-related factors (new enterprises, wages and skills, labour productivity), it may be interesting to seek to identify the sectors most affected by these changes and the geographic origin of the firms involved.

Trend in employment by sector of industry and geographic origin

The United States   During the period 1980–90, employment in domestically-owned firms in most manufacturing sectors declined, while in foreign affiliates it rose. The only exception was the motor industry (see Table 8.1). It is in that sector that the foreign penetration rate increases, but this is now in terms of capital; overall, few new jobs have been created. During this period,

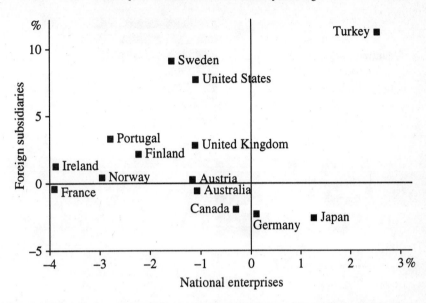

Note: The change is calculated over the periods 1980–86 for Australia and Canada, 1983–8 for Ireland, 1981–4 for Portugal, 1985–90 for the United Kingdom and 1986–90 for Turkey.

Source: OECD, EAS Division Industrial Activity of Foreign Affiliates data bank.

Figure 8.3   Trend in employment in the manufacturing industry (average annual growth rate, 1980–90)

it was above all in the chemicals, electrical and electronic machinery, paper, food, non-metallic minerals and basic metals sectors that employment in foreign affiliates progressed. In the chemicals sector, this progress is chiefly ascribable to the installation of new establishments by firms from Switzerland and the Netherlands and, to a lesser degree, from the United Kingdom, Japan and France. Nearly all the Swiss affiliates manufacture pharmaceuticals (53 600 jobs in 1990); British and Dutch affiliates were more often concerned with basic chemicals. German affiliates, although they still account for almost half the jobs in foreign-owned subsidiaries in the chemicals sector (95 200 in 1990), shed some 40 000 jobs between the beginning and the end of the 1980s.

Most of the growth in employment in foreign affiliates in the electrical–electronic machinery sector during the period was in subsidiaries owned by companies based in the United Kingdom (+28 000 jobs), Japan (+28 000), Germany (+22 000) and France (+16 000). Probably affiliates owned by companies in the Netherlands also contributed substantially to that growth, but

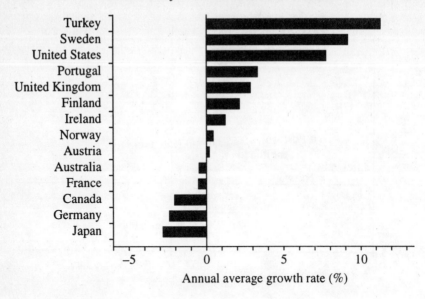

Annual average growth rate (%)

Note: The change is calculated over the period 1980–86 for Australia and Canada, 1983–8 for Ireland, 1981–4 for Portugal, 1985–90 for the United Kingdom and 1986–90 for Turkey.

Source: OECD, EAS Division, Industrial Activity of Foreign Affiliates data bank.

Figure 8.4   *Trend in employment in the manufacturing industry: foreign affiliates (average annual growth rate, 1980–90)*

the relevant figures are regarded as confidential and are therefore not available. Confidentiality is widely observed in the electronic components industry (see Table 8.1). In that sector, 18 per cent of all those employed by foreign affiliates work for firms based in Japan.

During the ten years under review, employment in foreign affiliates in the food sector increased by over 120 000, where subsidiary companies owned by firms in four European countries (the United Kingdom, the Netherlands, Switzerland and France) are predominant. Between 1980 and 1990, employment in British affiliates alone accounted for an increase in employment of around 46 000. Canadian affiliates created or saved more jobs than firms owned by any other non-European companies. Europe also led in the paper and printing sector, 57 per cent of all jobs of foreign-owned subsidiaries belonging to firms based in the United Kingdom and Germany, but also to Japanese and Canadian affiliates. The non-metallic minerals sector (stone, clay, glass) took on 76 000 more workers, recruited principally by affiliates of firms in the United Kingdom and France and, to a lesser extent, Germany

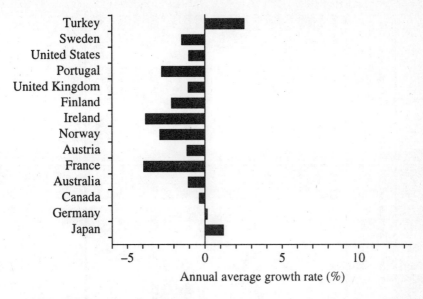

Annual average growth rate (%)

Notes:
1. For exact reference periods, see note to Figure 8.3
2. Domestically-owned firms: total number of figures, minus foreign affiliates.

Source: OECD, EAS Division, Industrial Activity of Foreign Affiliates data bank.

Figure 8.5   *Trend in employment in the manufacturing industry:*
            domestically-owned firms (average annual growth rate, 1980–90)

and Japan. Employment in the basic metals sector increased by 59 000, mainly in Japanese affiliates, since in this sector European firms (most of them German, British and French) did not recruit to any great extent.

Despite their strong representation in the motor industry, foreign affiliates increased their workforce moderately. Some 50 per cent of employment in foreign-owned companies is accounted for by affiliates belonging to firms in Japan, 8.5 per cent by German-owned firms. Companies based in other European countries have tended rather to shed labour over the past ten years.

Japan   Between 1980 and 1989,[8] foreign affiliates in Japan shed labour in every sector except 'other manufacturing industry' (see Table 8.2). While there has been some change in relation to the figures shown in that table as a result of the 1990 upturn in foreign investment, employment in manufacturing industry as a whole is still appreciably lower than in 1980. Between 1980 and 1990, the heaviest job losses in foreign affiliates were in the motor, chemicals, paper, non-metallic minerals, textiles and basic metals sectors. By

Table 8.1   United States: percentage of foreign affiliates by country of origin

Industry	Canada 1980	Canada 1990	Europe 1980	Europe 1990	UK 1980	UK 1990	Germany 1980	Germany 1990	France 1980	France 1990	Switzerland 1980	Switzerland 1990	Japan 1980	Japan 1990	Foreign subsidiaries' total employment 1980	Foreign subsidiaries' total employment 1990
Mining and quarrying	47.0	31.9	40.5	56.1	3.9	37.2	—	—	4.7	2.5	—	0.6	—	5.6	25 247	36 000
Food, beverages, tobacco	16.2	11.4	76.2	73.6	48.8	40.1	0.9	1.1	1.3	4.5	—	—	4.1	6.3	120 354	247 300
Textiles, leather, footwear	14.0	18.1	65.7	58.4	44.6	31.8	8.6	13.3	—	3.2	4.4	2.5	8.6	14.1	28 530	60 300
Wood, furniture	16.0	12.1	44.7	68.3	0.0	31.2	34.8	27.6	—	3.5	—	2.0	—	6.5	8 889	19 900
Paper, printing	—	33.8	50.8	56.7	—	23.3	—	9.4	—	—	—	—	—	—	78 452	170 500
Chemicals petroleum	2.7	—	93.7	69.1	17.4	—	46.0	—	5.0	8.5	—	9.8	1.1	—	307 079	626 000
of which:																
Drugs & medicines	0.0	*	79.6	88.0	14.2	27.9	3.3	3.7	—	—	3.8	46.6	—	6.1	33 056	115 000
Non-metallic mineral prod.	24.0	—	72.4	69.1	13.5	24.9	8.8	8.4	—	24.7	—	4.3	1.9	9.5	46 524	122 800
Basic metals	20.5	18.0	68.9	29.5	1.7	9.6	5.6	4.5	26.5	—	—	4.0	—	38.8	75 308	135 200
Machinery, Equipment	—	7.4	73.4	67.9	—	22.0	—	11.3	—	—	—	7.4	—	16.7	418 162	807 500
of which:																
Computers	—	1.1	—	46.0	—	16.6	—	4.4	—	—	—	1.5	—	45.0	—	61 300
Electrical mach.	17.6	12.1	62.3	71.1	9.9	15.6	9.7	13.3	1.6	6.6	4.1	—	4.1	12.2	172 507	290 100
Electronic comps	—	—	—	60.3	—	12.7	—	—	—	—	—	0.8	—	18.1	—	155 100
Motor vehicles	—	14.4	—	38.9	34.5	13.2	—	1.0	11.9	—	—	0.9	—	46.7	—	57 000
Other manufacturing ind.	2.9	2.9	69.4	79.5	—	—	—	—	—	—	4.9	8.0	—	7.4	21 662	31 200
Total manufacturing ind.	13.8	13.9	76.9	65.7	20.3	24.1	21.6	11.3	10.8	8.7	9.4	8.1	3.3	13.3	1 104 960	2 220 700
Commerce	9.7	21.9	71.4	56.3	—	12.4	—	19.4	—	5.8	5.6	—	11.2	15.7	521 442	1 174 600
Banking, insurance¹	—	—	55.7	54.6	32.7	23.9	3.2	2.0	—	0.5	—	11.5	—	15.0	106 840	230 400
Other services²	18.6	—	—	57.2	—	27.9	13.7	—	—	—	—	—	—	11.8	164 315	901 800

Notes:
1. Including services to enterprises.
2. Sectors 4+5+7+9 of ISIC.
* Less than 0.5 per cent.

Source: OECD, EAS, Industrial Activity of Foreign Affiliates data bank.

Table 8.2   Japan: employment of foreign subsidiaries by origin country or area (percentage of foreign subsidiaries' total employment)

Sectors	United States		EEC		Others		Foreign subsidiaries' total employment (natural persons)	
	1980	1990	1980	1990	1980	1990	1980	1990
Food, beverages, tobacco	79.0	86.6	20.9	12.1	0.0	1.2	3 020	3 455
Textiles, leather, footwear	28.3	0.8	0.0	6.4	71.6	92.8	2 246	1 630
Wood, cork, furniture	77.3	56.5	1.4	40.3	21.3	3.2	141	409
Paper, printing, publishing	77.4	45.8	1.9	32.6	20.6	21.5	2 334	1 026
Chemicals, petroleum	60.4	57.7	28.2	27.6	11.3	14.6	55 851	54 830
Non-metallic mineral products	86.2	41.4	10.7	35.2	3.0	23.3	6 307	1 621
Basic metals	29.6	4.0	0.5	2.2	69.8	93.7	11 150	4 812
Machinery, equipment	73.7	87.6	23.1	7.4	3.1	4.8	94 464	75 611
of which: Computers	—	—	—	—	—	—	—	—
Electric, electronic	95.6	93.7	4.3	5.4	0.07	0.8	31 710	53 670
Motor vehicles	98.6	53.9	1.3	40.6	0.04	5.4	26 260	2 990
Other manufacturing industries	83.2	33.4	10.8	58.5	5.9	7.9	2 549	1 327
Total manufacturing industries	66.9	71.1	22.1	16.0	10.9	12.8	178 062	144 721

Source: OECD, EAS Industrial Activity of Foreign Affiliates data bank.

133

contrast, employment increased, especially in 1990, in the electrical–electronic machinery industry and, to a lesser extent, in the timber and food sectors. Three-quarters of the jobs in foreign affiliates in the motor industry were lost in the space of ten years; their numbers fell from 26 260 to 2990. This very steep decline is wholly ascribable to disinvestment by US affiliates, whose turnover was divided by 17. European enterprises could by no means make up for this shrinkage of American affiliates. Even though their turnover increased tenfold, they created no more than 1000 new jobs. Labour shedding in the chemicals industry, the largest in Japan, is also ascribable to the retreat of American affiliates. Employment in European-based affiliates remained much the same.

Germany   Between 1980 and 1990, the number of foreign affiliates changed little, but they shed 162 000 jobs (see Table 8.3). The heaviest job losses were in the basic metals (53 000), chemicals (36 000) and electric–electronic machinery (31 000) sectors. In the basic metals sector, 44 000 jobs disappeared as European affiliates substantially reduced their capacity. In affiliates of non-European countries, fewer in size and number, there was little change. In the chemicals industry, American affiliates shed 18 000 jobs, European affiliates 8000. In the electric–electronic machinery sector, 38 000 jobs were lost in American and non-EC affiliates, whereas firms based in EC countries created 20 affiliates and employment increased by 33 000. Before 1980, all nine foreign affiliates in the computer sector were American. In 1990, ten new affiliates were established (six European, four American), creating 11 000 jobs, but this did not much alter the American/European employment mix.

France   Between 1981 and 1989, foreign affiliates in the manufacturing industry shed some 36 000 jobs. These losses were entirely attributable to minority-owned affiliates, employment in majority-owned affiliates having risen by 17 000 during the same period. It would seen that minority-owned affiliates were to be found in sectors in the process of being restructured, where employment has diminished sharply. As in Germany, foreign affiliates' heaviest losses were in the basic metals sector (–23 155) and were ascribable to capacity cutbacks by European firms. Foreign affiliates in the three other sectors (computers, electrical and electronic machinery and wood) also shed labour. In the first two sectors American affiliates have cut their workforces, and they have completely pulled out of the third (wood), so that since 1990 there have been no American affiliate in this sector.

The United Kingdom   Between 1985 and 1990, the workforce in foreign affiliates in the manufacturing industry increased by 98 000. About 59 000 jobs were held by EC firms, 34 000 by Japanese companies and 18 000 by enterprises based in other countries. American affiliates, while they still accounted for half of employment in foreign-owned firms, shed 13 900 jobs. Employment increased most substantially in the motor, computer, food and chemicals industries. In the motor sector, 67 per cent of new jobs in foreign-owned subsidiaries were created in European affiliates and 25 per cent in Japanese-owned subsidiaries starting from a low level, while employment in US affiliates changed little. In computer manufacture, it was the Japanese affiliates which chiefly accounted for the increase in employment. Employment growth in the agro-food sector was largely ascribable to firms based in some European non-EC countries (Switzerland in particular), that is, firms not based in a Triad (United States, EU, Japan) country (see Table 8.3).

Finland   There are not many foreign affiliates in the manufacturing industry in Finland (in 1990, 125 foreign affiliates employed 18 337 people). Between 1980 and 1990, foreign affiliate employment figures rose slightly, an increase ascribable to the establishment of subsidiaries, on the one hand by EC firms and on the other hand, probably, by Scandinavian-owned enterprises. Recruitment was highest in the paper, chemicals, non-metallic minerals and certain branches of the machinery sector. Jobs were lost, however, in the food, textiles and electrical machinery industries.

Norway   Between 1980 and 1989, the numbers of those employed by foreign affiliates overall changed very little. However, that apparent stability masked some major alterations in structure and geographical origin, above all cutbacks in the workforce of American affiliates in the electrical–electronic machinery sector (2914 job losses) and the arrival on the scene, in the same sector, of subsidiaries owned by firms in EC countries.

Turkey   There are still not many foreign-owned subsidiaries in Turkey (124 in 1990). However, a more open policy towards the end of the 1980s attracted some foreign investment. Between 1986 and 1990, the number of foreign affiliates, and their workforce, was multiplied by 2.5, and turnover by 13. Employment growth was largely ascribable to American affiliates (56 per cent) and to a lesser extent to subsidiaries owned by firms based in EC countries (37 per cent). The American firms, above all others, were responsible for the increase in electrical machinery, textiles and food sectors, the EC firms rather in the chemicals and motor industries.

Table 8.3   Foreign subsidiaries, employment by origin country or area

| | | Foreign subsidiaries, total employment | | Percentage of foreign subsidiaries, total employment | | | | | |
| | | All countries | | United States | | Japan | | EEC | |
Germany	ISIC	1980	1990	1980	1990	1980	1990	1980	1990
Mining and quarrying	2	5 000	0	0.00	—	—	—	100.00	—
Total manufacturing industries	3	779 000	617 000	47.37	44.89	0.13	2.27	23.62	28.36
Food beverages, tobacco	31	48 000	35 000	39.58	37.14	—	—	18.75	17.14
Textiles, leather, footwear	32	16 000	12 000	18.75	8.33	—	—	37.50	50.00
Wood and wood products	33	2 000	5 000	50.00	20.00	—	—	0.00	—
Paper, printing and publishing	34	13 000	18 000	15.38	5.56	—	—	7.69	16.67
Chemicals	35	155 000	119 000	35.48	31.09	—	1.68	31.61	34.45
Non-metallic mineral products	36	19 000	12 000	36.84	8.33	—	—	36.84	66.67
Basic metals	37	68 000	15 000	2.94	13.33	—	—	70.59	26.67
Machinery equipment	38	456 000	399 000	61.40	55.14	—	2.51	14.25	26.82
of which: Computers	3 825	36 000	47 000	100.00	89.36	—	2.13	—	6.38
Electrical machinery	383	130 000	99 000	46.92	23.23	—	5.05	17.69	56.57
Electronic components	3 832	—	—	—	—	—	—	—	—
Motor vehicles	3 843	136 000	124 000	84.56	87.90	—	—	—	—
Other manufacturing industries	39	3 000	2 000	33.33	100.00	—	—	0.00	7.26

France	ISIC	Foreign subsidiaries, total employment — All countries		Percentage of foreign subsidiaries, total employment — United States		Japan		EEC	
		1980	1990	1980	1990	1980	1990	1980	1990
Mining and quarrying	2	23 504	2 246	34.36	0.00	0.00	0.00	58.99	47.33
Total manufacturing industries	3	802 000	766 000	34.04	29.90	0.00	1.83	43.77	43.73
Food, beverages, tobacco	31	—	—	—	—	—	—	—	—
Textiles, leather, footwear	32	51 629	50 691	12.82	20.88	0.00	0.52	38.62	33.68
Wood and wood products	33	12 278	9 961	16.37	0.00	0.00	0.00	58.71	74.09
Paper, printing and publishing	34	43 047	50 264	33.25	30.40	0.00	0.00	40.61	37.01
Chemicals	35	158 325	178 732	36.90	32.79	0.00	3.46	46.40	43.88
Non-metallic mineral products	36	31 155	35 292	13.16	18.62	0.00	0.00	66.01	49.81
Basic metals	37	85 762	62 607	17.76	24.06	0.00	1.07	44.67	41.66
Machinery, equipment	38	377 548	361 873	40.07	31.64	0.00	0.96	33.74	41.95
of which: Computers	3 825	40 138	30 761	95.98	85.30	0.00	2.78	0.00	2.51
Electrical machinery	383	—	—	—	—	—	—	—	—
Electronic components	3 832	64 386	59 655	37.62	25.28	0.00	1.50	41.69	42.85
Motor vehicles	3 843	77 825	89 443	41.76	28.27	0.00	1.93	51.07	61.29
Other manufacturing industries	39	11 939	12 167	43.45	39.90	0.00	3.47	21.97	16.77

Table 8.3   continued

| United Kingdom | ISIC | Foreign subsidiaries, total employment | | Percentage of foreign subsidiaries, total employment | | | | | |
| | | All countries | | United States | | Japan | | EEC | |
		1980	1990	1980	1990	1980	1990	1980	1990
Mining and quarrying	2	—	—	—	—	—	—	—	—
Total manufacturing industries	3	677 100	775 100	61.44	51.88	0.93	5.28	14.15	19.97
Food, beverages, tobacco	31	57 700	73 400	66.55	48.77	0.00	—	10.92	—
Textiles, leather, footwear	32	15 900	—	50.94	—	0.00	—	20.13	—
Wood and wood products	33	4 800	5 900	27.08	35.89	—	0.00	43.75	64.41
Paper, printing and publishing	34	67 900	65 200	23.71	—	—	—	18.31	22.89
Chemicals	35	88 500	96 100	63.16	62.23	—	1.56	33.90	52.85
Non-metallic mineral products	36	11 800	19 300	45.76	26.42	0.00	—	5.56	—
Basic metals	37	21 600	23 600	33.80	21.61	0.00	—	—	—
Machinery equipment	38	359 500	417 200	71.71	57.55	1.64	8.17	11.79	19.15
of which: Computers	3 825	15 700	29 900	91.72	57.19	0.00	22.07	6.37	18.39
Electrical machinery	383	90 300	95 500	54.71	41.57	5.87	18.64	22.59	28.48
Electronic components	3 832	—	—	—	—	—	—	—	—
Motor vehicles	3 843	92 100	109 000	91.86	77.06	0.00	3.76	6.84	16.15
Other manufacturing industries	39	49 300	—	52.33	—	0.61	—	32.66	—

Source: OECD, EAS, Industrial Activity of Foreign Affiliates data bank.

Employment-related Factors

Skills and wages

A criticism that used to be levelled at foreign investment was that it could, in certain circumstances, encourage the creation of unskilled, assembly-type jobs,[9] to the detriment of skilled jobs. Empirical analysis of the facts soon blunted such criticism. Even if information relating directly to skills is not yet available, a certain amount can be learnt by looking at trends in the compensation of employees of foreign affiliates, which is well above host country averages. The theory that foreign investment depresses wages in the receiving country has been discredited by the empirical findings of this study, which demonstrate, on the contrary, that in all countries for which data are available, without exception, foreign firms offer wages which, overall, are higher than those paid by domestically-owned firms. These wage differentials can be explained in a number of ways. For example, foreign subsidiaries tend to concentrate on industries where wages per employee exceed the national average. The differentials may also reflect differences in skills, in the number of hours worked or in the organization of the labour market. They can also be explained by regional differences, the specific market conditions concerning

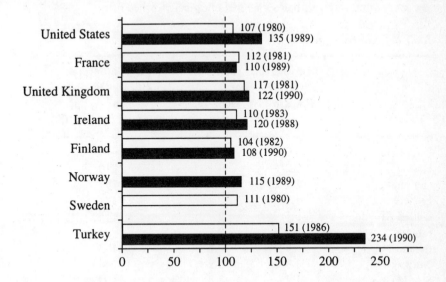

Source: OECD, EAS Division, Industrial Activity of Foreign Affiliates data bank.

Figure 8.6   Level of wages per employee in the manufacturing industry for foreign affiliates (national firms = 100)

foreign subsidiaries and probably by the size of these firms, which are often considerably larger than the average domestic firm. On the other hand, when wages per employee in foreign subsidiaries are compared with those of domestic firms of equivalent size which operate in the same sector and in the same locality and have a similar structure abroad, wage differentials tend to disappear.[10]

Figure 8.6 shows not only that the wages offered by foreign affiliates are invariably higher than those paid by domestically owned firms, but that between the beginning and end of the 1980s the differential widened still further. Wage differentials vary, too, even within a given sector, depending on the foreign affiliate's base country. These differences may be attributed to the factors mentioned above, such as the varying levels of productivity and skills. Where no information is available on these factors, the wage level could be a rough proxy.

Labour productivity

Looking at the trend of labour productivity in manufacturing industry (see Table 8.4 and Figure 8.7) in the 1980s, it can be seen that:

1. both the level and the rate of increase of labour productivity were usually higher in foreign affiliates than in domestically owned firms;

Table 8.4   Labour productivity in manufacturing industry

	Growth rate, 1980–90 (1985 prices)		Level of foreign affiliates in 1990 (when level in domestic firms = 100)
	Foreign affiliates	Domestic firms	
United States	4.0	—	—
Japan	0.2	4.1	210
Germany	2.7	2.2	197
France[1]	1.2	3.7	127
United Kingdom[2]	5.3	2.7	173
Finland	5.0	3.7	90
Ireland[3]	6.9	4.8	153
Norway	1.9	5.2	144
Sweden	1.7	3.8	109

Notes:
1. 1980–89.
2. 1985–90.
3. 1983–8.

2. in foreign affiliates labour productivity rises can be put down largely to higher output (see Figure 8.7) whereas in domestic firms they are ascribable rather to compressions in the number of employees;
3. only in Japan, Norway and Sweden does both the level and in half of the cases the rate of increase in labour productivity in domestic firms seem to be higher than in foreign affiliates.[11]

The higher productivity achieved by foreign affiliates in the majority of countries for which data are available is largely attributable to the sector of activity involved, but is also a matter of organization. One of the main competitive advantages enjoyed by multinational firms is their capacity to make use of having establishments throughout the world and to benefit from the comparative advantages offered by each individual market. By internalizing the many externalities available on these different markets, all the affiliates and firms in the same group or network are able to enjoy the relevant advantages.

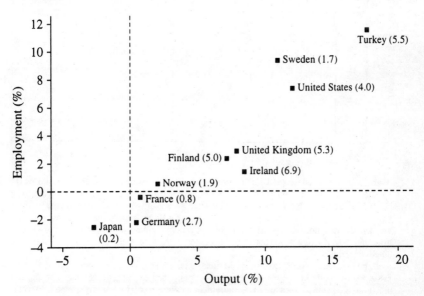

Notes:
1. The figures in brackets are the growth rates of productivity
2. Nearest years when 1980–90 unavailable.

Source: OECD, EAS Division, Industrial Activity of Foreign Affiliates data bank.

Figure 8.7   Trends in foreign affiliates' output, employment and productivity (average annual growth rate, 1980–90, 1985 prices)

Employment and changes in the number of enterprises
Numbers of jobs do not automatically increase when the number of foreign affiliates in a receiving country increases. Looking at the trend of the two variables, it can be seen that at the end of the 1980s the average size of

Size of Foreign Subsidiaries

		In growth	In reduction
Employees of Foreign Subsidiaries	In growth	United States Finland Sweden United Kingdom	Norway Ireland Portugal Turkey
	In reduction		Japan Germany France

Notes:
1. Average size increasing: (a) United States, Finland and Sweden. In all three countries the numbers employed grew faster than the number of firms. This may happen when the firms created or acquired by foreign companies are large, or when affiliates merge without shedding jobs, or when the foreign-owned firms that disappear are mainly small ones. (b) The United Kingdom is a special case in that numbers employed grew while numbers of firms *decreased*, suggesting that more affiliates merged or went under than in the three other countries.
2. Average size decreasing: (a) Japan, Germany and France. Numbers employed decreased faster than the number of firms. This may happen when existing firms shed jobs and any newly-created subsidiaries are of no more than medium size. (b) Norway, Ireland, Portugal and Turkey. Numbers employed grew faster than the number of firms. This may happen when large new foreign-owned companies are established (the most likely explanation) or when existing firms recruit.
3. Closer analysis of these trends would require additional information about mergers, acquisitions, creations or disappearance of foreign affiliates, broken down according to size.

Source: OECD, EAS Division, Industrial Activity of Foreign Affiliates data bank.

Figure 8.8 Size and employees of foreign subsidiaries

foreign affiliates (average number of employees per firm) grew in some countries (the United States, Finland, Sweden and the United Kingdom) whereas in others it shrank (Japan, Germany, France, Norway, Ireland, Portugal and Turkey) (see Figure 8.8). But whichever happened, the average size of foreign affiliates was invariably larger than the average size of domestically owned firms (see Table 8.5). Figure 8.8 ranks foreign affiliates according to change in size.

Table 8.5   Number of employees per firm

	Foreign affiliates		Domestic firms	
	1980	1990	1980	1990
United States	896	913	—	—
Japan	347	242	29	30
Germany	523	416	28	27
France	354	267[1]	—	—
United Kingdom	371	537	50	30
Ireland[2]	102	99	29	26
Sweden	146	193	38	22
Norway	110	90[1]	42	40[1]
Finland	122	146	74	69

Notes:
1.   1989.
2.   1983 and 1988

Source: OECD, EAS Division, Industrial Activity of Foreign Affiliates data bank.

THE IMPACT ON TRADE

The theoretical and empirical problems involved in analysis of the interaction between direct investment flows and trade flows are too numerous and complex to be considered in this chapter. Just two questions will be looked at here: (1) the extent to which foreign subsidiaries are at the same time exporting firms, and (2) what influence they have on the overall trade balances of host countries. However, a vast area of work could be under consideration here.

It is generally agreed that it is on trade that foreign investment has the most direct and possibly the biggest impact and, paradoxically, this is something that has received relatively little attention at either the theoretical or the empirical level. For this there are two possible reasons. The first has to do

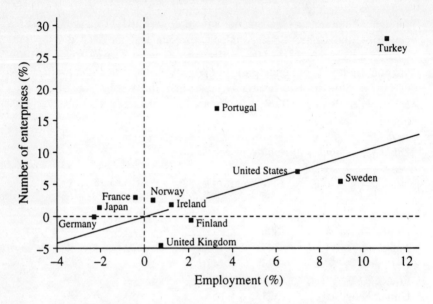

Source: OECD, EAS Division, Industrial Activity of Foreign Affiliates data bank.

Figure 8.9 *Average annual growth rate in the number of foreign affiliates and the number of their employees, 1980–90*

with the traditional theory of international economics and its basic assumptions which do not allow for the role of multinationals as major players in trade. According to the most conservative estimates, the latter account for more than a third of international trade, a growing proportion of which takes place within their 'internalized' area but remains 'off market' in the sense that the prices of the goods and services which make up these trade flows (intra-firm flows) are 'transfer prices'. In 1990, some 75 per cent of imports to the United States by foreign subsidiaries derived from the foreign parent company, while 41 per cent of these subsidiaries' exports went to the parent company.

The second major reason is the lack of sufficiently detailed and comparable data on direct investment flows and trade flows.

Foreign Subsidiaries and their Export Performance

It might reasonably be supposed that the main task of foreign subsidiaries is to meet local demand in the host country, exports being only a secondary objective. The fact is, however, that the vast majority of them export and import more than domestic firms (see Table 8.6). This is mainly because

Table 8.6   *Exports and imports by employee of foreign subsidiaries and total economy, 1989 (thousands of dollars)*

	Exports by employee		Imports by employee	
	Foreign subsidiaries	Total economy	Foreign subsidiaries	Total economy
United States (1990)	14.8	11.7	20.5	16.9
Japan	32.7	21.7	12.8	11.1
France	49.9	38.1	—	52.2
Sweden	66.1	50.4	—	50.8
Finland	47.0	56.1	—	53.3
Portugal (1984)	11.0	7.7	10.3	7.2

Source: OECD, EAS Division, Industrial Activity of Foreign Affiliates data bank.

foreign subsidiaries are big companies with a dominant position in their sector. However, two other reasons can explain this result.

First, foreign subsidiaries are much more fully integrated in world trade than are domestic firms. When a foreign subsidiary is set up, irrespective of whether it is entirely new or involves the acquisition of an existing firm, close ties are immediately established not just with the parent company, but also with a network of related firms operating at world level. Even where acquisitions are concerned, being able to obtain commodities, intermediate products and services from a multitude of foreign sources at a lower price increases the degree of dependence on imports from overseas, and especially from the parent company when new investment is involved. Where exports are concerned, too, links with the parent company can be just as strong, particularly in the case of products subcontracted by the subsidiary and re-exported to the parent company, or high-technology products to be marketed worldwide.

Second, the majority of foreign subsidiaries belong to sectors which are highly exposed to foreign trade. Many acquisitions are made because of the strong propensity of the firms concerned to import, which will be of benefit to the parent company. This is why it is preferable to make comparisons between manufactured products which, from the trade standpoint, are similar. However, it is difficult to establish comparisons even between manufacturing products because of classification problems. Foreign subsidiaries' trade figures are classified, in their entirety, according to the main activity of the subsidiary in question; this includes products deriving from their secondary activities.[12] The result is that, when these secondary activities concern services (examples being distribution, marketing, and so on), exports of manufactures are overestimated. Conversely, when the secondary activities are in manufacturing, that sector's trade will be underestimated, for example, in the motor industry.

Economy-wide comparisons of the propensities to export and import of domestic firms and foreign subsidiaries can introduce further distortions, inasmuch as part of the output of domestic firms may not be traded, whereas virtually the whole of the production of foreign subsidiaries is. Figure 8.10 shows that foreign subsidiaries' propensity to export manufactures is greater than that of domestic firms in the United States, France and Sweden, and slightly lower in Japan and Finland. While not losing sight of the limitations of such comparisons, the result for Japan and Finland could be explained by the low level of foreign investment which has not yet reached the critical threshold at which the focus can be switched to foreign markets. It may also be the case that some of this investment concerns sectors which are not very export-oriented. In Japan, for example, foreign subsidiaries' propensity to import is between five and seven times greater than that of domestic firms.

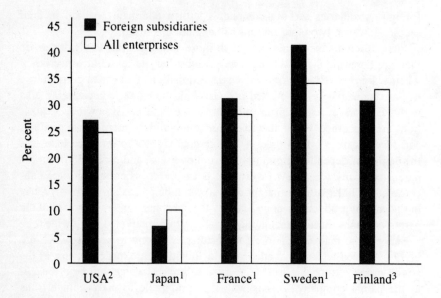

Notes:
* Exports/turnover.
1. 1989.
2. Exports/value added.
3. Exports/production.

Source: OECD, Industrial Activity of Foreign Affiliates data bank.

Figure 8.10   Export propensities* in manufacturing, 1990

Some caution should be shown, however, in interpreting the foreign subsidiaries' marked propensity to import. Most of the imports simply pass through the subsidiaries prior to dispatch to other producers or local consumers. Foreign subsidiaries may sometimes carry out minor processing operations or assembly work on the imported products for which they are not the real consignees. Even if these firms did not exist, the imports would probably continue and the impact on an economy's total deficit would be less significant.

At the sectoral level, the target for the majority of foreign firms is the host country's domestic market. However, exports can also become an objective when investment reaches a certain level. In the United States, for example, it is in the sectors where the presence of foreign firms is greatest (computers, electronics, chemicals) that the propensities to export are the highest (see Figure 8.11). In the motor, textile, paper and food industries, on the other hand, foreign firms are mainly there to meet domestic demand.

In Japan, the situation is somewhat different inasmuch as it is in the textile industry, with few foreign firms but a high level of import penetration (see

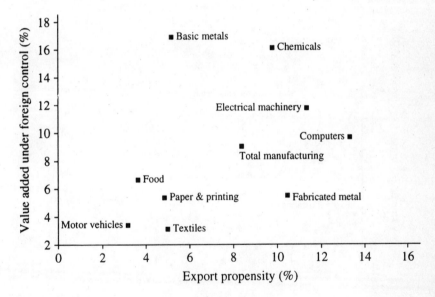

Notes:
1. Penetration: value added of foreign subsidiaries/value added of all firms.
2. Export propensity: exports/turnover of foreign subsidiaries.

Source: OECD, EAS, Industrial Activity of Foreign Affiliates data bank.

Figure 8.11   United States: penetration of foreign subsidiaries and export propensity, 1990

Figure 8.12 and Table 8.7), that the propensity to export is greatest. Foreign subsidiaries in this industry appear rather to aim at overseas markets in order to reduce the sector's import dependence, unlike the chemicals industry, where they aim more at the domestic market.

In France penetration by foreign subsidiaries is greatest in the data processing and electronics industries which aim at the domestic and foreign markets to an equal degree (see Table 8.8). In Sweden and Finland, even though their presence is fairly modest, foreign subsidiaries export a large proportion of their output. This is striking in the case of the paper industry, where these countries enjoy big comparative advantages, but the propensity to export is also quite high in the wood, basic metals and motor industries.

Foreign Subsidiaries and Trade Balances

Analysis of the contribution that foreign subsidiaries make to the overall trade balance comes up against both the difficulties referred to above, and

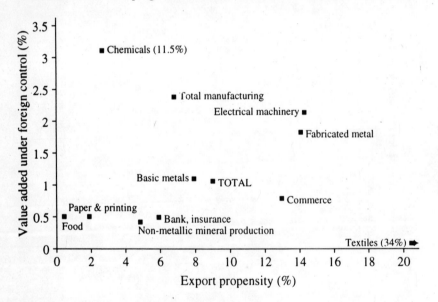

Notes:
1. Penetration: turnover of foreign subsidiaries/turnover of all firms.
2. Export propensity: exports/turnover of foreign subsidiaries.

Source: OECD, EAS, Industrial Activity of Foreign Affiliates data bank.

Figure 8.12   Japan: penetration of foreign subsidiaries and export propensity, 1989

Table 8.7 Trade balance and export and import propensities* of foreign affiliates in Japan (millions, of yen)

Sectors	Trade balance		Export propensity		Import propensity	
	1980	1990	1980	1990	1980	1990
Food, beverages, tobacco	−24.6	−20.0	0.0	0.4	14.4	10.8
Textiles, clothing, leather	2.6	−0.3	18.0	34.0	10.1	36.4
Wood, furniture	0.4	−0.3	28.9	—	13.5	26.4
Paper, printing	−12.0	−57.3	0.7	1.9	16.4	41.9
Chemicals, petroleum	−4 854.9	−1 703.5	3.4	2.7	58.6	35.6
Non-metallic mineral products	−0.9	−7.7	8.0	4.8	8.6	16.8
Basic metals	−46.5	−52.1	4.1	7.9	13.1	25.1
Machinery, equipment	273.9	−1.4	22.7	14.0	11.3	14.1
of which: Electric, electronics	−58.6	—	15.9	—	24.1	—
Motor vehicles	255.4	—	29.6	—	0.8	—
Other manufacturing industries	0.0	−2.3	4.9	6.0	4.8	7.5
Total manufacturing ind.	−4 662.0	−1 845.4	7.3	6.8	45.4	26.8
Trade	−702.0	−1 022.2	5.7	13.0	19.0	35.5
Banking, insurance, real estate	4.7	14.7	5.2	5.8	2.4	13.6
Construction, energy, other services	13.8	19.9	12.4	62.1	0.4	14.8
Grand total	−5 345.5	−2 862.4	6.8	8.9	36.8	29.4

Note: * Exports and imports on turnover

Source: OECD, EAS Division, Industrial Activity of Foreign Affiliates data bank.

Table 8.8 Penetration rates of foreign affiliates and export propensities

Sectors	France (1990) Foreign penetration[1]	France (1990) Export propensity	Sweden (1989) Foreign penetration[2]	Sweden (1989) Export propensity	Finland (1990) Foreign penetration[2]	Finland (1990) Export propensity
Food, beverages, tobacco	—	—	11.6	13.4	1.9	8.2
Textiles, clothing, leather	15.8	29.5	6.7	19.5	3.9	32.6
Wood, furniture	10.3	13.9	2.5	31.3	0.7	31.8
Paper, printing, publishing	26.4	17.7	8.2	50.7	0.9	48.3
Chemicals, petroleum	44.5	28.7	30.1	38.2	9.2	27.8
Stone, clay, glass	25.5	18.9	32.7	19.3	3.6	7.1
Basic metals	18.7	31.6	11.4	61.9	2.6	37.2
Machinery, equipment	28.0	36.5	17.4	47.1	8.8	43.0
of which: Computers	73.6	45.0	—	—	—	—
Electric, electronics	31.3	36.7	—	—	1.4	46.4
Motor vehicles	18.9	30.5	—	—	—	—
Other manufacturing industries	21.2	30.3	13.3	19.1	5.2	34.7
Total manufacturing industries	28.4	28.3	15.3	33.8	4.3	32.5

Notes:
1. Weight of foreign affiliates in the sector's turnover.
2. Weight of foreign affiliates in the sector's gross output.

Source: OECD, EAS Division, Industrial Activity of Foreign Affiliates data bank.

also a lack of information – especially concerning imports. At present, just two countries have provided data on both the exports and imports of foreign subsidiaries – the United States and Japan – but only the American data are broken down by both sector and country of origin. In 1990, foreign subsidiaries in the United States accounted for 23 per cent of the country's total exports and 36 per cent of its imports, compared with 3 and 14 per cent, respectively, in the case of Japan.

A first breakdown of the US trade deficit between 1977 and 1990 shows that, 1984 and 1985 apart, foreign subsidiaries had a consistently bigger deficit than did other American firms (see Figure 8.13). Another breakdown in the United States shows that the bulk of the deficit throughout the 1980s was attributable to trade by non-manufacturing firms, and in particular firms in the distributive sector (wholesaling and retailing). The chemicals industry is the only major sector in surplus, while 90 per cent of the motor industry deficit is accounted for by commercial firms (–$40.8 billion). The scale of intra-firm trade has increased subsidiaries' deficits, in particular because of the sharp rise in imports after 1983.

A breakdown of the deficits of foreign subsidiaries by geographical origin shows that they widened after 1983, this being attributable to Japanese and to a lesser extent European subsidiaries (see Figure 8.14). In 1990, Japanese

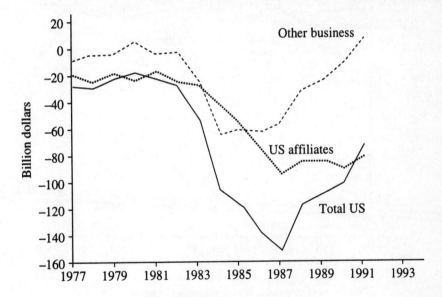

Source: US Department of Commerce, Bureau of Economic Analysis.

Figure 8.13 United States: breakdown of the trade deficit

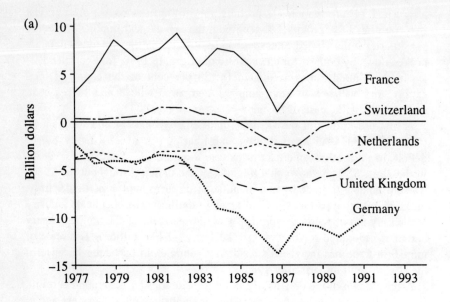

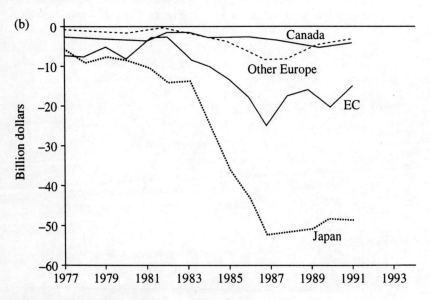

Source: US Department of Commerce, Bureau of Economic Analysis.

Figure 8.14   *United States: trade balance of foreign subsidiaries by
             geographical origin (billions of dollars)*

subsidiaries recorded the bulk of their deficit ($48.5 billion) in wholesaling, and more especially in the motor vehicle and electronic products industries ($28 and $16.1 billion, respectively). The deficit was entirely attributable to imports from parent companies. The deficit recorded by German subsidiaries in 1990 ($10.8 billion) was also attributable in intra-firm trade, but the vast bulk of it concerned the motor industry. The deficit posted by British subsidiaries ($5.3 billion), which is relatively modest, is notable for the existence of small deficits in many sectors, none predominating. French subsidiaries are the only ones (together, to some extent, with Swiss subsidiaries) to have recorded a surplus for most of the 1980s. This was attributable to exports of agricultural products to third countries.

In Japan, the trade deficit posted by foreign subsidiaries shrank considerably following the fall in foreign investment, narrowing from ¥5.3 billion in 1980 to ¥2.8 billion in 1990. This decrease was almost entirely attributable to trade in manufactures, and more particularly to the chemicals industry, whose exports fell by half and its imports by two-thirds.

An Alternative Method of Calculating Trade Balances

Because of the globalization of the economy, the traditional measurement of market shares based on firms' activity within national frontiers is no longer entirely satisfactory. When a production subsidiary is established on a foreign market, it is in response to a desire to win that market by a means other than exports. Multinationalization is a clear extension of an export policy. Also, setting up abroad is often the best way to preserve an earlier flow of exports or to replace it with other flows which complement the previous ones.

While exports and imports are the basic variables used in macroeconomic analysis of a country's production and employment, it is being recognized increasingly that, to have a complete picture of firms' global activities, sales by their foreign affiliates need to be taken into account. In the case of the United States, for example, the overwhelming majority (85 per cent) of sales by American multinationals to unaffiliated foreign firms in 1991 were in the form of local sales by their affiliates and only 15 per cent were the result of direct exports by parent companies. Clearly, therefore, sales via affiliates is a factor that needs to be taken into consideration during trade negotiations and, of course, when analysing the global activities of multinational firms.

In the traditional balance of payments approach, foreign affiliates' purchases and sales are not recorded in the accounts of host countries, except indirectly if these transactions affect revenue from direct investment and can indirectly influence exports and imports. In balance of payments accounts the activities of foreign affiliates are classified in the host country 'residents' category, rather than in that of the country which owns the capital. Thus direct investment income (retained earnings, interest and dividends) is re-corded by the investor country as revenue from abroad and by the host country as a payment to abroad. In contrast, foreign affiliates' local sales are not recorded, being regarded as transactions between residents of the same country. It follows that foreign affiliates' profits are included in the GNP of the investor country, but excluded from its GDP, while their output is in-cluded in the GDP of the host country and excluded from the GDP of the investor country. Similarly, goods and services for export are included in both the GNP and GDP of the exporting country, irrespective of the country of destination and the links between the firms involved in the transactions (af-filiate with parent company, for example). Likewise, imported goods and services are excluded from the GDP and GNP of the importing country.

On the basis of this information, various alternative methods have recently been developed which incorporate both cross-border sales, as defined in the balance of payments framework (based on the notion of 'residence') and foreign affiliates' sales in their country of location (notion of 'ownership'). The major principle of these methods is that they exclude sales between entities belonging to the same owner country. Borders are no longer geo-graphical, but are determined by the origin of the capital's ownership. These new methods of calculation are confined to goods and services transactions and those involving direct investment. Transactions concerning portfolio

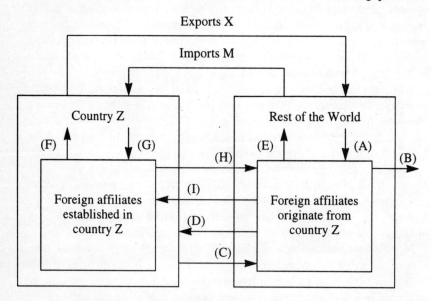

*Figure 8.15 Calculation of the trade balance for a country Z according to
          the nationality of its firms*

investment and other capital transfers are not taken into account. Analysis of a country's trade transactions based on the ownership of its productive assets throughout the world may be presented as follows (see Figure 8.15).

Exports X' of country Z, according to the nationality of its firms:

$$X' = X + A + B - C - H - E$$

where

X = exports of country Z goods services, residence basis,
A = sales by foreign affiliates from country Z to unaffiliated foreigners,
B = exports of country Z's affiliates to their foreign affiliates,
C = exports of country Z's firms to their own affiliates abroad,
H = exports of foreign affiliates established in country Z to the rest of the world,
E = local (non Z's) purchases of goods and non-factor services by foreign affiliates of Z's companies.

Imports M' of country Z, according to the nationality of its firms:

$$M' = M - D - I + F - G$$

where

M = imports of country Z goods and services, residence basis,
D = imports from foreign affiliates of country Z companies,
I = imports by country Z affiliates of foreign companies, less imports of country Z's affiliates from their foreign affiliates,
F = sales by country Z affiliates of foreign companies less their exports (H),
G = local purchases of goods and non-factor services by country Z affiliates of foreign companies (country Z sales).

The trade balance according to firms' nationality will thus be:

$$B' = X' - M' = (X + A + B - C - H - E) - (M - D - I + F - G)$$

In the case of the United States and Japan, these calculations would give the following results:

United States: 1991
Traditional trade balance of goods and services:
B = $X - M$
B = \$(581.2 − 609.1) billion
B = − \$28 billion
Trade balance based on firms' nationality:

$$B' = X' - M' = (X + A + B - C - H - E) - (M - D - I + F - G)$$
$$B' = \$[(581.1 + 1\ 188.4 + 8.4 - 139.9 - 108.4 - 713.4)$$
$$- (609.1 - 108.7 - 182.2 + 1\ 065.6 - 731.5)]\ \text{billion}$$
$$B' = \$(816.2 - 652.3)\ \text{billion} = \$US\ 164.1\ \text{billion}$$

In these calculations affiliates' purchases of goods and services from foreigners are deducted from their sales, but their payments to foreign capital and labour are not. (See also National Academy of Sciences study panel, Table 8.9.)

Japan: 1991

Traditional trade balance of goods only:

$$B = X - M$$
$$B = \$(314.5 - 236.7)\ \text{billion} = \$77.8\ \text{billion}$$

Trade balance based on firms' nationality:

$$B' = B' = X' - M' = \$(503.9 - 368.4)\ \text{billion} = \$135.5\ \text{billion}$$

In this approach, with respect to local sales and purchase, only purchased goods and non-factor services are included.

Global trade transactions based on the ownership of the firms show a positive trade balance for the United States and an increase in the Japanese surplus. However, these calculations still have an experimental side, as certain methodological difficulties have not yet been satisfactorily resolved. Amongst the problems still awaiting a satisfactory methodological solution are the following:

1. Inclusion of the sales of minority foreign-controlled firms (between 10 and 50 per cent) can pose problems of double counting in calculating overall totals. One solution might be to calculate all transactions proportionately to the percentage of control, of else to confine the calculations to majority-owned firms.
2. Identifying the investor country. Double counting can also occur when the country of ultimate ownership is not the country of the parent company. This difficulty could be eliminated by taking account only of ultimate ownership and not of the origin of the parent company.
3. Transactions between affiliates controlled by the same foreign country, but whose parent companies are not the same. In order to determine whether or not to include these transactions when calculating the affiliates' net sales, it is necessary to know the country of origin of each firm with which the affiliates have done business, and this information is not always easy to obtain.

That said, these calculations give a fuller picture of the globalization of multinational firms' activities and provide an idea of the capacity of a country's firms to be competitive on world markets. Also they throw light on the nature of certain transactions (deficits or surpluses involving affiliates, the importance of intra-firm trade,[13] and so on).

Similar studies have recently been carried out in the United States by the National Academy of Sciences (NAS),[14] and also by DeAnne Julius.[15] These studies indicate, for 1991, a net United States balance on global sales and purchases of goods and services of $24 billion (the Julius proposal) or $164 billion (the NAS proposal), compared with a $28 billion deficit on traditional balance of payments definitions (see Table 8.9). A recent US Department of Commerce study reviewed these proposals and, in addition, suggested a set of supplemental accounts that, while providing additional information on ownership, retained residency as their basis of organization.

These calculations, like the preceding ones, regard foreign affiliates located in host countries as foreign firms, and affiliates of domestic firms abroad as domestic firms in so far as they are controlled by domestic capital. In the National Academy of Sciences framework, global net sales (foreign sales less foreign purchases) are defined as the sum of the following three components: (1) net cross-border sales[16] by US-controlled domestic firms, (2) net foreign sales by US foreign affiliates, and (3) net sales by US firms to foreign affiliates in the United States.

The main differences between the NAS method and that proposed by Julius concern the calculation of affiliates' net sales, that is, their sales less their purchases. Whereas in the NAS method purchases include payments to foreign capital and labour,[17] in the Julius method these are excluded. The NAS measure, by not regarding foreign supplied labour and capital as a 'purchase' of the investor country, includes in the investor country's 'net sales' to foreigners the returns to foreign-supplied factors of production. This may be appropriate from the standpoint of analysis of the affiliate's productive activity in the host country, but it may give misleading signals if used as a general country-level macroeconomic indicator, since it commingles returns to factors of production supplied by the host country with those supplied by the investor country. The Julius method (as well as the alternative residency-based approach, see Table 8.9) avoids the problem of commingling of returns to factors of production supplied by different countries and thus could be said to be more consistent with traditional macroeconomic indicators, though it could be argued that it may be less useful for some other purpose (for example, as an indicator of company performance).

Another difference between the two approaches concerns the way information is recorded. In the NAS approach, net sales and net purchases are registered separately for inward and outward investment. Julius, on the other hand, proposes that local purchases of goods and services by foreign affiliates be seen as a component of sales by foreigners to the United States (instead of subtract-

Table 8.9　International economic performance of the United States, 1991 (billions of US dollars)

	Residency-based frameworks		Ownership-based frameworks	
	Cross-border trade in goods and services	Alternative residency-based approach, including both cross-border trade and net sales through affiliates	National Academy of Sciences proposal	Julius proposal
US sales to foreigners	581	632	816	2 523
US purchases	609	608	652	2 499
Balance	−28	24	164	24

Source:　*Survey of Current Business* (December 1993).

ing them from American affiliates' total sales), using ratios based on estimates of the supposed local content. (The *Survey of Current Business* article provides real information, not estimates of local content.) This also explains why sales are higher in the Julius approach than in the NAS method.

Also presented in Table 8.9 are the results of another alternative approach which is closer to conventional calculations of direct investment income. The trade surplus is identical to that in the Julius approach, even though the latter starts with much higher flows. Compared with the NAS approach, the surplus is much smaller because of differences in the way net sales of foreign affiliates are calculated, and also owing to the fact that American firms' foreign affiliates obtain more factors of production outside the United States than do foreign affiliates inside.

CONCLUSIONS

This chapter has provided an admittedly incomplete but nevertheless fairly novel overview of the influence of foreign investment on industrial activity in the host country. It has been shown that, in the great majority of cases, such investment is very important to host country economies because it brings tangible and intangible assets which make it possible to mobilize those countries' own resources – in particular manpower. The level of foreign subsidiaries' skills and productivity is above the national average, while at the same time these subsidiaries hasten the pace of technology transfers. In so doing, they generate positive externalities from which the whole of the host country's industrial system can benefit.

Foreign subsidiaries' propensities to export and import are greater than those of domestic firms, but the increase in imports from source countries, which is mainly apparent in the United States in the case of new investment, ought not to affect host countries' competitiveness in view of all the other positive effects and of a continuing high level of competition.

It hardly needs pointing out that the focus in this chapter has been only on the influence of foreign investment on the domestic economy. Another aspect to be investigated, which is harder to tackle but is also very topical, is that of the impact on the investor country's economy of the relocation of production units abroad. No such study has been included in this analysis because of the lack of information, but it will doubtless need to be given priority in the near future.

NOTES

1. For a more general presentation, see 'The Performances of Foreign Affiliates in OECD Countries', (OECD, 1994).
2. John H. Dunning, 'The Eclectic Paradigm of International Production: a Personal Perspective', in Christos N. Pitelis and R. Sugden (eds), *The Nature of the Transnational Firm*, London: Routledge, 1990.
3. O.E. Williamson, *The Economic Institutions of Capitalism*, New York: The Free Press, 1985.
4. Frédérique Sachwald 'Les Entreprises Japonaises en Europe. Motivations et Stratégies' (IFRI), Paris: Masson, 1993.
5. E. Graham and Paul Krugman, *Foreign Direct Investment in the United States*, 2nd edn, Washington, D.C.: Institute for International Economics, 1991.
6. It is often considered that relocation abroad (subject related to the 'outward' investments) adversely affects employment in that jobs go to another country. Although, by using input–output tables, the indirect effects of redeploying labour from one sector to another can be calculated, there is no way of taking into account, at the microeconomic level, the positive effects on employment that may come about because of the parent firm and industrial group concerned increase their competitiveness and earn more as a result. And while it is often assumed that, if there had been no relocation abroad the parent company would have created or maintained the same number of jobs in the original country, this may well be a false assumption, given the need to be competitive internationally.
7. Currently no country established a direct correlation between the trend in the different types of investment as categorized above and the effect brought about by each separate one of them. Apart from the United States, few countries make any distinction as regards job creations or losses relating to those types of investment. This was done in the United States for the period 1980–90 (see the country study). However, the findings were partially aggregated, so that some estimates have to be made. Moreover, all the jobs in firms acquired by foreign companies are regarded as new jobs. The data in this section concern the manufacturing sector only. As matters stand at present, few countries make service job figures available, and then only in a highly aggregated form. So, although the question of how services are affected by international investment is an interesting one, it cannot be treated systematically in this chapter.
8. The period for which comparable data on the activities of domestically owned firms are available.
9. Obviously, this charge would be meaningless if the labour market were perfect. In such a

market, wage differentials would reflect workers' performance rather than 'good' and 'bad' jobs. As pointed out in a study on labour economics (Carl Shapiro and Joseph E. Stiglitz, 'Equilibrium unemployment as a worker discipline device', *American Economic Review*, Vol. 84, No. 3, June 1984, pp. 433–44), wage differentials can be the result of market failures. Certainly, as international integration proceeds, foreign firms can have a negative influence on the receiving country's economy if they offer only unskilled, low-paid work and keep the best-paid jobs at home. In the medium term this will tend to depress wages – and therefore the standard of living – in the receiving country.

10. See also 'Payroll per Employee of Foreign and US-owned Manufacturing Establishments', in *Foreign Direct Investment in the United States: An Update*, US Department of Commerce, June 1993, pp. 56–7.

11. This may be attributable, in Japan, to the steep fall in foreign affiliates' output (despite their higher productivity) and in Sweden, France and Norway to heavy job-shedding by domestic firms.

12. In the United States, however, Benchmark Survey data are collected 'by product' for 12 SITC categories at the enterprise level. Additional product detail may be available in the future from a project to link Bureau of Economic Analysis data on foreign direct investment in the United States with Census Bureau data on US trade by detailed product at the establishment level.

13. Marcus Bonturi and Kiichiro Fukasaku, 'Globalisation and intra-firm trade: an empirical note', OECD Economic Studies No. 20, Spring 1993.

14. J. Steven Landefeld, Obic G. Whichard and Jeffrey H. Lowe, 'Alternative Frameworks for US International Transactions', *Survey of Current Business*, December 1993.

15. DeAnne Julius, *Global Companies and Public Policy*, New York: Council on Foreign Relations Press, 1990.

16. [Total exports of American firms to their affiliates minus exports of foreign affiliates in the United States], less [total imports of American affiliates abroad minus imports of foreign affiliates in the United States].

17. The American economy can obviously be differently affected, depending on where its affiliates make their purchases. If, for example, an engineering study is carried out in the United States by the parent company of an American multinational on behalf of its affiliate in Germany, the impact on the American economy will be different from what it would have been had the study been conducted by the affiliate in Germany on its own behalf.

9. 'Managed' growth, relocation and restructuring: the evolution of Japan's motor industry into a dominant multinational player

Terutomo Ozawa

INTRODUCTION

Japan's motor, electronics and office equipment industries, in particular, are noted for their technological prowess in the world market. Although the overall productivity of the Japanese economy is still at a lower level than that of the United States (since the former has many inefficient industrial and service sectors), the above-cited Japanese industries dominate the world in productivity. There are many sources of competitiveness, but what underlies their competitiveness is Japan's technological achievement in the form of what is popularly known as 'lean' or 'flexible' manufacturing, which originated in Japan's motor industry as a new alternative to the conventional paradigm of mass production.

In fact, Japan's current huge trade surplus can be largely accounted for by the three main categories of industry: motor vehicles and car parts, electronic goods (mostly audio-video and communications equipment and semiconductors) and general machinery (mostly office and data-processing equipment and machine tools). In 1992, for example, Japan's motor industry registered a trade surplus of as much as $71.3 billion ($79.2 billion of exports and $7.9 billion of imports, a ratio of 10:1), while Japan's overall merchandise trade surplus was $106.6 billion. Moreover, no less than half of Japan's trade surplus with the United States is attributable to this industry alone.

How significant the new manufacturing paradigm of lean production is in Japan's motor industry as the major source of its global competitiveness seems to be not fully appreciated in general or even grossly underestimated with respect to its distinctive competitive characteristics (that is, its capacity to raise productivity and quality and to facilitate product development), perhaps because of its very newness and because of a lack of information to – hence ignorance on the part of – the public.[1]

This chapter analyses why it was Japan's motor industry (not America's or Europe's) that initiated and innovated such a dramatic change in motor manufacturing, and examines its impact on the growth of the industry in Japan and its evolutionary path from a home-based exporter to a multinational operator. In this connection, the government's role in industrial development will also be touched upon, since the motor industry was once promoted as a strategic industry in Japan. And the notion of what may be called 'reserved competition' will be explored as a unique institutional feature (a dynamic version of 'infant industry' protection) in Japan's successful development of the motor industry. The leitmotif of this chapter is that *the evolutionary process of multinationalization of Japan's motor industry is an emanation of its past developmental experiences which witnessed the origination and spread of lean production*. The present dominance of Japan's motor industry as a global player is thus explained in terms of its historical dynamics.

LEAN PRODUCTION: AN INDUSTRIAL MILIEU-MOULDED ORGANIZATIONAL INNOVATION

The revolutionary nature of lean production is well articulated and publicized in Womack *et al.* (1990):

> After World War II, [Toyota Motor in Japan] pioneered the concept of lean production. The rise of Japan to its current economic preeminence quickly followed, as other Japanese companies and industries copied this remarkable system.
>
> Manufacturers around the world are now trying to embrace lean production, but they're finding the going rough. The companies that first mastered this system were all headquartered in one country – in Japan. As lean production has spread to North America and Western Europe under their aegis, trade wars and growing resistance to foreign investment have followed... Many Western companies now understand lean production... However, superimposing lean-production methods on existing mass-production systems causes great pain and dislocation.
>
> But why should we care if world manufacturers jettison decades of mass production to embrace lean production? Because the adoption of lean production, as it inevitably spreads beyond the auto industry, will change everything in almost every industry – choices for consumers, the nature of work, the fortune of companies, and ultimately, the fate of nations. (Womack *et al.*, pp. 11–12)

Some qualifications are in order. Womack *et al.* may have gone somewhat overboard in asserting that lean production 'will change everything in almost every industry'. As will be explained below, lean production is rather specific to, and originates and thrives in, what I call 'components-intensive, assembly-based' industries (Ozawa, 1991, 1992) which by nature can and need to produce differentiated products for competitive reasons.[2] It is true that 'The companies that first mastered this system were all headquartered in one country – in Japan', but those companies are mostly in motor vehicles, electronics and certain types of machinery – and not in food processing, chemicals and other traditional (material-transforming) sectors. In fact, this explains the 'unevenness' of productivity in Japanese industry.

As will be discussed below, cars, electronics and certain types of machinery are the industries where a high degree of precise 'interstitial coordinations' among a myriad of parts, components and accessories (PCAs) is required. Although 'other companies and industries copied this remarkable system', they only adopted more or less in a fragmentary fashion some methods of lean production, such as the 'just-in-time' (JIT) delivery system, in-process quality control, on-the-job training of shopfloor workers for multi-skilling via job rotation, and teamwork-based *kaizen* (constant improvement) efforts. In other words, the lean production system is not as effectively applicable to them in its totality as it is to assembly-based industries. Their production is mostly centred on a physical transformation of inputs (say, flour) into processed products (say, cakes) without involving the confluence of separately produced parts and components in a great variety to be sequentially assembled at different work stations from upstream to downstream operations. The need for, and degree of, interstitial coordination are thus much lower, if not insignificant. On the other hand, Japan's competitiveness in the assembly-based industries clearly stems from the widespread adoption and continuous upgrading of lean production, whose methods are *most* suitable for them. The nature of this new manufacturing system will be detailed later on.

THE MOTOR INDUSTRY

The Reserved Competition Paradigm

As a latecomer seeking to catch up with the advanced West, especially after the Second World War, Japan pursued an import-substituting but simultaneously export-focused approach of developing domestic industries and export competitiveness, an approach which can be conceptualized as, in an ex post sense, a 'reserved competition' paradigm of industrial development.[3] It is a dynamic version of the infant industry strategy. Such an approach was not always applied across the board, but it can be traced out in the experiences of those industries considered 'strategic' – and hence promoted – by the Japanese government, such as computers.

The key feature of this catching-up approach is that a new selected industry was initially heavily protected from both imports and FDI, but that, within that protected industry, a large number of domestic entrants were attracted to enter the industry and compete vigorously with each other in a fierce market share-grabbing contest. This multi-entrant formula is diametrically opposite to the 'national champion' strategy pursued by some European nations, especially by France.

The reserved competition approach does not reduce the rigour of competition in such a protected industry; on the contrary, there will be fierce competition among the domestic firms. Theoretically speaking, the effectiveness of this 'infant industry' approach depends on the conditions under which a fostered increase in the intensity of domestic competition needs to be greater in absolute terms than the reduction in foreign competition caused by protection so that a net competitive effect would be positive; otherwise, the surviving domestic firms would never be able to compete in the global markets:

Domestic competition	Foreign competition	Net competitive effect (NCE)
+	− =	NCE > 0

There is no doubt that competition is the mother of efficiency and technological progress. Thus what is protected is not only an industry itself but, more importantly, an *efficiency-inducing mechanism* (the 'survival of the fittest' principle) that can nurture world-class manufacturers, instead of letting only a few privileged firms effortlessly enjoy 'protection rents'. The winners from this unique brand of protection are *always* national firms and not foreign firms.

As will be seen below in terms of Japan's motor industry, by restricting imports and inward FDI, the government created protection rents (immediate as well as expected) for the domestic firms, inducing multiple entries and thereby turning the industrial environment into an extremely rivalry-driven one at home. This 'condensed' domestic competition then generated all the more pressure for export (to compensate for the overcrowded domestic market), forced the entrants to raise efficiency via technological progress (initially by way of absorbing the advanced technologies from the West) and compelled them to innovate the techniques of lean production (initially at Toyota, where an engineering genius, Taiichi Ohno, strove to create – and succeeded in introducing – the new system). The soon widespread adoption of lean production made all the Japanese carmakers formidably competitive, and their exports soared. But such an export blitz soon led to trade frictions, and the carmakers were then forced to resort to overseas assembly operations via foreign direct investment (FDI).

In the meantime, the successful exports of cars (along with those of electronic goods, in particular) led to Japan's huge trade surplus, exerting upward pressure on the yen, which inevitably began to appreciate at a rapid rate. Japan's industrial expansion as a whole caused labour shortages, particularly those of factory workers, and a continuous rise in labour costs at home. The appreciating domestic currency and the rising labour costs continued to erode the price competitiveness of Japanese car exports. In response, Japan's carmakers began to shift assembly operations and production of parts, components and accessories overseas (to be described in detail later on). These sequential developments are schematically summarized in Figure 9.1.

The sequence of events outlined above clearly demonstrates that the emergence of Japanese carmakers as powerful multinationals emanates from their industry's growth trajectory 'managed' by both Japanese government and industry. In what follows, more detailed examinations of the developmental path of Japan's motor industry will be made.

The Government Role

Although Japan's motor industry had existed before the Second World War, and in fact was promoted as a strategic industry, it was basically in the post-war period that it began to manufacture passenger cars. In the prewar days, the industry was concentrating its production in utility/commercial vehicles such as trucks, jeeps and buses, especially under the government promotion policy for military purposes. As early as the 1920s, Ford and General Motors were the first foreign carmakers who set up knockdown-assembly operations in Yokohama and Osaka, respectively, to supply passenger cars: Model T and Chevrolet.

The 'reserved competition' phenomenon of post-war industrial development for cars is illustrated in Figure 9.2. The post-war government policy consisted of three approaches: first, *protection*: (a) tariffs, (b) a tax system favourable to (small) domestic cars and unfavourable to large cars (imports), and (c) controls on inward FDI; second, *promotion*: (a) technology imports, (b) financial assistance, (c) domestic demand creation and infrastructural support (highways); and third, *trade dispute mediation* with other governments, such as the voluntary export restraint agreements with the United States and Europe.[4]

In fact, the 'Basic Automotive Industry Policy' was established in October 1948 for the purpose of encouraging expansion of the industry. The Law on Temporary Measures for Promoting the Machinery Industries (Machine Industry Law) of 1956 specifically selected the motor-parts industry as one of the 17 industries for promotion, which qualified for special funding from the Japan Development Bank. The law was designed to build a streamlined

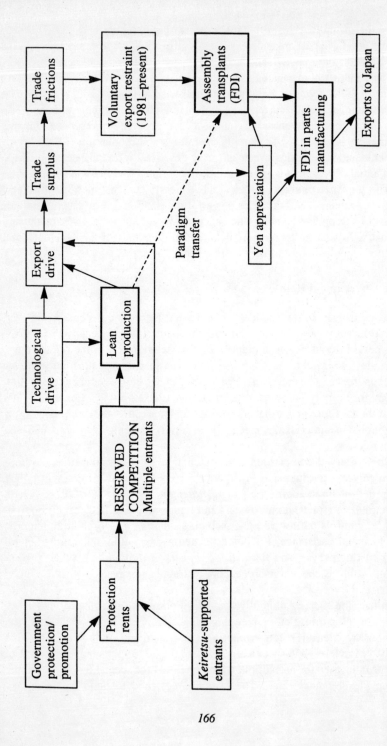

Figure 9.1 · The sequential development of Japan's motor industry as a multinational player

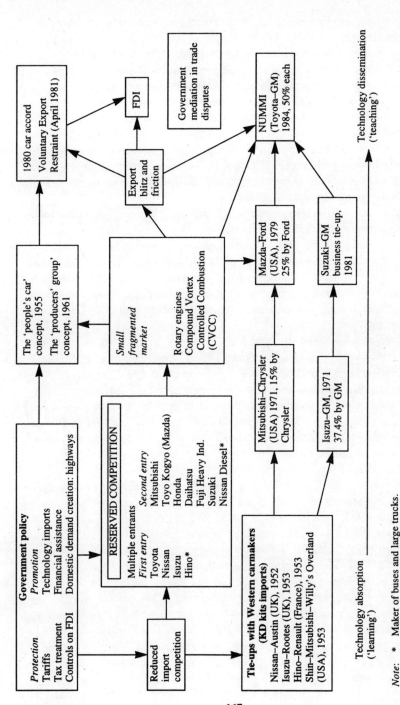

Note: * Maker of buses and large trucks.

Figure 9.2 The 'reserved competition' paradigm of industrial development: Japan's motor industry

production system by modernizing/rationalizing manufacturing facilities (for example, via special depreciation measures), promoting exports, assisting technological progress and formulating overall raw materials policies.

In order to overcome the initial quality and cost disadvantages of Japanese carmakers, the government allocated then scarce foreign exchange to promote technology imports via knockdown-assemblies of foreign models in collaboration with Western carmakers: the four approved ventures were a Nissan–Austin (UK) tie-up in 1952; an Isuzu–Rootes (UK) contract in 1953; a Hino–Renault (France) tie-up in 1953, and a venture between Shin-Mitsubishi Heavy Industries and Willy's-Overland (USA) in 1953. These knockdown-assembly ventures helped Japanese carmakers learn the basic techniques of modern passenger car manufacturing.

At the start, Toyota, Nissan, Prince, Isuzu and Hino were the first entry group that began to manufacture domestic passenger cars, but were quickly followed by the second entry group of other carmakers: Mitsubishi, Toyo Kogyo (Mazda), Honda, Daihatsu, Fuji Heavy Industries and Suzuki. Thus, as many as 11 carmakers soon crowded the Japanese market, but Nissan soon absorbed Prince (1966), thereby reducing the number to ten. They vied vigorously with each other in expanding productive facilities and raising output at a phenomenal pace.

This growth is vividly illustrated in Figure 9.3. From 1960 to 1965, the output expanded by 322 per cent (from 165 000 passenger cars to 696 000); from 1965 to 1970, it expanded by 357 per cent (from 696 000 to 3 179 000) – overtaking European carmakers and emerging as the second largest passenger carmaker after the United States; from 1970 to 1975, there was a 43.7 per cent jump (from 3 179 000 to 4 568 000); and from 1975 to 1980, a further 54.1 per cent growth (from 4 568 000 to 7 038 000), with Japan finally catching up and unseating the United States as the world's largest car manufacturer in the late 1970s.[5]

At the same time, Japan became the world's largest exporter of passenger cars. Its dependency ratio on exports rose from 4.2 per cent in 1960 to 14.5 per cent in 1965, 22.8 per cent in 1970, 40.0 per cent in 1975 and to 56.1 per cent in 1980. During the course of this precipitous growth, MITI ironically tried to curb what it perceived as 'an excessive competition' among the multiple entrants by introducing two policies: (1) the 'People's Car' concept in 1955, and (2) the 'three-producer group' concept in 1961. The People's Car programme aimed at introducing a low-priced minicar for both domestic and export markets with its production concentrated in one firm so as to reap scale economies, a plan modelled on Germany's VW. All entrants produced small sub-compacts anyway, but MITI's attempt to force production concentration did not work because of fierce rivalries among the domestic carmakers.

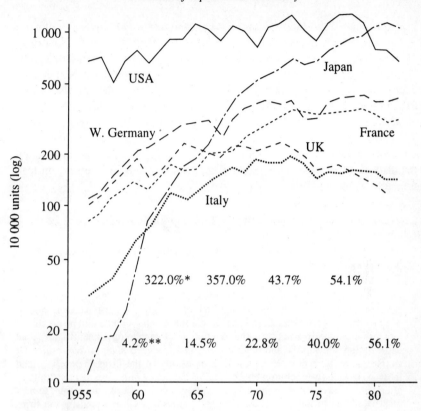

Notes: * 5-year average growth rates of Japan's car output; ** Japanese car exports as a proportion of total output.

Source: Adopted, with modifications, from Mutoh (1988, pp. 308, 319).

Figure 9.3 Passenger car production by major countries

The three-producer group plan of 1961 was introduced as a way of strengthening the competitiveness of the Japanese motor industry, since Japan was forced to liberalize car imports, for commercial vehicles in 1961 and for passenger cars in 1965. The government scheme would divide the domestic carmakers into groups of two to three firms each, with one group specialized in mass-producing passenger cars (with a monthly output of at least 7000 vehicles), with a second group producing speciality vehicles (a monthly output of 3000 luxury and sports cars) and a final group manufacturing minicars. The industry strongly resisted this administrative interference and the plan failed to be legislated.

It was against the intense competition at home that Mitsubishi Motors, a newcomer, manoeuvred to tie up with Chrysler, then a powerful American carmaker, in 1971, despite MITI's opposition. In the same year, Isuzu similarly concluded a capital link-up with GM, which acquired a 32 per cent equity interest. Another new challenger, Toyo Kogyo (Mazda) also established close relations with Ford, which culminated in the sale of 25 per cent equity to Ford in 1979. These Japanese makers were still in the learning stage and gained from partnerships with their American affiliates – perhaps most importantly, learning about not only the basic techniques of mass-production but also its weaknesses as a production system. (More will be said on lean production below.)

Effectiveness of Industrial Policy and Oligopolistic Rivalries

As regards the effectiveness of the Japanese government's industrial policy, Mutoh (1988) concludes:

> promotion policies were advanced with the recognition of the infant industry status of the Japanese automotive industry. It was not a great mistake in and of itself to have targeted it as an industry of the future, and with certain reservations, the initial import restrictions, the promotion of technology licensing, special depreciation allowances, and other policies *did produce some positive results.* Of course, there were also the rationalization efforts of the firms themselves, and these were able to function well *because of the heavy initial protection.* Policies after 1965, however, when the infant industry status had been overcome, unnecessarily served to delay liberalization and were not well accepted by the firms themselves. (Mutoh, 1988, p. 330, emphasis added)

Thus the initial protective and promotional measures did have a 'desirable' effect from Japan's industrial policy perspective, since they provided a 'greenhouse' for the infant industry. And interestingly, this greenhouse fostered what I call 'reserved competition' because

> The firms in the 'greenhouse' avoided *unnecessary* price reductions, which gave rise to *excess profits.* In the long term these excess profits lowered the barrier to entry, making it possible for *numerous firms to coexist.* It is ironic that *cooperation* among domestic makers in fact worked to prevent increasing concentration in the industry. (Mutoh, 1988, p. 324, emphasis added).

Although not elaborated in this quotation, 'cooperation' meant an implicit agreement (or collusion) among the participants not to resort to 'disorderly' price competition but instead to compete in terms of cost reduction efforts through technological improvement. This production cost-focused rivalry allowed all the participating firms to retain a substantial portion of productivity growth (since they did not pass on such a gain to consumers at lower product prices at home) and to reinvest in productive capacities.

Why there were so many eager entrants into the motor industry – for that matter, in any growth industry in Japan – needs to be examined, since protection alone, and the protection rent thus offered, is only a necessary condition for the reserved competition phenomenon to occur. The competitive effect needs to be generated in a magnified manner so as to spur technological progress. The reason for the ready existence of multiple entrants can be found mainly in Japan's unique institution, the *keiretsu* groups (closely knit industrial groups).

Indeed, in the early developmental phase of Japan's motor industry the groups vied fiercely with each other in securing and setting up any promising industry within themselves, a phenomenon popularly known as the 'one set' principle,[6] since this tendency resulted in each group having a complete set of major industries. In this connection, the core *keiretsu*-affiliated banks played an active role in financing the group's advance into key sectors. All the Japanese carmakers were therefore supported by their own group banks when they entered car manufacturing;

Carmakers	Keiretsu	Banks
Toyota	Mitsui	Mitsui Bank
Nissan	Fuyo	Fuji Bank
Isuzu	Dai-Ichi Kangyo	Dai-Ichi Kangyo Bank
Mitsubishi	Mitsubishi	Mitsubishi Bank
Toyo Kogyo	Sumitomo	Sumitomo Bank
Daihatsu	Sanwa (Toyota affiliation, 1967)	Sanwa Bank
Honda[7]	Mitsubishi	Mitsubishi Bank

The attraction of cars as a new growth industry was especially strong for the *keiretsu*, since this is an industry with numerous industrial linkages, notably backward (input) linkages with steel, tyres and plastics. Since each major group was simultaneously building up these key (upstream) industries under the one-set principle, it was naturally eager to have the motor industry as an outlet for these industries.

Industrial Retention at Home and Relocation Abroad

Two types of Veblenian 'interstitial coordinations'
The motor industry is intensive in the use of parts, components and accessories (PCAs) to be assembled into final products. Hence it requires precise coordination among the operating constituent sub-units if a myriad variety of PCAs is to be put together precisely in the most efficient way. Although it is

not widely known, it was Thorstein Veblen (1927) who first emphasized the significance of *interstitial coordinations* in modern manufacturing;

> By virtue of this concatenation of processes, the modern industrial system at large bears the character of a comprehensive, balanced mechanical progress. In order to achieve (*sic*) an efficient working of this industrial process at large, the various constituent sub-processes must work in due coordination throughout the whole. Any degree of maladjustment in the *interstitial coordinations* of this industrial process or any industrial plant will do its work to full advantage only when due adjustment is had between its work and the work done by the rest. The higher the degree of development reached by a given industrial community, the more comprehensive and urgent becomes this requirement of interstitial adjustment. (Veblen, 1927, p. 16, emphasis added)[8]

Here Veblen is clearly referring to relational or transactional efficiency or what may be alternatively called 'interstitial efficiency'[9] – in addition to the widely known concept of 'specialization efficiency' attainable from the division of labour, whose very progression all the more necessitates a higher degree of interstitial coordinations.

No doubt the components-intensive, assembly-based industries are exactly that particular type of manufacturing where interstitial coordinations are most strongly called for, because their production processes are vertically divided up into numerous stages involving a large number of PCAs (as many as 7000 per vehicle, though it depends upon how you classify PCAs). Interstitial (inter-process) coordinations are thus as important as, or perhaps even more critical than, the conventional gains that can be derived from the Smithian division of labour and specialization (which culminated in Fordism-cum-Taylorism).

In this regard, Japan's carmakers have been pursuing through internalization (via organizational means) both the Veblenian interstitial efficiency and the Smithian scale-based division of labour in as synergistically optimal a combination as possible, whereas the American carmakers in the past tended to focus mainly on the Smithian efficiency through hierarchies and leave the assembler–supplier relations to the market mechanism (that is, purchasing PCAs from independent suppliers in the 'open' markets).

In contrast, two types of the Veblenian interstitial efficiency are being actively exploited by Japan's carmakers in the form of lean production. One may be called '*intra-shop* interstitial efficiency', the other '*intra-industry* interstitial efficiency'. The former refers to the efficiency of inter-process coordinations on the assembly line within a given car plant, and the latter to that of inter-process coordinations between the assemblers and their PCA suppliers in the product development and delivery system of the motor industry.

Intra-shop interstitial (inter-process) coordinations: the 'pull' system[10]

As is already well known, Japan's carmakers, initially Toyota which innovated the methods of lean production, adopted a so-called 'pull' system of assembly operations. As illustrated in Figure 9.4, the conventional Fordist-cum-Taylorist paradigm of mass production is characterized as a 'push' sys-

A The 'push' system

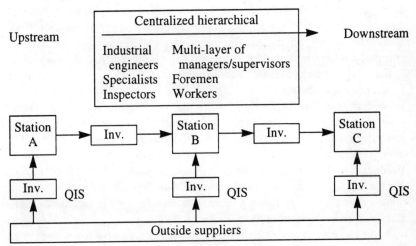

B The 'pull' system

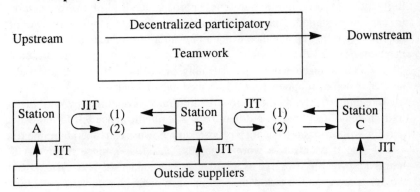

Notes: Inv.: inventory; QIS: quality inspection/sampling; JIT: just-in-time.

Source: Ozawa (1993, p. 173).

Figure 9.4   Conventional mass production (a 'push' system) v. Toyota's flexible production (a 'pull' system)

tem, for work-in-process is *pushed downstream* from one station to the next, whether the latter needs a particular piece of work right away or not, since any work done at one station is forwarded downstream and piled up in an inventory at the next station. Quality control is centrally implemented and exogenously exercised by inspectors (specialists), usually at the end of an assembly line, and is thus not the job assigned to assembly workers themselves (that is, a clear-cut Smithian division of labour and specialization between assembling and inspecting). As a rule, therefore, a given tolerable rate of defect, say, 5 per cent is set, and considered 'good enough',[11] and workers can rely on the portion of good parts available in the station's inventory. After all, inventories are meant to be for the 'just-in-case' contingencies. If the defective rate exceeds tolerance, specialist engineers try to figure out the problems.

In sharp contrast to Detroit's traditional 'push' process with the 'just-in-case' inventories, what Toyota eventually succeeded in creating is a diametrically opposite, new approach, that can reduce inventories to the bare minimum or even eliminate them altogether. Work-in-process and parts are produced *as they are needed* by *a downstream station*, that is, 'just in time' for use as they are needed. The famous *kanban* (a piece of paper indicating a 'pull' order and/or a production order) was initially used as a communication device from a downstream to an upstream station.

Indeed, the *kanban* (which is now increasingly 'computer-programed') is an instrument to achieve Veblenian interstitial coordinations along the assembly line, an instrument that proved more efficient than the use of inventories. In its ultimate form, the 'just-in-time' approach can lead to a zero inventory for each work station. This saves physical space, time and motion (no work is required for piling up and then using up inventories) and the cost of financing inventories, if all the sub-works of the entire production process are completely synchronized within the assembly plant, as well as with its multi-layered group of suppliers (to be described in detail below).

More importantly, as they strove to minimize inventories by way of the 'pull' method, they discovered that there was no allowance left for defective parts or work-in-process being passed on to a downstream operation; the line would stop if a defective work-in-process was found, since there was no longer an inventory to serve as a buffer. In fact, under the new system, each worker is assigned the task of inspecting each piece he receives ('pulls out') from upstream – in addition to making sure that what he produces in his station is defect-free. The worker is no longer a mere assembler (automaton), mindlessly putting and adding pieces together as instructed – as appropriately depicted in Charlie Chaplin's *Modern Times*; he now is a quality inspector, as well, *responsible* for the quality of what he produces and of what he receives from an upstream station – and from outside suppliers. Thus assembly workers have to do 'thinking' as well as 'doing' (whereas they do only 'doing' under the Fordist-cum-Taylorist approach).[12]

As will be discussed below, the above system of intra-shop interstitial coordinations can be transplanted into other countries most effectively through the medium of FDI under Japanese management.

Intra-industry interstitial (inter-firm) coordinations: the pyramidal structure

The motor industry is vertically deep in the structure of manufacturing activities (the chain of value-added operations). Accordingly, as will be seen below, the pattern of industrial retention and relocation in this phase of economic growth is shaped along the vertical characteristics of integrated production. In organizing and managing such vertically integrated production, the industry has formed an *externalized* pattern of the vertical division of labour along the lines of different wage levels, factor intensities and technological sophistications: that is, a vertical division of labour among (1) several major assemblers (large-sized oligopolistic firms) at the top, (2) their closely affiliated primary suppliers of sub-assemblies, parts and components in the middle, and (3) a large number of secondary and tertiary subcontractors (small-sized firms) operating in a highly competitive market down the hierarchy and at the bottom.

Toyota, Nissan, Honda, Mazda and other Japanese carmakers reign as the main assemblers, each thus constituting its own *keiretsu*. About 60 to 70 per cent of car parts and components are normally 'outsourced' to their primary suppliers (about ten to 15 in number for each *keiretsu*, totalling 168 shops), who in turn farm out some portion of work to their own secondary subcontractors (4700 shops for the motor industry as a whole), who again in turn depend on the lower-echelon producers, and so on, down to the bottom of the hierarchy (such lower-echelon shops numbering as many as 31 600 in the entire industry).[13]

The industrial pyramid thus formed by the *keiretsu* is schematically illustrated in stylized form in Figure 9.5. Actually, this multi-layered organization has many more layers than three. The top segment is highly capital-intensive and large scale-based (that is, exploiting scale economies) in market structure, its intermediate segment less capital-intensive and medium scale-based, and its bottom segment labour-intensive, with the lowest wage scale. Hence the relative capital–labour ratios largely determine the relative wage ratios: $(w/r)a > (w/r)b > (w/r)c > \dots (w/r)n$. In other words, the whole organization of vertically linked production is hierarchically built on what is popularly known as the 'dual structure' (though 'multitudinous' is a more appropriate adjective).

The top-echelon firms (main assemblers) are thus able to employ large-scale, capital-intensive methods of production, thereby exploiting internal scale economies, *which may otherwise be impossible to do if scarce capital is*

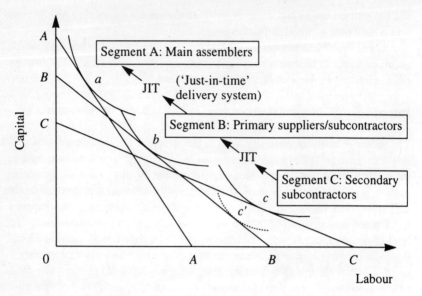

Figure 9.5   A multiple division of labour in the vertically integrated stages of production

evenly distributed throughout the industry.[14] The workers in such firms are 'elite' employees who can enjoy lifetime (guaranteed) employment and high wages; they are usually recruited fresh from college. On the other hand, the lower-echelon firms specializing in labour-intensive parts, components and accessories can remain price-competitive by employing low-wage workers (who are usually graduates from high schools) in an 'open' labour market and using highly labour-using methods of production.

This vertical division of labour is designed to exploit an *intra-industry pattern of comparative advantages* along the lines of both the Heckscher–Ohlin theory of factor proportions and the Ricardian model of different technological (labour productivity) levels. Such an intra-industry (intra-*keiretsu*) cultivation of comparative advantages is then translated into Japanese carmakers' competitive (or absolute) advantages in the world markets, reinforcing their competitive advantages emanating from the intra-shop interstitial efficiency described above.

Furthermore, the transactions between the assembler/procurers and sub-contractors are based on long-term, trust-based, reciprocal relationships. As might be expected, the 'terms of trade' between them tend to favour the higher-echelon firms that place orders, but the relationship is, on the whole, mutually beneficial. In fact, the large firms usually give managerial and technical guidance and assist their subcontractors financially, whenever necessary, so that the latter would be able continually to improve quality and productivity. After all, the existence of stable, reliable and efficient suppliers is a must for the JIT delivery system. (It should be noted, however, that the JIT delivery system is mainly between the main assemblers and their primary suppliers, and that it tends to decline as subcontracting moves down the hierarchy, since the lower-echelon producers are engaged more in standardized work.)

It is not unusual for the main assemblers to demand a cut in price for parts, say, as much as 10 per cent, on occasions of intensified competition, but this is not totally one-sided exploitation of smaller firms, since whatever help is necessary is also usually provided to raise efficiency and cut costs.

Thus this *keiretsu*-based pyramidal organization has been one of the major – and rather distinct – sources of Japanese carmakers' competitiveness, but as will be analysed below, ironically their very competitive prowess (emanating from the lean production methods) has resulted in a self-dismantling (self-dissolution) of this cooperative structure, especially at the bottom of the pyramid.

Export expansion, trade conflicts, yen appreciation and transplants abroad

The combination of Veblenian interstitial efficiencies at both the plant and the industry levels crystallized into Japanese-style lean production gave Japan's carmakers a formidable competitiveness, not only in price but also in quality, product development and delivery. As already seen and reflected in Figure 9.3, Japanese production and exports of cars recorded an explosive growth in the global market. This has led inevitably to two dramatic changes in the market conditions that affect corporate decisions as to the location of production. One is the rising incidence of trade conflicts with the countries at whose markets Japanese exports of vehicles were aimed, notably the United States and Europe; the second is the sharp appreciation of the yen *vis-à*-vis the American dollar, which is caused by Japan's huge trade surplus with the United States, 60 per cent of which is accounted for by the export of cars and car parts. An appreciated yen weakens Japanese carmakers' price competitiveness and the profitability of their exports. Hence these two developments are self-induced and self-inflicting, in the sense that the very effectiveness of Japanese-style lean production is basically responsible, that is to say, Japanese carmakers are being 'handicapped' by their own success.

In response, Japanese carmakers began to establish assembly operations ('transplants') in North America and Europe in the mid-1980s, as illustrated in Figure 9.1. These are the markets Japanese carmakers captured by initially exporting small-sized, fuel-efficient compacts (for which the demand was also increasing rapidly at home as Japan entered the stage of motorization with the sharp rise in per capita income). Hence the assembly segment of Japan's pyramidal structure (segment A in Figure 9.4) began, in part, to be transplanted abroad.

However, to counter the criticism that these transplants were merely the 'screwdriver plants' designed to assemble imported kits in the local markets and to meet the demand for the local content requirements, Japanese parts makers quickly followed suit by setting up parts-manufacturing ventures, in many cases as joint ventures with local interests (that is, segment B in Figure 9.4 started to be transplanted in tandem with segment A). But the establishment of these overseas outposts also contributed to Japan's exports of plant equipment, machinery (especially robots) and sub-parts which were usually specifically developed for firms by the carmakers in connection with their innovation of lean production techniques – hence the negative 'hollowing-out' effect has been so far largely cancelled out by the positive 'new export-creating' effect of FDI.

Given the *internalization* (via the *keiretsu*) of interstitial coordinations between the main assemblers and their parts suppliers, it is easy to understand why Japan's carmakers (main assemblers) initially could not depend on local parts producers. In fact, the quality of local parts was early on unacceptably low, with a high defective rate and unsuitable for their highly differentiated models. Japanese carmakers at home developed a system of 'design-in parts production' in which parts producers work closely with their carmakers from the very beginning of a product development. Hence it has taken a considerable amount of time to recruit and mould some local suppliers into Japanese-style design-in parts manufacturing and JIT delivery.

The above type of overseas production of cars, introduced for the purpose of skirting trade conflicts and escaping from the appreciating home currency, involves the relocation abroad of low-end, low-profit-margin models and the retention of high-end, high-profit-margin models at home. Toyota is transplanting the production of Tercels, Corollas and Camries abroad but retaining (and expanding) the production of Lexuses at home; Nissan is producing the Sentra-class models overseas but produces Infinities only at home; and Honda is increasingly shifting Civics and Accords for overseas production but manufactures at home Preludes and Accuras – and NSXs ($60 000 sports cars). Japanese carmakers' concentration on high-end, high-profit-margin models is turning them into structurally more profitable producers, whose profits can be parlayed into further R&D.

The low-end models produced overseas are increasingly exported to third-country markets – and back to Japan as well. Japanese car transplants in the United States are now responsible for at least 30 per cent of the recently booming exports of vehicles made in the United States and Canada![15] As Japanese carmakers concentrate on high-end models for export and import, those produced by their overseas transplants, *inter-model* trade is thus shaping up as a sub-set of intra-company trade.

The appreciated yen is also making overseas-produced PCAs cheaper to procure for Japanese carmakers. While some parts are still produced at home and exported, the increasing imports of PCAs are creating another type of trade: *inter-process* trade. Japan exports higher value-added, more sophisticated PCAs, while it imports low value-added, standardized (hence, more price-sensitive) PCAs. Now that many PCAs have been transferred to overseas production to be imported back to Japan, the recent series of yen appreciations is bringing back the benefits of exchange gains, since Japanese carmakers are able to procure at lower prices. This is one important reason why Japanese carmakers have not been completely entrapped by the soaring yen. (They no longer need to ask their suppliers to make price cuts as they once did at home; such price cuts are now automatically granted through the currency exchange mechanism!)

In the meantime, in addition to this string of overseas investments pushed by the currency appreciation, another development has been forcing the relocation of upstream (PCA manufacturing) operations abroad because of the rising wages at home.

Rising labour costs and shortages
The rising labour costs and shortages are the inevitable outcome of successful economic growth. These phenomena are more pronounced in the lower/bottom sections of the pyramid, that is where relatively young, low-wage workers (mostly junior-high-school graduates) are most intensively employed for standardized, highly labour-intensive and low-skill work. Japan's youth, spoiled by economic prosperity and a relative abundance of job opportunities, eventually began to characterize such work as '3-Ds' (dirty, demanding and dangerous), hence a sharp decline in the supply of such workers.

A wage increase can be illustrated in terms of Figure 9.5. CC is the initial wage line paid in the labour-intensive sector C, whose production takes place at point c. Now the wage rate rises (that is, the wage line becomes steeper from CC to BB), closing the wage gap. This necessarily raises the production costs of a good C (as indicated by a decline in output from c to c'). So how should this situation be coped with? One possible measure is to make a technological improvement of the Hicksian type (that is, a proportionate, factor-neutral downward shift of the isoquant curves) so that the same quantity of output could be maintained as before (via across-the-board rationalization efforts). A second approach is to make a labour-saving technological progress so that the C production function now becomes more capital-intensive and identical, say, to its B counterpart (that is, using automation to reduce labour use). Other than these technological solutions, another avenue is to *relocate C* production to a developing country where a low wage (at least the *CC* wage line or even a flatter one) still prevails. All three measures have been vigorously pursued by Japan's car parts makers.

The net result is the scaling up and 'flattening-out' of Japan's industrial pyramid, as the lower-echelon activities are transplanted abroad while Japanese manufacturing is increasingly concentrated on higher-echelon segments, in terms of both vehicle models and PCAs. This is not really a 'hollowing-out' of the entire industry, but a 'restructuring' ('house-cleaning' or 'upgrading') of the industry in net terms and in the long run, although there are no doubt some short-term resource reallocation problems associated with the declining sectors.

At the same time, the host countries are given the transfusions of new industrial knowledge. Thus FDI is serving as an instrument of structural upgrading for both the home and host economies. Moreover, Japan's FDI in cars and car parts is, as seen above, leading to the emergence of two types of new trade: inter-model trade and inter-process trade.

Behavioural differences in international business activities: established firms v. newcomers

One interesting question related to the reserved competition phenomenon is whether there are any behavioural differences between the dominant firms (Toyota and Nissan) and the latecomers or challengers (such as Honda, Mazda and Mitsubishi) with respect to their international business activities, and, if so, in what way, and why, they have acted differently.

It has already been observed that all of them became strongly export-driven, simply because of the necessity to do so for survival in the face of the over-crowded domestic market. And the degree of export orientation is expected to be much higher for newcomers; in fact, this tendency is demonstrated by Mazda's 69.5 per cent and Honda's 64.0 per cent in comparison with Toyota's 52.5 per cent and Nissan's 56.6 per cent.[16] Mitsubishi's relatively low 51.6 per cent is an exception. (Mitsubishi's exports have been constrained because of its marketing agreement with Chrysler, a 15 per cent equity holder of Mitsubishi at the time of its tie-up in 1971, whose business performance deteriorated in the late 1970s, hence adversely affecting Mitsubishi exports as well. The 1981 Voluntary Export Restraint (VER) imposed by the United States locked in Mitsubishi's export performance, although the company began to set up its own direct distribution channel later on. As discussed below, however, Mitsubishi is particularly aggressive in its direct overseas operations throughout Asia – perhaps to compensate for its relatively unfavourable position in the United States.) As for direct overseas business activities, the newcomers are also expected to be more active in setting up market-seeking types of overseas investment and forging strategic alliances with foreign firms.

It was Honda – ahead of any other Japanese carmakers – that, as early as 1982, began assembly production of its most popular model, the Accord, in the United States. This move was a logical extension of its successful assembly production of motorcycles at the same location in Ohio. Honda America now produces both Accords and Civics (totalling 475 000 cars in 1992) and engines – and exports back to Japan its American-designed Accords.

Mazda, on the other hand, has been strengthening its operation by establishing a close relationship with Ford, which owns a 24.4 per cent equity interest in the former. Its export strategy has largely been to pursue an OEM (original equipment manufacturing) arrangement under which Mazda produces small trucks, passenger cars and car parts for Ford. But most recently Mazda began a joint assembly venture with Ford in the United States (at Flat Rock, Michigan).

In the meantime, Mitsubishi is especially active in moving into the Asian countries. It has a 15 per cent equity in, and a close technical assistance tie-up with, Hyundai (South Korea) and has a 30 per cent equity interest in Proton, Malaysia's 'national car' project. Doner (1991) makes the following pertinent observation:

> competition for ASEAN market shares is intensified by the importance of the ASEAN countries to certain Japanese firms, especially the Mitsubishi Motors Corporation (MMC), undoubtedly the most aggressive of the Japanese firms in the region. This is in part because of MMC's desire to compensate for its fifth-place standing in the Japanese domestic market through successful foreign operations. But Mitsubishi has seen its market opportunities in the developed countries reduced by distribution problems with Chrysler and by Voluntary Export Restraint agreements in the United States that have adversely affected the smaller Japanese firms. Consequently, the Far East and Australasia account for between 30 and 37 percent of the company's total exports, second only to those of Isuzu among the Japanese firms with regard to the significance of Asian markets. Finally, the interests of the broader Mitsubishi group may encourage highly aggressive strategies on the part of Mitsubishi Motors. (Doner, 1991, p. 79)

Indeed, Mitsubishi's entry into the passenger car market has been strategically supported by the Mitsubishi group; for example, car electronics is provided by Mitsubishi Electric, assembly and automation equipment by Mitsubishi Heavy Industries and overseas sales by Mitsubishi Corporation (a trading firm).[17]

On the other hand, Toyota, Japan's largest carmaker, had until recently been relatively slow in taking up local production abroad; for example, it was behind Honda and Nissan in establishing assembly operations in the United States. Although a more detailed study is called for, the above brief illustrations do point out some behavioural differences between the dominant firms and their challengers in multinational operations.

Management as a transplanter of a mini-home community

No doubt the origination of Japanese-style lean production was decisively influenced by Japan's distinctive socioeconomic–cultural milieu. After all, it is an *organizational* technology designed to raise interstitial efficiency at both the plant and industry levels, as seen above. Indeed, this is why this new manufacturing paradigm was born in Japan – and not in the United States and Europe. In other words, the provenance of lean production has been clearly embedded in Japan's location-specific factors, particularly the government protection and promotion policy, the *keiretsu*-supported multiple entries and Japan's many centuries' tradition, to mould imported technologies to suit specific local conditions that resulted in the reserved competition phenomenon, as described above.

In this connection, Gittelman and Dunning (1992) zeroed in on the important question as to how such a high location-specificity of the competitive advantages of Japanese carmakers might affect their effectiveness as multinationals:

> Will the competitive advantages of Japanese firms be modified now that they are increasingly exploiting these advantages from a foreign production base? To what extent will they be able to 'export' their competitive, or ownership-specific, advantages which owe much to the institutional, economic and cultural environment of their country of origin?
>
> ... Unlike many American multinationals which have O [ownership] advantages in strong brand names (Coca-Cola) or the common governance of a range of related activities (American Express) or superior technology (IBM), the O advantages of Japanese firms are not easily internalized in an overseas location; they are, in this sense, more location-bound. Part of the reason for this is that it is initially more difficult to transfer any intra- or inter-firm organizational structures than it is to transfer production or marketing techniques across national boundaries... And, as Porter points out..., nowhere are the elements underlying the comparative advantages of a country, which help to create and sustain the competitive advantages of its firms (factor conditions, demand conditions, related and supporting industries, and domestic competition) more closely linked to one another than in Japan, where they function as an organic system.
>
> While such a situation is ideal for a country building up its competitive advantage through exports, as Japan had done until recently, difficulties may arise when such a country's firms are compelled to replicate their successes internationally (or internalize the markets for their O advantages through fdi) in different national cultures. In this scenario, the main challenge is to move the entire system to the target market. The risks inherent in such a move are high, since the firm's original O advantages and the conditions which make for their internal use, i.e. the I [internalization] advantages, are bound to change once transplanted to foreign soil, as indeed are the O advantages of the host country's firms which are now given an opportunity to compete – and cooperate – with their overseas rivals on familiar territory (Gittelman and Dunning, 1992, pp. 256–7).

Although Gittelman and Dunning correctly pointed out the inherent difficulties involved, their concern is justified more as regards the intra-industry *keiretsu* (assembler–supplier) system,[18] which nowadays is becoming increasingly difficult to retain even at home. Surprisingly, however, the *intra-shop* assembly efficiency (in which the 'just-in-time' delivery system equally exists among the operating units down the assembly line, as detailed earlier) is being transplanted and replicated abroad quite effectively.

Some evidence is provided by the most recent (1994) comprehensive study made by Harbour & Associates Inc. on the relative efficiencies (as of late 1993) of American assembly plants and Japanese transplants in the United States, as reported in *The Wall Street Journal*.[19] The study was 'designed to correct for differences in levels of vertical integration'; that is, to correct for difference in intra-industry interstitial efficiencies and to focus on their comparative intra-shop efficiencies alone. The results are as follows:

	Per vehicle labour requirements	Relatives
Nissan, Smyrna, Tenn.	2.29 workdays	58
Toyota, Georgetown, Ken.	2.44 workdays	62
GM (the least efficient reported)	3.94 workdays	100

Nissan and Toyota's transplants are thus as much as 42 per cent and 38 per cent, respectively, more efficient than GM![20] (Certainly, these differences in assembly efficiency alone do not determine their competitiveness, since other operations such as product development are also critical competitive factors. In fact, Chrysler is cited as the least-cost producer in connection with Neon because of 'the use of relatively simple and inexpensive components'.)

How on earth, then, can these Japanese transplants achieve as they do such an exceptionally high level of intra-shop assembly efficiency – a level that cannot be attained by their American competitors on the latter's own home turf? The answer lies in the effective adoption of the shopfloor techniques of lean production (that is, intra-shop interstitial coordinations) applied under Japanese management, since Nissan's Smyrna plant and Toyota's Georgetown plants are wholly owned and managed by the Japanese.

This reveals the critical linkage between lean production and management techniques. Japanese-style lean production involves management of workshop organization, involving the whole structure of industrial relations (labour-management nexus) as well as that of assembler–supplier relations; hence it is inseparably linked in functional terms with the managerial philosophies and practices and the social organization specific to it.

There is no doubt that Japanese-style management can serve as a cultural shell, so to speak, or as a transplanter of a mini-home community (a carrier of home-originated factors). Indeed, management is culture/tradition-intensive in organizational ideologies and routines. But, surprisingly, intangible location-specific factors, such as culture, traditions and values, can be internalized within the hierarchy and transferred across borders (although tangible locational factors cannot). They are surely 'embedded' in a particular home country's socio-cultural milieu, but when such a milieu is replicated as a microcosm in terms of managerial ambience, such seemingly location-bound factors as culture, traditions and values can be rather effectively transplanted across borders. Wholly owned overseas operations thus become an extended locational capsule, so to speak, in which a home-embedded value system can still prevail.

But the workers overseas need to be selected carefully to make sure that their characteristics match the special nature and needs of such a community. As is widely known, therefore, Japanese multinationals, especially in cars and electronics, spend an extraordinary amount of time and care screening potential employees. Once hired, they are then trained for teamwork as multi-skilled flexible workers – indeed, as *interstitial coordinators* – whose brawn and brains become inputs on the assembly lines. Effective lean production thus requires the cocoon of a specific managerial system (Figure 9.6).

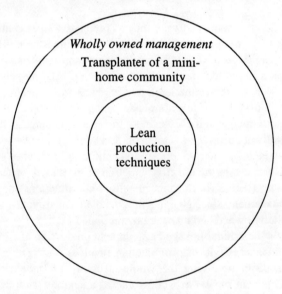

Figure 9.6   Japanese-style management and lean production

CONCLUSIONS

This chapter has shown that, during Japan's unique process of catching-up development (here identified as the 'reserved competition' phenomenon), its motor industry (initially Toyota) stumbled upon the 'discovery' of a radically new way of organizing manufacturing – lean production – whose techniques were then quickly adopted by other components-intensive, assembly-based industries, notably electronic goods. Japan is currently in the very forefront of this new manufacturing revolution, just as the United States was once with its Fordist/Taylorist mass-production, and Europe with its craft-based factory production. 'These companies have provided an invaluable gift to the world by pioneering a new way of making things that really is superior' (Womack *et al.*, 1990, p. 272).

One distinctive difference of the reserved competition phenomenon as compared with the conventional 'infant industry' scheme is that, thanks to the vigorous inter-*keiretsu* rivalries, a protected domestic market had to be shared (competed for) by multiple entrants, thereby causing fierce competition among the 'infant' producers, so that protection rents were never monopolized (as often is the case with the 'national champion' model) but were made to serve as an incentive for organizational-cum-technological innovatory efforts. Moreover, the already small domestic market was even more fractionalized, making it impractical to depend on the conventional methods of mass-production. Efficient multi-variety, small-lot flexible manufacturing had to be innovated to satisfy the diversified needs of the fragmented small market. Their ownership advantages thus came to be lodged in the new manufacturing system.

The emergence and evolving patterns of Japanese carmakers as multinationals are, therefore, the emanations of their industry's technological progress, fostered against the unique background of Japan's post-war experiences and the dynamics of the *keiretsu* rivalries.

Japan's huge trade surplus will diminish as the techniques of Japanese-style lean production spread to the rest of the world. In other words, such an external disparity is a decreasing function of the global dissemination (emulation) of Japan's new manufacturing paradigm. Such dissemination may take time, although Detroit has been catching up quickly. In the meantime, during the very course of such a gradual process of paradigm transfer, Japan's FDI will most likely expand even further, even when its trade surplus begins to show a declining trend. For more home-based production for export is now being transplanted into other countries via FDI – and transformed into both *inter-model* and *inter-process* trades (which increases Japan's intra-firm imports in net terms) in cars and car parts as an increasing segment of Japanese carmakers' manufacturing structure crosses national borders.

NOTES

1. Surprisingly, some cynics even say that there is no such thing as lean production. For them it is basically no different from mass production. As will be shown below, lean production has a set of distinctive features.
2. A myriad of parts, components and accessories mean that they can be combined in a large number of variations for the purpose of product differentiation. The components-intensive, assembly-based industries thus have a built-in structural proclivity to differentiate products – seemingly to an excessive degree. This is especially typical of motor vehicles.
3. Japan's Ministry of International Trade and Industry (MITI) was the major protector and promotor of import-competing and subsequently export-competitive manufacturing. But MITI itself did not perceive the effectiveness of its protection policy in the way conceptualized in this chapter. As will be demonstrated below, in fact, on a couple of occasions MITI tried to weaken the mechanism of 'reserved competition'.
4. This section on the motor industry draws on Mutoh (1988), Shimokawa (1985) and Shirasawa (1979).
5. These figures and others shown below are from the Japan Automobile Association, *Jidosha tokei Nenpo* [Automotive Statistics Annual], as cited in Mutoh (1988, p. 319).
6. This phrase was popularized by Miyazaki (1967).
7. Honda is rather independent, without any formal membership in the Mitsubishi group's council of presidents, but still maintains a close relationship with the Mitsubishi Bank.
8. The author is indebted to his colleague, Dennis Black, for pointing out Veblen's writings on this topic. For an analysis of the relevance of Veblenian economics to Japanese industry, see Ozawa and Phillips (1994).
9. According to the *Oxford Dictionary*, 'interstice' means 'an intervening space; chink, crevice'. This relates to the connecting points in flow of an integrated work process rather than to transactions or exchanges between disparate economic units. 'Interstitial efficiency' seems, therefore, preferable to 'transactional efficiency' to describe the quiddity of lean production, which after all focuses on the total flow efficiency of a production process.
10. This section draws on the comparative analysis of mass production and lean production made in Ozawa (1993).
11. Womack *et al.* (1990) observe: 'Perhaps the most striking difference between mass production and lean production lies in their ultimate objectives. Mass-producers set a limited goal for themselves – "good enough", – which translates into an acceptable number of defects, a maximum acceptable level of inventories, a narrow range of standardized products. To do better, they argue, would cost too much or exceed inherent human capabilities. Lean producers, on the other hand, set their sights explicitly on perfection; continually declining costs, zero defects, zero inventories, and endless product variety. Of course, no lean producer has ever reached this promised land – and perhaps none ever will, but the endless quest for perfection continues to generate surprising twists' (pp. 13–14).
12. To prevent any defective work from being passed down and assembled into a final product, therefore, each station is equipped with a stop button on the assembly line. When the stop button is pushed at a particular station, the entire factory floor is able to tell where the trouble has occurred by looking at a huge display of a work flow chart on a big factory-ceiling board above their heads. In such a situation, the workers at the troubled station are compelled to solve the problem as a team as quickly as possible, helping each other. This teamwork also means that each worker needs to be familiar with – hence to be trained for – a multiple variety of related work in his station.

    Furthermore, in order to prevent any recurrence of a given problem, the team will get together and find out its root causes. For this purpose, each station has a quality control (QC) circle. After a day's regular work, they discuss any problem they have encountered or expect to encounter and make suggestions as to the possible ways of improving their productivity. They usually receive pecuniary rewards for those suggestions adopted by management. These direct rewards are perhaps not of primary importance, however. As workers' productivity rises, thereby making their company more profitable, not only do their wages increase but they can also expect a larger bonus, which all the Japanese companies pay twice a year as a profit-sharing custom, which as a rule results in additional three to four months of compensation. Thus the bonus system serves as an important incentive mechanism for workers' brain inputs. See Ozawa (1993, p. 176)

13. The numbers cited are based on 1985 statistics, as presented in Shimokawa (1985, p. 23). In contrast, American carmakers once used to produce about 70 per cent of parts and components internally. Their in-house production has come down considerable as they have adopted the Japanese-style subcontracting approach.

14. For instance, assume that the economy has a given overall factor endowment ratio, say, a capital–labour ratio, but a certain sector needs to be more capital-intensive than the overall ratio to be an economically viable industry, and a certain other sector happens to be more labour-intensive than the overall ratio. If available factors are all proportionately allocated for the two sectors, they will not be able to produce efficiently, since such a factor allocation does not match the optimum factor intensity of each sector. In this case, more capital should be allocated to the capital-intensive sector and more labour to the labour-intensive sector. Each sector, then, can exploit its comparative efficiency in factor use.

15. *The Wall Street Journal*, 27 June 1994, p. A2. In 1993, exports of US-assembled vehicles numbered 356 261, of which 48 549 were exported by Toyota's transplants, and 41 694 by Honda's. Hence these two Japanese transplants alone accounted for 25.3 per cent. If other major transplants operated by Nissan, Mitsubishi and Mazda are added, the share will be well over 30 per cent.

16. Shimokawa (1985, p. 15). These percentages represent the 1984 statistics.

17. Shimokawa (1985, p. 198).

18. Dunning (1993) re-emphasizes this point: 'the question as to whether [Japan] can transfer those competitive advantages that arise specifically from the organizational culture is still to be resolved. One example is the kind of relationship that Japanese firms have with their suppliers, which explains much of the success of the Japanese auto and electronics suppliers. When these sectors are transplanted into an alien culture, can they succeed?' (p. 298).

19. *The Wall Street Journal*, 24 June 1994, p. B8.

20. Unfortunately, other carmakers' per-vehicle labour requirements are not cited. It is reported, however, that 'GM pays $2.2 billion a year in excess labor costs because its plants are substantially less efficient on average than Ford's... In the past two years several GM assembly plants posted productivity improvements of more than 20%, while Ford improved little... Separately, Ford's cumbersome product development, which includes redundant engineering in the U.S. and Europe, cost Ford $400 to $500 a vehicle... Chrysler Corp. isn't as efficient at vehicle assembly as Ford or Nissan, but manufacturing efficiency gives the best producers in North America only about a $200-a-vehicle edge over Chrysler. And that is more than offset by Chrysler's highly efficient product development... Taking that into account made Chrysler the low-cost producer among the manufacturers in the Harbour report... Chrysler's product development process gives it a $357-a-vehicle cost advantage over Ford. Chrysler gets additional savings over Ford and over Japanese auto makers from the use of relatively simple and inexpensive components... One reason the Japanese manufacturers have higher-cost products than Chrysler is that Japanese vehicles are built with expensive sound dampeners and other amenities designed to give them a high-quality feel... Toyota Corollas with four-speed electronic automatic transmissions, while Chrysler's Neon has an inexpensive three-speed transmission.'

BIBLIOGRAPHY

Doner, Richard F. (1991), *Driving a Bargain: Automobile Industrialization and Japanese Firms in Southeast Asia*, Berkeley: University of California Press.

Dunning, John H. (1993), *Multinational Enterprises and the Global Economy*, Reading, Mass.: Addison-Wesley.

Gittelman, Michelle and John H. Dunning (1992), 'Japanese Multinationals in Europe and the United States: Some Comparisons and Contrasts', in Michael W. Klein and Paul J.J. Welfens (eds), *Multinationals in the New Europe and Global Trade*, Berlin and New York: Springer-Verlag, pp. 237–67.

Miyazaki, Yoshikazu (1967), 'Rapid Economic Growth in Post-war Japan – with Special Reference to "Excessive Competition" and the Formation of "Keiretsu"', *The Developing Economies*, V, (June), pp. 329–50, as reproduced in Kazuo Sato (ed.), *Industry and Business in Japan*, New York: M.E. Sharpe, pp. 53–73.

Mutoh, Hiromichi (1988). 'The Automotive Industry', in R. Komiya, M. Okuno and K. Suzumura (eds), *Industrial Policy of Japan*, Tokyo: Academic Press, pp. 307–31.

Ozawa, Terutomo (1991), 'Japanese Multinationals and 1992', in B. Burgenmeier and J.L. Mucchielli (eds), *Multinationals and Europe 1992: Strategies for the Future*, London: Routledge, pp. 135–54.

Ozawa, Terutomo (1992). 'Foreign Direct Investment and Economic Development', *Transnational Corporations*, Vol. 1, No. 1 (February), pp. 27–54.

Ozawa, Terutomo (1993), 'The Provenance of Japan's Flexible Production: The Role of Milieu-Locational Factors in Organizational Technology', *Development and International Cooperation*, Vol. IX, No. 16 (June), pp. 167–86.

Ozawa, Terutomo and Ronnie Phillips (1994), 'Persistence of the Veblenian "Old Japan": Organizational Efficiency as a Wellspring of Competitiveness', *Rivista Internazionale di Scienze Economiche e Commerciali*, Ano XLI, N. 9 (Settembre), 721–40.

Shimokawa, Koichi (1985), *Jidosha* [Motor vehicles], Tokyo: Nihon Keizai Shimbunsha.

Shirasawa, Teruo (1979), *Jidosha Gyokai* [The Motor Industry], Tokyo: Kyoikusha.

Veblen, Thorstein (1927), *The Theory of Business Enterprise*, New York: Charles Scribner's Sons.

Womack, James P., Daniel T. Jones and Daniel Roos (1990), *The Machine that Changed the World*, New York: Rawson Associates.

10. MNEs and technology diffusion: a Southeast Asian experience[1]

F. Harianto and A.E. Safarian[2]

Following the Asian newly industrializing economies (NIEs), ASEAN economies have also pursued an export-led growth strategy in the past two decades. ASEAN exports of manufactures have grown significantly since the 1980s, albeit less spectacularly than the Asian NIEs. The openness of ASEAN economies, measured as the share of total trade (exports plus imports) in GDP has also increased markedly, well above international norms.

The export performance of the ASEAN economies in the past few decades has been characterized by the shift in the revealed comparative advantage (RCA) of each economy. In the capital-intensive industries, the five ASEAN economies (Singapore, Thailand, Malaysia, the Philippines and Indonesia) exhibit a similar pattern (Figure 10.1). Their exports in this category were growing quite rapidly and, in 1991, Thailand and especially Malaysia achieved a similar level of RCA to that of the Asian NIEs. In the science-intensive sectors (Figure 10.2) such as electronics and basic chemicals, Singapore and Malaysia have since 1980 been substantially above the world average and, in the case of Malaysia, the RCA has grown very rapidly. Malaysia has now become the world's largest exporter of semiconductors, the second largest exporter of room air-conditioners and a major player in VCR markets. Thailand was able to develop its electronics industry almost overnight by further liberalizing its trade and investment regimes in 1987. In 1991, Thailand's exports in this category surpassed the world average. Both the Philippines and Indonesia are lagging in the science-intensive sectors. Nevertheless, the Philippines indicated a consistent and rapid growth in the period 1980–91, while Indonesia was left behind by its neighbours.

Singapore and Malaysia showed a declining export performance in the low-skill, labour-intensive sectors (Figure 10.3), although their positions were still above the world average in 1991. This reflected the tightening of their labour supply in the late 1980s. Thailand and, more recently, Indonesia showed a rapid growth of exports in this category and, by 1991, both countries also surpassed the world average. The Philippines also indicated a

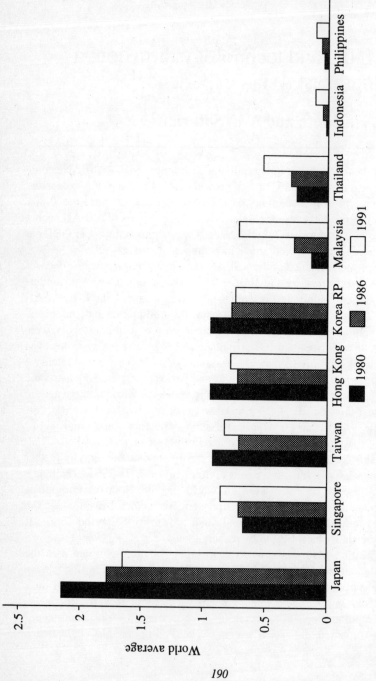

Source: Calculations from Statistics Canada World Trade Database.

Figure 10.1 Revealed comparative advantage for capital-intensive industries, 1980–91

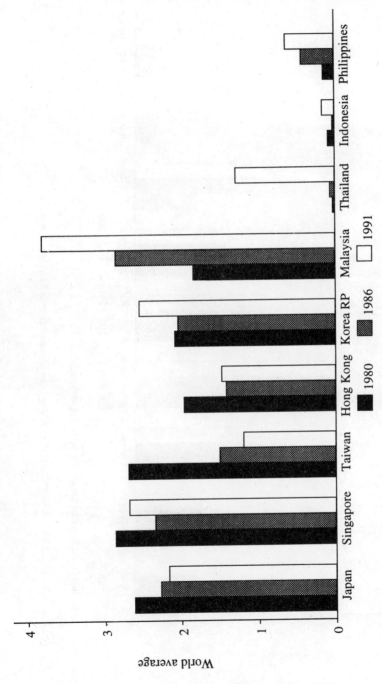

Source: Calculations from Statistics Canada World Trade Database.

Figure 10.2 Revealed comparative advantage for science-intensive industries, 1980–91

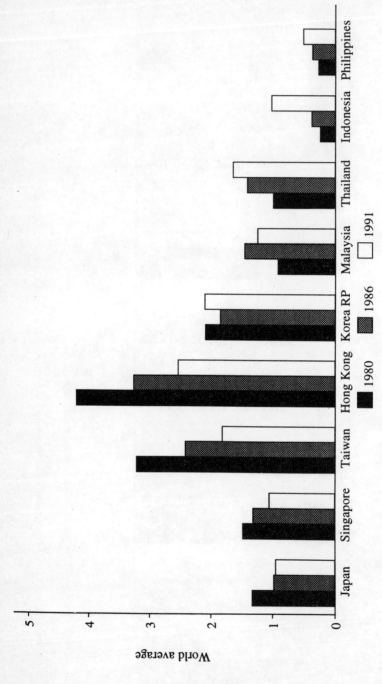

Source: Calculations from Statistics Canada World Trade Database.

Figure 10.3 Revealed comparative advantage for labour-intensive industries, 1980–91

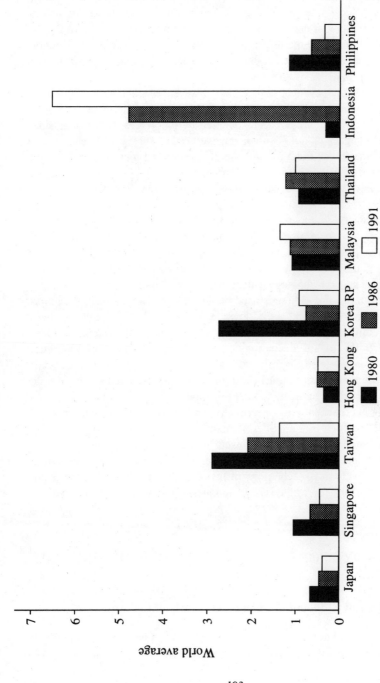

Source: Calculations from Statistics Canada World Trade Database.

Figure 10.4 Revealed comparative advantage for resource-intensive industries, 1980–91

strong growth but its position was still below the world average. Finally, Indonesia has led its neighbours in the resource-intensive sectors, which is consistent with its vast natural resources endowment (Figure 10.4). Malaysia also indicated growth and a position above the world average in 1991, while Singapore, Thailand and the Philippines showed a declining position in this industrial category.

Despite these achievements, there has always been a lingering question about the sustainability of ASEAN's export-led growth. The more developed economies in the region have been squeezed by two forces. On the one side, other developing economies with a relatively large supply of cheap labour (such as China, India and Vietnam) are also becoming more export-oriented and have started to compete more vigorously. On the other side, developed economies have created advanced, automated production techniques that enable them to regain competitive advantage in some of the traditional labour-intensive products.[3] In the meantime, technological advances in new materials may continue to reduce demand for some of the region's traditional natural resource-based commodities. It is within this context of 'reindustrialization' of the West and the 'catching-up' process of the developing economies that the issues of growth and technology diffusion are considered.

The term 'technology' here is used broadly in its generic sense; it encompasses all forms of physical assets, knowledge, human learning and organizational capabilities that enable the firm to produce products and services efficiently. In this regard, technology covers not only manufacturing/production activities and related R&D, but also the whole array of business processes, including improvements in marketing and distribution, finance, accounting, human resource development, and organization.

This chapter concentrates specifically on the role of multinationals in diffusing technology in the ASEAN countries. First, it will present a framework for technology diffusion, followed by a survey on the role of foreign direct investment and technology in the region. The chapter then describes the emerging patterns of technology diffusion at the firm level, from in-depth case studies of firms in Malaysia and Indonesia. Discussions of implications follow.

FRAMEWORK FOR TECHNOLOGY DEVELOPMENT AND DIFFUSION

Technology and Economic Development

The process of technological change can be usefully considered as involving three phases: invention, innovation and diffusion (Schumpeter, 1942;

Stoneman, 1987). Invention refers to the generation of new scientific ideas or knowledge, while innovation refers to the development of these new ideas or knowledge into marketable products. Finally, diffusion refers to the adoption of these new products or processes by economic agents in and across economies. As has been widely documented (for example, Mensch, 1979), it often takes a very long time before a new idea can be transformed into marketable products.[4] In this chapter, we are more interested in technological innovation than invention per se.

The development and diffusion of new technology can be framed within a simple *technology gap* model of economic growth. This Schumpeterian model portrays economic growth as a disequilibrium process characterized by the interaction of two conflicting processes: 'innovation', which tends to increase economic and technological differences between economies, and 'diffusion', which tends to reduce the gap between economies (Fagerberg, 1988). The technology gap model assumes that the benefit of technology diffusion follows a logistic curve, meaning that the benefit of the diffusion depends on the gap between the receiving country and the technology frontier: the less developed an economy, the bigger the benefit gained from technology diffusion, assuming the other conditions for growth are favourable.

This technology gap model indicates that there are two basic approaches for technology policy[5] (Ergas, 1987). The first option is to push forward the technology frontier by developing leading-edge techniques (a *mission-oriented* policy). The focus of this policy is, essentially, to put a heavy emphasis on the generation of new scientific ideas and their development into new marketable products and processes (that is, on invention and innovation). The second option of policy is to foster technology diffusion so as to close the gap between the actual and the best available practices (*diffusion-oriented* policy). It should be noted that, whatever the path of technology policy pursued by a country, in the process the country should also develop its absorptive capacity to sustain and exploit the benefit of the knowledge generated by the innovation, regardless of the origin of the technological innovation.

Technology diffusion takes place through foreign direct investment, import of various kinds of capital goods, formal cooperation between firms (such as licensing) and informal trading of knowledge. Movements of people, both as immigrants and to secure education, can spread technology. International trade can facilitate the diffusion of technology across economies, for several reasons. First, the participation of economic agents of a particular country in world markets will allow them to gain access to a larger pool of technical knowledge. In international trade, sellers may provide buyers with technical assistance on how to use their products more productively, and buyers often advise the sellers on how to design or modify their products to meet their domestic requirements (Grossman and Helpman, 1991; also compare von

Hippel, 1988). Second, international competition will discipline the firms and at the same time induce them to generate ideas that are competitive internationally. Finally, the integration of an economy into world markets can expand the size of the potential customer base which, in turn, may further the incentive for industrial research (Rivera-Batiz and Romer, 1991). International trade brings with it the technological know-how embedded in capital goods or intermediate inputs (Grossman and Helpman, 1991) and, more importantly, the transmission of new ideas (compare Romer, 1992).

Grossman and Helpman (1991) have noted, however, that the role of international trade in promoting technological invention and innovation is not unambiguous. There are several conditions under which opening up an economy to international trade may discourage domestic R&D. Their models show, for example, that a country endowed with relative abundance of natural resources and unskilled labour but lacking skilled workers (as in Indonesia) may be induced under international trade to specialize in the production activities that make use of those relatively abundant resources, at the expense of R&D activities which are crucial for the sustainability of the country's long-run growth.

Technology Development at the Firm Level

The technology gap model can also capture the process of technological development at the firm level. The firm can be depicted as a bundle of resources which embodies two types of activities: (1) operating activities applying knowledge to production, marketing, distribution and finance, and (2) activities to increase the knowledge base of the firm. As both of these activities involve people, a significant part of the firm's resources is embodied in people working for the firm. Firms, in their pursuit of better knowledge and technology – including but not limited to products and production technologies – are continuously and gradually improving their technological skills from a set of technological possibilities. Much of the innovative activities of the firm take place within a specific context (for example, product or plant) through 'learning by doing' (Arrow, 1962) or 'learning by using' (Rosenberg, 1979). In this view, the accumulation of technological skills can only take place within the realm of practical experience, through the process of trial and error.

Technological advancement at the firm level follows the nature and evolution of technology (that is, the technology regime) which varies across industries. In essence, the production structure of the firm dictates the various inputs including new technology know-how – and hence the source of technology learning – required by the firm. In certain industries, it is the suppliers of the firm that dominate and provide the critical source of technology for the firm. In other industries, it is the users or the firms themselves. Whichever is the case, these external sources of general knowledge and specific technology have to be supported by and combined with in-house skills if they are to be effectively adopted (Pavitt, 1984; von Hippel, 1988). It is the existing stock of know-how within the firms, in tandem with its organizational capacities, as a product of cumulative learning, which drives and at the same time limits the area of improvements that the firms can effectively carry out. In addition, firms also face external influences in the form of competition, dominant technology regimes and potential synthesis of inter-industry linkages. It is the interaction between the two, the internal dynamics of the firms and the external inducements, that eventually shapes the direction of technological advancement that firms will undertake.

MNEs and Technology Diffusion

It has been argued that any additional unit of capital investment not only increases the stock of physical capital but also increases the level of techno-logical knowledge for all firms in the economy through knowledge spillovers (for example, Arrow, 1962). In the case of foreign investment, multinational enterprises (MNEs) have firm-specific advantages in their ability to generate, develop and organize the application of specific technologies across national borders. Thus they bring in with their investment a bundle of technologies embedded in their financial, production, management and marketing capa-bilities. Usually, MNEs can transfer this knowledge to their foreign subsidiar-ies, although not without cost (Teece, 1977). The MNEs could also affect the local economy through their decisions to purchase raw materials and inter-mediate products locally, and through their technical linkages with both the domestic suppliers and buyers.

The domestic suppliers and buyers can gain directly from MNEs through various forms of technical linkages. These include, among others: (1) informa-tion linkages, whether specific technical information about machinery, materi-als, parts and components or general information about markets and govern-ment regulations; (2) technical assistance, in the areas of plant design and layout, tooling, machinery selection, maintenance, troubleshooting and product design; (3) managerial and organizational assistance; (4) financial assistance; and (5) procurement assistance (Lall, 1980). Certainly, the end results – how much the local firms can benefit from the MNEs – depend on the quality of their workforce, their age and experience in dealing with MNEs and their existing technological and organizational capacities, as well as on the nature of the MNEs themselves and on the host country regulatory framework.

In the specific area of technological innovation by MNEs in their host countries, some notable patterns have emerged. First, the proportion of MNEs'

R&D activity outside their home countries is generally quite small and, in the case of Japanese firms, negligible.[6] Second, the MNEs' R&D activity is heavily directed towards the adaptation of specific products, production techniques or organizational practices of the firm rather than towards basic research (for example, Pearce, 1990; Pearce and Singh, 1992). Such adaptations are made necessary by the host country-specific conditions in terms of availability of materials, supply capabilities, human capital capacities and organizational practices. Third, basic research undertaken by MNEs' subsidiaries in the host countries, if any, usually involves: (1) immobile inputs for the research (for example, plantation or mining), and (2) heavy interaction with domestic customers and/or local government (for example, pharmaceuticals). In any case, such basic research requires the availability of scientists and engineers and will be most likely to flourish when the host countries have developed proper innovatory infrastructure.

In general, the relatively new industrializing countries such as ASEAN are in no position, at the moment, to push forward the technology frontier. The national technology base of these countries has just developed; their R&D expenditure is relatively very low (ranging from about 0.2 per cent of GDP for Indonesia and Thailand to about 1 per cent of GDP for Singapore) and the institutional framework for promoting R&D is not in place yet. In addition, the technological capacity of the private sector is still shallow and its ability to invest in R&D is limited. Therefore the natural technology policy will be to emphasize the effective diffusion of foreign technology and, at the same time, to build up absorptive capacity in the forms of effective learning, adaptation and possibly improving upon available foreign technology to gain competitive advantage. As these countries move up the technology ladder over time, the emphasis can then be shifted toward new knowledge creation – particularly knowledge relevant to each individual country's condition. Diversification and specialization can then be expected to develop in the region. With this in mind, our analysis will be focused more on the diffusion aspect of technology development. In particular, we will examine the role played by MNEs in the ASEAN countries in technology diffusion and in the development of domestic absorptive capacity.

THE ROLE OF FOREIGN DIRECT INVESTMENT AND TECHNOLOGY

All the ASEAN countries have now adopted export-oriented development policies. The success of their export drives, however, can be largely attributed to the investment of multinationals operating in the region. The share of multinationals in total country exports ranges from 22.3 per cent for Indonesia to 34.7 per cent for the Philippines, 48.6 per cent for Thailand and as high as 59.6 per cent for Malaysia and 88.1 per cent for Singapore (Table 10.1). Compared to the other ASEAN countries, Indonesia seems to be lagging behind in capitalizing on multinationals in its drive for industrial and export development.

The ratio of FDI inflows to GDP in ASEAN increased significantly in the 1980s, from 1.3 per cent in to 3.3 per cent, while its ratio to gross domestic capital formation also increased, from 5.1 per cent to 9.4 per cent (Table 10.2). Among the ASEAN countries, Singapore is the most dependent on FDI, followed by Malaysia which is catching up rapidly. The success of ASEAN countries in attracting FDI can be attributed largely to a combination of the following factors: political stability, rapidly growing domestic markets,

Table 10.1   The role of multinational corporations in the host economy

	Year	Employment (per cent)	Exports (per cent)	Value added (per cent)
Singapore	1988	59.5	88.1	71.7
Malaysia	1988	48.7	59.6	n.a.
Thailand	1986	8.8	48.6	n.a.
Indonesia	1990	18.8	22.3	27.6
Philippines	1987	27.3	34.7	9.0

Sources: Various country studies.

Table 10.2   Foreign direct investment ratios

	FDI inflows/GDP (per cent)		FDI inflows/domestic capital formation (per cent)	
	1980	1990	1980	1990
Singapore	9.7	9.6	21.0	24.5
Malaysia	3.8	7.1	12.5	21.9
Thailand	0.6	2.9	2.2	7.9
Indonesia	0.3	0.9	1.2	2.5
Philippines	0.0	0.6	−1.1	3.3
ASEAN total	1.3	3.3	5.1	9.4

Source: Asian Development Bank, *Key Indicators of Developing Asian and Pacific Countries*, 1992.

favourable resource endowments (natural resources and labour supply in ASEAN-4, and human capital and infrastructure in Singapore) and development-oriented governments with generally FDI-friendly policies (see Chia, 1993). It should be noted that, although all ASEAN countries tend to have broadly similar investment incentives (for example, tax facility, export incentives and import duty exemptions), they differ quite substantially in terms of bureaucratic efficiency, restrictive rules (on ownership of equity and of land, and other restricted sectors) and performance requirements (export, local content, technology transfer and training). In the past few years, however, with the continuing liberalization of trade and investment in the region – particularly with the conception of the ASEAN Free Trade Area and also in response to ever-increasing competition from China and Vietnam in attracting FDI – there has been a tendency for policy convergence on FDI in the ASEAN countries.

Japan has emerged as a major investor in ASEAN in the 1970s, followed by the East Asian NIEs in the post-1987 period. Japanese FDI in ASEAN grew significantly in the 1980s, reflecting its domestic structural transformation, increasing labour and land costs in the 1970s and the appreciation of the yen in 1985. The Japanese FDI in ASEAN tends to concentrate in selected manufacturing sectors, such as electrical and electronic products, chemicals and, to a lesser degree, machinery and metal products.[7]

While ASEAN's success in attracting FDI has contributed significantly to the local economies, in terms of providing employment and promoting exports, the ASEAN countries are still in the process of learning how to diffuse the foreign technology to local firms. With only a few exceptions, foreign multinationals have generally not developed significant linkages with local firms, despite various attempts by governments to promote subcontracting schemes involving large and small enterprises in the region. The industrial sectors in Thailand, Indonesia and the Philippines are still relatively shallow: there is only a small base of reliable local suppliers; many key industrial inputs still have to be imported; also there is only an embryonic, albeit growing, local capital goods industry. The industrial structure of Thailand and of Indonesia,[8] for example, is dominated by a small number of large conglomerates and a large number of very small enterprises. As a result, particularly in the protected sectors, the large firms tend to be vertically integrated. The local content requirements generally promote only inefficient local producers protected by government regulations.

Another source of foreign technology is through imports of capital goods (Figure 10.5). During 1965–87, the pattern of capital goods imports did not change much in terms of ranking. Singapore was the highest in terms of capital goods importation. The ratio of its capital goods import to GDP was 129 per cent in 1965 and increased slightly to 163 per cent in 1987.[9] Malaysia

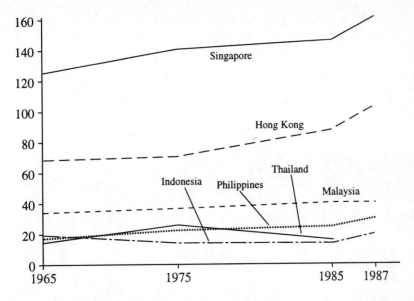

Source: Dahlman and Brimble, *Technology Strategy and Policy for Industrial Competitiveness: A Case Study of Thailand*, World Bank Report, 1992, p. 22.

Figure 10.5   Imports of capital goods as a ratio to GDP (%)

was next, with the ratios of 35 per cent and 39 per cent, respectively, in the same period. Thailand increased significantly its use of capital goods imports; the ratios were 17 per cent in 1965 and 27 per cent in 1987. Indonesia and the Philippines were the lowest; their imports were about 15 per cent of their GDP, and the figures did not change much in the period 1965–87. It could be that Indonesia, the Philippines and, to some extent, Thailand, suffered from the relatively high import duties for capital goods, particularly for non-exporting firms or for firms which did not enjoy import duty exemption. As a result, firms in these countries were not able to take as much advantage of importing foreign technology embedded in capital goods as were their counterparts in the East Asian NIEs.

Table 10.3 summarizes the comparative features of the trade and investment regimes in ASEAN, and their export and industrial performance. It suggests a relatively strong correlation between the rankings of industrial and export performance indices and trade and investment regime indices. The better export and industrial performances were noted earlier and are shown in Table 10.3 by the revealed comparative advantage in capital- and science-intensive sectors, as well as by the role of metal products and machinery sectors in manufacturing value added. This superior performance is correlated

Table 10.3 *Comparative indices of trade and industrial regimes and industrial performance in ASEAN*

| | Indices of industrial performance | | | Trade and investment indices | | |
| | Sectoral ranking of RCA | | Ranking of the role of metal products and machinery | FDI inflows/GDP | Ranking of: | |
	Capital-intensive	Science-intensive			Imports of capital goods	Effective tariff rate
Singapore	1	2	1	1	1	1
Malaysia	2	1	2	2	2	2
Thailand	3	3	4	3	3	3
Indonesia	4	5	3	4	4	4/5
Philippines	5	4	n.a.	5	5	4/5

Notes:

1. Sectoral rankings of RCA are derived from Figure 10.1 and 10.2.
2. Rankings of FDI inflows/GDP and imports of capital goods/GDP are obtained from Tables 10.2 and 10.3, respectively.
3. Ranking of the role of metal products and machinery in manufacturing value added is derived from the World Bank, *The East Asia Miracle: Economic Growth and Public Policy*, p. 305. Specifically, the ratios of metal products and machinery in manufacturing value added for each economy are 61 per cent for Singapore, 27 per cent for Malaysia, 14 per cent for Indonesia, and 11 per cent for Thailand. No similar data are available for the Philippines.
4. Ranking of the effective tariff rate (unweighed) is obtained from the IMF Data (1992) and Sri Kumar (1992). Specifically, the ETR is 0 per cent for Singapore, 11 per cent for Malaysia, 14 per cent for Indonesia, and 19 per cent for both Thailand and the Philippines.

positively with better flows of imports and investments in each of the ASEAN economies, as measured by the ratios of high FDI inflows and of capital goods imports to GDP and a low effective tariff rate.

If one is willing to make a crude rank order of technology development in ASEAN based on the indices of export and industrial development above, then a case can be made that Singapore is leading the way, followed by Malaysia and then Thailand, albeit at some distance. Indonesia and the Philippines are unambiguously lagging compared to the other three. An argument can be made that, in the case of ASEAN, the most relevant technology policy for the region is the one which promotes the diffusion of foreign technology. More specifically, it can be argued that the more permeable the trade and investment regimes of a country are, the further the country will be able to move up the technology ladder.[10]

In the following section descriptive case studies are presented, in an attempt to account for the emerging patterns of technology diffusion at the firm level.

PATTERNS OF TECHNOLOGY DIFFUSION AT THE FIRM LEVEL

This section reports three case studies of host country firms in Indonesia (two companies, at Batam and Bandung) and Malaysia (one firm) in the semiconductor sector.[11] It attempts to delineate the domestic firms' approach to technology acquisition through various linkages they have with their buyers, equipment suppliers and principals or foreign partners, within a given production structure of the firm.

The Production Structure

The major value-adding activities in this particular sector consist of design and mask making, wafer fabrication, assembly or packaging, and final testing (see Ernst, 1983, for a fuller description). Each production stage requires different levels of skills, different factor intensity and different sources of know-how. The design of semiconductors is highly knowledge-intensive, involving proprietary know-how about the functioning of the chips, knowledge about basic material sciences and intimate knowledge about the production process involved. Naturally, this activity requires very high-level design and production engineers, including basic material scientists.

The wafer fabrication stage is very capital-intensive and requires high standards of precision and product quality control, often employing the latest technology in CNC (computerized numerical control) equipment. Some numerical adjustments of the equipment are required to fit into the parameters of each design (types, density and dimension). The packaging stage is more labour-intensive than the wafer fabrication, although it also employs many state-of-the-art CNCs. The last stage of semiconductor manufacturing, the final testing, requires skilled labour and considerable investment in capital goods. The testing itself involves the use of proprietary software to evaluate the functioning of the chips as specified by their design. Interestingly, while the software is proprietary, it is nevertheless highly codified and transportable, requiring only certain features/specifications in the testing equipment to run it.

As our interviews reveal, the wafer fabrication and assembly stages tend to be increasingly more automated and more capital-intensive.[12] A new venture in Batam Island in Indonesia, which started in 1992 with a capacity of 50 million units of various types of chips per month, took a total investment of about $US 60 million. To produce the wafer (as its input), the estimated total investment required is about $US 200–250 million. A senior engineer of the Malaysian plant gave an illustration of the increasing use of automation in its packaging operation. In 1983, the assembly operation was very labour-intensive. The worker–machine ratio was about 1:1. In 1985, this firm replaced its old equipment with equipment which was five to six times faster, but the worker–machine ratio was still at the 1:1 level. Since 1986 it has selectively introduced fully automated assembly operations, and the worker–machine ratio is now about 1:3.

Apart from its functional design, there are two parameters in semiconductor production which are of critical importance and have become a standard measure of efficiency and customer satisfaction. The first, the 'cycle time', refers to the amount of time taken to deliver the final product to the customers' door. The semiconductor business is marked by a rapid proliferation of new product innovation, and competing in time becomes imperative. The second parameter, 'production yield', and its twin, 'production defects', are self-explanatory. These two parameters underscore the importance of the overall approach of a company in its semiconductor business. Motorola, for example, puts heavy emphasis on its 'operational expectations': (1) to strive for one-tenth of the previous level of defects in every two years (in the five year period 1988–92, Motorola reduced its worldwide work-in-process defects to about 0.6 per cent of the previous level, resulting in a manufacturing cost saving of $US 2.2 billion); (2) to achieve a 90 per cent reduction in cycle time in the next five years, by applying cycle-time reduction techniques to all elements of its businesses, and (3) to maintain quality services by developing indices and continuously monitoring 'customer satisfiers' in each business (Motorola, 1992).

The two semiconductor assembly operators in Indonesia being studied indicated their preoccupation with both the cycle time and the production yield. In terms of production yield, it is believed that there is a tremendous learning curve effect in assembly production. The Bandung plant has been in operation at least since 1986 when the current owners, a joint venture between a Singaporean firm and two Indonesian partners, took it over from National Semiconductor. Currently, its annual output averages about 450–500 million units. With a cumulative output since 1986 of about 3.5 billion units, its production yield is close to the target of 99.5 per cent (that is, defects of only 0.5 per cent) which is an acceptable yield in the industry. The Batam plant, on the other hand, only started its operation in April 1992. With its current output at about 20 million units per month, it has accumulated output in the range of 250–350 million units. Its current yield is between 97 and 98 per cent, which is much below the industry standard.

For the two Indonesian assemblers, there are two elements involved in their cycle time performance. One element, in-plant production time, reflects the production capability of the firm (including production engineering, organization and control of production process, and the management of interaction with upstream, downstream and ancillary activities). Normally, one would also expect there to be a strong learning curve effect in this regard. The Batam plant managers indicate that its current production cycle is about seven to eight days, compared with five to six days for its Bandung counterpart. The second element involves externalities in the form of transport and custom clearance time. Here, government bureaucracy matters greatly. In general, those involved in the two Indonesian plants claim that, compared to their Malaysian counterparts, for example, they are victims of bureaucratic inefficiency, despite Batam's status as a free trade zone. In Batam it takes about six to eight hours to clear customs, compared with one to two hours in Malaysia, and it takes an even longer time for the Bandung plant.

The nature of semiconductor production, as described above, gives some indication of the relationship among chip makers, the users and equipment suppliers in the various stages of chip production. These relations in a sense also reflect the sources of learning and innovation, as summarized in Table 10.4.

The pursuit of productivity improvement (cycle time and production yield) also reflects technological progress within the firm. The progress seems to follow an S-curve: once a basic innovation emerges, it is followed by a series of incremental improvements with an accelerating rate which slows down when the potential for additional improvements is exhausted. Further improvements are not only difficult technically but also very costly. At this juncture, technological progress faces a stalemate which can only be offset by other developments in basic invention (compare Mensch, 1979). The Motorola experience is telling in this regard. After it set up a 'new' approach in 1983, it proceeded incrementally by introducing full automation, albeit

Table 10.4   Production structure and sources of learning and innovation in the semiconductor sector

	Structure	Sources of learning and innovation
Design	Knowledge-intensive (skilled design and production engineers; material scientists)	Company labs; users (for ASIC)
Water fabrication	Highly capital-intensive; high standard of precision and product quality control	Company labs; equipment (CNC) suppliers; own learning curve
Assembly	Less capital-intensive; skilled operators	Company labs; equipment suppliers; own learning curve; other assembly operators
Final testing	More labour-intensive; proprietary software;	Company labs

selectively, and by concentrating on bottlenecks in every element of its businesses. In 1992, Motorola realized that such small, incremental changes were not sufficient any more. It declared that it needed to 'totally change the way it does the business, and it may also require a major cultural change within Motorola' (Motorola, 1992).

For the two Indonesian semiconductor assemblers, technological progress takes place incrementally through their learning curve or learning by doing, as noted earlier, and also through interaction with their buyers (semiconductor firms such as Motorola) and equipment suppliers. It is clear that the various linkages/networks that emerge in the semiconductor sector are structured by the nature and pattern of the production itself. This is one of the reasons why technological advancement may differ significantly across industrial sectors.

The Domestic Firms' Approach to Technology Acquisition

Another factor that shapes cross-border technology diffusion is the strategy pursued by host firms. Strategy includes the role of this particular semiconductor unit in the host firm's portfolio, hence the weight the firm puts behind investment in technology, and its approach to technology acquisition.

The firms interviewed reveal rather striking differences in their overall strategy and approach to technology acquisition (Table 10.5). The Batam venture is a major, and the most ambitious, diversification for the company. The semiconductor assembly and testing operation is considered as its future growth potential and is built upon the cash flows made available from its old businesses (selling and servicing office equipment, notably copy machines). At the same time, the company is building the largest Indonesian distribution network and service points for its office equipment and systems products, including copy machines, computer, printing and telecommunication equipment. This is achieved through combining the extensive distribution system just noted with good products with a known brand name, a service programme of exemplary quality, and skilled and dedicated employees.[13]

The most salient characteristic of the firm's diversification strategy is seen in the various modes of entry it used. As of 1993, there were 14 diversifica-

Table 10.5   Host firms' strategies and approach to technology acquisition

	Semiconductor A (Batam)	Semiconductor B (Bandung)	Semiconductor C (Malaysia)
Status	Wholly subsidiary (greenfield)	Joint venture (Singapore plus two Indonesian partners)	Wholly subsidiary to a leading US multinational
Major thrusts	Build a dominant distribution network in Indonesia	Stand-alone investment, net cash-flows	Build a dominant plant outside the USA
	Aggressive diversification	Possible learning platform for future expansion	Source of expertise for assembly operation
	Combination of greenfield and alliances		
Approach to technology acquisition	Dual approaches: incremental (for old business) and aggressive investment (using turnkey contracts for its semiconductor unit)	Conservative and incremental	Incremental, with a strong pattern of increasing capital intensity

tion ventures, seven of which were still at their planning stage. Out of 14 ventures, five are joint ventures involving partners from Taiwan, South Korea and Singapore-based companies, and the other nine are internally developed. As described earlier, the company also has marketing agreements with foreign firms to distribute their products in Indonesia. The CEO of the company indicates that the key success factor in managing its various alliances with various foreign partners is to secure their support and at the same time to let his company take the initiative to build and nurture the business ('We lead with ideas, they back up fully').

The second company, the Bandung joint venture, is focusing on the assembly of 'application-specific integrated circuits (ASIC)' through original equipment manufacturing (OEM) arrangements with US and Japanese multinationals. The company carefully builds its customer base and establishes its reputation as a reliable provider of assembly operations by maintaining close relations with its customers. Future investments are incremental, carefully designed to fulfil its customers' future requirements. Even within the next ten years, the firm does not have any plan to diversify itself into downstream activity, that is to provide testing services. While the venture mainly serves as a stand-alone investment that generates net cash flows, particularly for its two Indonesian partners, it can also be seen as a learning platform for the partners' future expansion. This is particularly the case for the Singaporean partner, a computer firm. Just recently, the Singaporean partner also established a similar operation in Malaysia, acting as an independent subcontractor for semiconductor packaging.

The different strategies pursued by the host firms are also accompanied by different approaches in their technology acquisitions. As described earlier, the Bandung assembly operation is rather conservative in terms of its investments, including technology investment. Most of its near-term capital outlays are undertaken in close consultation with its customers, so as to fit into their near-term production plans. The two major sources of technological know-how of the firm are its customers and suppliers.

Generally speaking, the parent company of the Batam venture is a marketing and distributing enterprise, and only lately seriously ventured into manufacturing operations. The establishment of semiconductor assembly and testing in Batam Island is unusual in the sense that it was done by contracting with experienced foreign managers to run the company. The venture has produced only since April 1992, and it is too early to assess its performance and, particularly, its ability to absorb technology successfully. Nevertheless, some progress has taken place. By December 1992, after only eight months in operation, the level of output reached about 10 million units per month, generating a revenue of $US 1.75 million per month. In 1993, the output was about 20 million units, and expected to climb to 40–50 million units in 1994.

In 1992, the Batam venture was only offering PDIP (8-40 LD) and PLCC (28-84 LD) packaging. In 1993, it added SOIC (8-28 LD) and QFP Gull Wing (80-208 LD), and in 1994 QFP (256-304 LD) and Thin QFP (1.4mm, 48-176 LD).[14] So far, it has about 25 customers, three of which also give the venture contracts for both assembly and testing, using its testing facility. Current monthly output of the testing facility is 2.5 million units.

Emerging Technology Linkages

Given the above production structure, it appears that there are six types of technology linkages that can be discerned from our case studies, as follows.

Buyer linkages

In general, most MNEs in semiconductors are relatively highly vertically integrated. Subcontracting, if any, is used to accommodate fluctuations in worldwide demand and/or to produce smaller, older-style chips which have lower value added but nevertheless need to be provided as a part of their service to their customers. Motorola Malaysia, for example, subcontracts only about 10 per cent of its output to six local/regional contractors for packaging and testing. Another company, Intel Malaysia, subcontracts a higher proportion of output, 20 per cent, externally. Consequently, each individual subcontractor needs to have more than one customer to utilize its production capacity and to survive. For example, the Bandung assembler has about 20 customers (70 per cent American and 30 per cent Japanese multinationals) and the Batam assembler has 25 customers, which are mainly American multinationals.

From the multinational semiconductor firms' viewpoint, the use of subcontractors involves substantial initial investment in terms of identifying and finding the right candidates. Initially, a potential customer will send their quality assurance people to inspect various facilities, personnel and the performance of the subcontractor plant, followed by a trial production of a very small lot (a 'qualification lot'). This first test usually takes two to three months. If it succeeds, another trial run follows with a bigger batch of 2000–5000 units and then 10 000 units, particularly to test the consistency of production quality and efficiency. If the potential buyer is satisfied, it will send another team to audit the whole process and to decide whether it will place the order or not. Two important implications arise from this process. The first is that there is a substantial initial investment of both parties in getting to know each other, although the larger investment is by the potential buyer seeking to know more about the subcontractor's facility, technical ability, performance and, particularly, its personnel. This means that, once a buyer agrees to enter a contract, this usually entails a long-term relationship.

The second implication, further underscoring the importance of this initial stage, refers to the technical exchange occurring during the qualification process. The trial runs and quality assurance audits usually involve discussion about problems which have occurred and how best to deal with them in ways which may become normal practice later on.

As the two semiconductor assemblers are involved mainly in the OEM market, significant amounts of technology diffusion occurred through this arrangement. From the buyers' perspective, the use of local subcontractors helps to absorb demand fluctuations and requires substantial investment in choosing the subcontractors. Given the magnitude of their initial investments, it is imperative that the buyers commit themselves to providing technical support for the subcontractor whenever necessary. Also they need to consider the opportunity costs involved. As an example, Motorola once experienced a serious problem with one of its subcontractors: there was a 'micro crack' in the units produced. A team of Motorola experts from Taiwan was assigned to help the subcontractor, to no avail. The advice from the equipment supplier was also sought. This accident also led to discussion within the worldwide Motorola organization and, as a result, one solution was offered which solved the problem. Such an incident is very costly; it includes not only the cost of the error but also the opportunity costs due to the unfulfilled deadline. It is imperative, therefore, that both parties develop close long-term relations to minimize such problems.

The exchange of technical and production information with its customers provides a basis for the firm to learn about new products and processes, and to gain insights into users' evaluations of specific technology embedded in capital goods. The two assemblers have developed very good relationships with their customers. To support interface with its customers, the Batam assembler provides real time access to its computer systems as well as e-mail. Its computer systems (using DEC VAX 6310) allow customers to learn, on-line, about the status of their work-in-progress, inventory level, the yield level and any statistical report, from any part of the world at any particular time. The customers can then interact with the Batam venture using this data. In another case, one of the Bandung plant's customers, an American multinational, has for several years consigned its testing equipment at the Bandung plant to testing the chips produced by the plant. This American customer then trained the local operators to handle the proprietary equipment for its own use.

Most of the two assemblers' customers visit the plant four to six times a year to inspect it and ensure that their quality assurance programmes have been put in place. During the visits the customers' engineers usually hold meetings with their counterparts in the host firm to discuss any technical matters of mutual concern. Often they also provide on-the-job training to the host firm's operators and engineers. The visiting customers also commonly provide relevant information on their medium-term production plan, including product specifications and quantities. This rather informal exchange of information is used by an assembler to prepare its own planning, including near-term investment outlays. Before investing in any capital goods, it discusses this with its customers and seeks their advice on the type and the supplier of the equipment. In effect, the company has used this process to cement long-term relations with its customers.

Interestingly, the buyers, which are multinational firms, often become a source of technology diffusion through mobility of their engineers to local subcontractors. Many Motorola engineers, for example, resigned and then joined Motorola Malaysia's local subcontractors, or even established new ones. In one case, Motorola Malaysia spun off one of its production activities involving mature products, specifically small-sized chips, and sold the asset to its engineers while retaining them as a new subcontractor. Spillover of technology to other firms occurred through this process of inter-firm mobility of engineers. From Motorola's perspective, though, this incident can be seen as an efficient way of finding new subcontractors.

Supplier linkages

Semiconductor assembly involves substantial investment in capital goods. The purchase of capital goods also brings with it disembodied know-how in the form of technical and training manuals and technical support from the suppliers. Exchange of information on the latest development of process technology is usually also provided by equipment suppliers.

The two assemblers show different approaches to their acquisition of capital goods. The Bandung venture is very conservative; it invests only incrementally, using inputs from its customers. The key criterion in choosing equipment has been the availability and reliability of the technical support from the equipment suppliers. The Batam venture, on the other hand, is more aggressive. Although its progress (in terms of output produced, cycle time and yield rate) is slower than expected, it has considered doubling its capacity in the next few years. The venture puts a strong emphasis not only on the suppliers' technical support but also on the level of sophistication of the technology (most of its equipment is state-of-the-art) and on its capacity for upgrading. For example, it experienced a problem with one of its very sophisticated machines from Intercon of the USA, used for dejunking/trimming/forming SOIC and PDIP. The supplier agreed to send its expert technician, to remain on site for a year, in order to train the local operators to operate, adjust and maintain the equipment, including troubleshooting.

The key materials for semiconductor assembly (leadframe, gold wire, mould and epoxy) are commodity-type goods imported from Japan, the United

States and Switzerland. The availability of these standard direct materials in the venture is continuously communicated to its customers. The technical exchanges with the suppliers of these standard materials are limited to the exchange of information about technical specifications, delivery time and prices.

Inter-firm informal linkages

Another important avenue of technology diffusion to the firms is through informal exchange of know-how among engineers from other semiconductor firms (that is, competitors: compare von Hippel, 1988, chap. 6).

The plant manager of the Bandung assembler expressed his concern that, while the company has developed competence at the shopfloor/operator level, he is not as satisfied about its engineers and managers. One problem is that its engineers represent less than 2.5 per cent of total employees (compared to the Motorola Malaysia figure of about 10–15 per cent) and the number will not change dramatically in the near future. He feels that the development of the company's business hinges upon the technological deepening of the semiconductor industry in Indonesia. There are two problems related to this issue. The first is what the management of this firm terms the 'lack of critical mass' in the Indonesian semiconductor industry, and in the electronics industry in general. The government is viewed as not giving enough support for the acquisition of foreign technology; the investment regulations in general and industrial relations in particular are blamed for this problem.[15] The second, related, problem pertains to the weakness in upstream activity: there is almost no design capability, not even a wafer foundry, in Indonesia. As a consequence, the company is very much dependent on its customers in terms of technology acquisition and diffusion. The plant manager gave an example of how difficult it is for him to get local support if he encounters technical problems. Again, using Malaysia as a reference, he pointed out that there is extensive communication and exchange of technical know-how among the Malaysian engineers of various firms, even if the firms are competing with each other. He claimed that the large number of engineers in the Malaysian electronic industry provides a basis for technical exchange and hence technological learning.

In Malaysia, there are now 725 companies in the electronic and electrical industry, including about 27 in the semiconductor sector, of which 19 are multinational companies and eight are local subcontractors (*Business Times*, 1993). The annual growth rate of industry output is about 30 per cent. The industry employs 171 000 workers, representing 12.4 per cent of total employment in manufacturing, and contributes 60 per cent of total manufactured exports. The inter-firm mobility of engineers is quite noticeable. The turnover rate for Motorola, for example, is about 10 per cent. In addition, a significant proportion of the engineers in Malaysia have had working experience with other electronics firms in Singapore. It is of interest to note that, in the 1970s, the Singapore government ruled that Malaysian engineering students enrolled in Singaporean universities should work in Singapore for several years to fill in its own human capital needs. In the aggregate, with thousands of engineers and technicians working in this industry, the impact of the mobility of engineers within and between firms has been quite significant for the diffusion of technology in the country. The inter-firm mobility is not restricted to multinationals, but occurs also from multinationals to local firms, as indicated by the Motorola case above. It appears that there has developed a strong, albeit informal, network among the electronic engineers in Malaysia and, to some extent, Singapore.[16] They discuss many aspects of their professional life, including career paths and opportunities, as well as current issues in the industry. It is not at all unusual for them to exchange information on a certain piece of technology or equipment, or on technical problems.

As the plant manager of the Bandung assembler indicated, his technology network is very limited. In Indonesia there are only two assemblers and two government/educational laboratories for wafer fabrication and both of these are practically defunct. Even the two assemblers are geographically separated and the communication between them is almost non-existent. Compare this to the Malaysia plants, which are closely clustered and also close to Singapore. In aggregate, there are less than 150 engineers in the two separate Indonesian assembly plants, which makes it difficult to achieve the critical mass needed to make informal trading of know-how among them useful. In the case of the Batam venture, besides their proximity to Singapore, the contracted engineer-managers bring with them their own network of professional engineers as a source of technical know-how, as described more fully below.

Turnkey contract
The Batam venture is a good example of how the firm acquires technology through contractual arrangements, such as management and turnkey contracts, and also through disembodied technology embedded in the imports of leading-edge capital goods. To run the venture, the company hired 115 experienced engineers (about 60 per cent Filipinos, 20 per cent Malaysians and the rest American and Singaporean) through such contracts. These foreign engineers and executives take almost all managerial and other senior positions within the company. All of these expatriates have a minimum experience of ten years with major electronic firms (TI, Motorola, NS, Hitachi, RCA and Swire, among others), while the senior managers have an average experience of more than 20 years. These senior foreign executives were responsible for every aspect of the venture: the design of the plant, selecting

equipment and vendors, training the engineers and operators, obtaining certification and marketing the products/services.[17] The company is still in the process of learning how to manage these expatriates. It appears that a natural, ethnic-based grouping emerged among the expatriates that often creates its own cultural problems. On another front, the recruitment of these expatriates also poses a challenge to the management, on how to learn and absorb knowledge, attitude and skills embedded in both the individuals and in the organizational practices of this unique venture. The senior management hopes to double its production capacity within the next few years. With a limited supply of experienced engineers within the country, they doubted that they will be able to replace these expatriates with local engineers. On the contrary, the company sees them as the critical asset that needs to be maintained to sustain its survival.

The management of the firm noted that this particular mode of technology acquisition can be very costly. Initially, it was expected that this venture would be able to break even in 1993, but it now remains to be seen whether it will be able to do so in 1994. Meanwhile, some progress did take place, as noted earlier; its output is increasing steadily. The 'excellent quality' objectives of zero customer return and 99 per cent yield rate were not quite achieved, since the 1993 yield was 98 per cent. The actual cycle time of eight to nine days needs to be improved. As the bulk of its expenses are in the cost of materials (standard, commodity-type available competitively in international markets), the company does not consider cost or price as a critical issue at the moment, except in the case of major manufacturing errors. Rather, the two previous issues, quality and cycle time, are more pressing at the moment.

Technology cooperation
In 1993, the Batam venture launched an alliance with a Singaporean semiconductor laboratory, to offer a full turnkey solution of wafer fabrication, assembly and testing. The Singaporean laboratory is a joint venture between a Singapore private firm (20 per cent) and the Singapore government (80 per cent), specializing in wafer fabrication, particularly for application-specific chips. It is currently expanding to the third unit of wafer fabrication. Another new wafer manufacturer, a joint venture involving Japanese and US multinationals and the Singapore government, is now being established in Singapore. It is conceivable that the Batam venture will also be able to forge an alliance with this new wafer manufacturer to strengthen its position in the market. If these alliances do take off, it is expected that some joint design will take place, involving the partners and the buyer(s).

Intra-firm linkages

Significant amounts of technology diffusion occurred within the firms interviewed. This intra-firm diffusion of technology pertains to the basic and general knowledge transferable across various businesses, such as quality control circles (the Batam venture), customer services (the Malaysian and Batam ventures) and basic supervisory and managerial knowledge (all firms interviewed). In the case of the Batam venture, the implementation of QCC (quality control circles) and customer services is supported by a special task force within the parent holding company. The success of the photocopy business in promoting excellent quality services can be attributed to this intra-firm technology diffusion. Currently, the Batam venture is also in the process of implementing both the QCC and customer services programmes with the help of a consulting firm based in Hong Kong and Australia. In addition, the Batam venture also employs a sophisticated statistical technique as an integral part of its QCC programmes and also as a basis for communicating with its customers.

Much of the diffusion of technology within the company is through various forms of in-company training programmes, ad hoc programmes such as QCCs, internal mobility of employees, and on-the-job training and interaction with foreign engineers and managers. All the three firms studied have very good and systematic training programmes. In the case of the Batam venture, an employee who is about to be promoted to a certain position, for example, has to attend the general training programmes for that managerial level, and a specific programme for the position. In addition, all of its operators and engineers have to go through specialized training programmes and be certified. The training includes product specification, operating procedures, 'do's and don'ts' and statistical control procedure. The certification of operators is re-evaluated and recertification is granted on a periodic basis.

CONCLUDING COMMENTS

As has been well documented, multinationals have for some time relocated some of their facilities to the production platform countries in Southeast Asia. Usually, these multinationals began by relocating their most labour-intensive operation (such as assembly) to the region. Since the mid-1980s, however, the relocation has also included other activities (such as components), more capital-intensive processes such as wafer fabrication, and knowledge-intensive processes (such as design) to the region as well. As of 1993, Malaysia has become the centre of several multinationals' manufacturing operations in this industry, while Singapore has been involved in certain design activities. Motorola and National Semiconductors, for example, now produce more than half of their semiconductor output in Malaysia. Motorola, and also Texas Instruments, now rely on their Malaysian subsidiary in terms of manufacturing expertise; they often send their Malaysian engineers to the United States to solve problems there.

Following Singapore, both Malaysia and Thailand have gradually upgraded their electronics industry to more skill-intensive activities and abandoned their low-skill labour-intensive manufacturing operations. Despite a general trend to increasing relocation of low-skill labour-intensive operations to China and Vietnam, there is some indication that Indonesia is also considered by the Japanese MNEs for FDI in such operations. Several Japanese firms have now submitted their letter of intent to expand or produce components (CRT, for example). The Indonesian minister of industry is now aggressively inviting electronics firms, including Toshiba, Philips, Mitsubishi and Samsung, to expand their manufacturing operations, including component production. NEC is in the negotiation process with the Indonesian government to establish semiconductor production in Indonesia. Sony is planning to use Indonesia as a production platform to quickly build further export markets of low-end technology consumer electronics, particularly for North American and European markets. Current output is about one million units per year and is expanding. By 1996, Sony plans to produce four million units in Indonesia, with an export value of $US 400 million, which is about 20–25 per cent of Sony audio sales worldwide. While current product lines only cover radiocassettes and home audio equipment, the company plans to produce walkman and minidisc next.

This chapter suggests that multinational enterprises are important agents for promoting exports and developing internal markets, employment and technology transfer for the ASEAN economies. Our analysis of technology diffusion suggests that the friendlier the policy regime of a country, the more numerous the benefits which can be gained from the multinationals in terms of technology diffusion. The actual diffusion of technology to local firms follows the production structure of the firm, which determines the sources of the technological know-how and the various linkages used for transmitting the know-how. The various inter-firm linkages, from a firm's viewpoint, can be viewed as a vehicle for securing access to new technology and skills or for absorbing spillovers from developmental activities of other firms or other industrial sectors.

NOTES

1. This study is funded by ADSGM/CIDA. Partial support from the Centre for International Studies, University of Toronto, is gratefully acknowledged. We thank Matthew Sell for his research assistance.

2. The authors have benefited from comments made by Hal Hill, Sylvia Ostry, and participants of the conference at the University of Paris I, Sorbonne.
3. One study on the use of microelectronics in textile and garment industries suggests, for example, that developed countries will regain their competitiveness in this particular industry within about ten years, through their extensive use of robotics, CAD (computer-aided design) and CAM (computer-aided manufacture) (Hoffman and Rush, 1988).
4. It is also important to add that there are significant links and 'feedback' mechanisms among the three phases and the sub-steps involved in each. See Kline and Rosenberg (1986).
5. 'Technology policy' here refers to a set of policies that promote the creation of new ideas, the development of such ideas into marketable product and process technologies, and the diffusion of the technologies in a particular economy.
6. The proportion abroad is about 15 per cent for US multinationals and much higher for those from other developed countries, but appears to be largely concentrated in other developed countries which have a high degree of technological competence. For surveys, see Dunning (1993a); Eaton *et al.* (1994, pp. 91–9).
7. The concentration of Japanese FDI in electronic and electrical industries is not unique to ASEAN. Dunning (1993b) also reported that, while American FDI in the United Kingdom showed no particular pattern of concentration in the 1953–83 period, Japanese FDI was concentrated in electrical and electronic equipment (75.6 per cent of total FDI inflows in 1982 and 52.6 per cent in 1988).
8. For two country studies, see Dahlman and Brimble (1992) for Thailand, and STAID and BPPT/Ministry of Technology, Indonesia (1993) for the Indonesian case.
9. The reason for these percentages being so large is the entrepot trade through Singapore.
10. See Harianto (1993) for a fuller exposition of this argument.
11. A study was also carried out for another sector, consumer electronics, but these results are not reported here. As it happens, there are pronounced differences between the sectors (compare Pavitt, 1984), due particularly to the differences in their production structure.
12. The information which follows is based largely on interviews, unless otherwise indicated.
13. In 1992, its share in Indonesia of the copier market was 43 per cent; of the telefax market 19 per cent, while its computer sales grew by 25 per cent.
14. The letters used to specify integrated circuits are international standards. Basically, they refer to the size/dimension of the chips and to the types of plate/frames being used. PDIP is the oldest type; to mount it onto printed circuit boards (PCB) requires holes to insert its 'legs' onto the PCB. Both PDIP and QFP use surface soldering to mount them, while PLCC requires a special socket to mount them onto PCB. The letters LD following a number behind the product category indicate its dimension, and the number of the 'legs' of the chip.
15. The experience of Fairchild, which pulled out of Indonesia in the 1980s, is often cited as a case in point. Fairchild proposed to modernize its semiconductor plant in Jakarta, using the most advanced production technology, but was rejected by the government of Indonesia on the ground that such a technology would reduce the number of people employed. As a result, Fairchild relocated to Malaysia. Another company, National Semiconductor, followed.
16. When we interviewed the Malaysian engineers, they offered to arrange meetings with their friends in Japanese or American firms of our choice.
17. When we asked why these expatriates were willing to join the new venture, we were told that they are not getting shares of the equity. Their motivation was rather to earn better pay and at the same time to build a reputation for running a relatively large and sophisticated operation assembling and testing semiconductors.

BIBLIOGRAPHY

Arrow, K.J. (1962), 'The Economic Implications of Learning by Doing', *Review of Economic Studies*, 29, pp. 155–73.

Asian Development Bank (1992), *Key Indicators of Developing Asian and Pacific Countries*, Manila.

Business Times (1993), 'Malaysia Electronics & Electrical Industries', Kuala Lumpur: Business Times.

Chia, S.Y. (1993), 'Foreign Direct Investment in ASEAN Economies', *Asian Development Review*, Vol. 11, No. 1, pp. 60–102.

Dahlman, C.J. and P. Brimble (1992), *Technology Strategy and Policy for Industrial Competitiveness: A Case Study of Thailand*, Washington, D.C.: World Bank Report.

Dunning, J.H. (1993a), *Multinational Enterprises and the Global Economy*, Reading, Mass.: Addison-Wesley, Chap. 11.

Dunning, J.H. (1993b), 'The Governance of Japanese and U.S. Manufacturing Affiliates in the U.K.: Some Country-specific Differences', in B. Kogut (ed.), *Country Competitiveness*, New York: Oxford University Press.

Eaton, C., R.G. Lipsey and A.E. Safarian (1994), 'The Theory of Multinational Plant Location: Agglomerations and Disagglomerations', in L. Eden (ed.), *Multinationals in North America*, Calgary: The University of Calgary Press, pp. 79–102.

Ergas, J. (1987), 'The importance of technology policy', in P. Dasgupta and P. Stoneman (eds), *Economic Policy and Economic Performance*, New York: Cambridge University Press.

Ernst, D. (1983), *The Global Race in Microelectronic Innovation and Corporate Strategies in a Period of Crisis*, Frankfurt: Campus Verlag.

Fagerberg, J. (1988), 'Why growth rates differ', in G. Dosi *et al.* (eds), *Technical Change and Economic Theory*, London: Pinter Publishers.

Grossman, G.M. and E. Helpman (1991), *Innovation and Growth in the Global Economy*, Cambridge, Mass.: MIT Press.

Grossman, G.M. and E. Helpman (1994), 'Endogenous Innovation in the Theory of Growth', *Journal of Economic Perspectives*, Vol. 8, No. 1, pp. 23–44.

Harianto, F. (1993), 'Technology Policy: An ASEAN Experience', working paper, Centre for International Studies, University of Toronto.

Hoffman, K. and H. Rush (1988), *Microelectronics and Clothing: The Impact of Technical Change on a Global Industry*, New York: Praeger.

IMF (1992), *Issues and Developments in International Trade Policy*, Washington, D.C.: IMF.

Kline, S.J. and N. Rosenberg (1986), 'An Overview of Innovation', in R. Landau and N. Rosenberg (eds), *Positive Sum Strategy: Harnessing Technology for Economic Growth*, Washington, D.C.: National Academy Press.

Kumar, S. (1992), 'ASEAN Free Trade Area: Issues for Policy', working paper, Institute of Southeast Asian Studies, Singapore.

Lall, S. (1980), 'Vertical Interfirm Linkages: an empirical study', *Oxford Bulletin of Economics and Statistics*, 42, pp. 203–16.

Mensch, G. (1979), *Stalemate in Technology*, Cambridge, Mass.: Ballinger.

Motorola Inc (1992), *Annual Report*, Rolling Meadows, Illinois.

Pavitt, K. (1984), 'Sectoral patterns of technical change: Toward a taxonomy and a theory', *Research Policy*, 13, pp. 343–73.

Pearce, R.D. (1990), *The Internationalisation of Research and Development*, London: Macmillan.

Pearce, R.D. and S. Singh (1992), 'Internationalization of R&D among the world's leading enterprises', in O. Grandstrand, S. Sjolander and L. Hackanson (eds), *Technology, Management and International Business: Internationalization of R&D and Technology*, Chichester: Wiley.

Rivera-Batiz, L.A. and P.M. Romer (1991), 'Economic Integration and Endogenous Growth', *Quarterly Journal of Economics*, Vol. 106, No. 2, pp. 531–56.

Romer, P.M. (1992), 'Two Strategies for Economic Development: Using Ideas and Producing Ideas', *Proceedings of the Annual World Bank Conference on Development*, Washington, D.C. Reprinted as Supplement to the *World Bank Economic Review*, March 1993, pp. 63–91.

Rosenberg, N. (1979), *Perspective on Technology*, New York: Cambridge University Press.

Schumpeter, J.A. (1942), *Capitalism, Socialism and Democracy*, New York: Harper and Row.

STAID and BPPT/Ministry of Technology, Indonesia (1993), *Science and Technology and Industrial Development: A Plan of Action*, Jakarta: BPPT.

Stoneman, P. (1987), *The Economic Analysis of Technology Policy*, Oxford: Clarendon Press.

Teece, D.J. (1977), 'Technology transfer by multinational firms: The resource cost of transferring technological knowhow', *Economic Journal*, 87, pp. 242–61.

Thailand Development Research Institute (1993), *The Development of Thailand's Technological Capability in Industry: Final Report*, Bangkok.

UNDP (1992), *Human Resource Development Report*, Oxford: Oxford University Press.

UNESCO (1990), *Statistical Yearbook*, New York.

von Hippel, E. (1988), *The Source of Innovation*, New York: Oxford University Press.

Wong, P.K. (1991), 'Singapore's Technology Strategy', mimeo.

The World Bank (1993), *East Asia Miracle: Growth and Public Policy*, Washington, D.C.: World Bank.

11. Exit of Japanese multinationals in US and European manufacturing industries

Hideki Yamawaki

INTRODUCTION

During the second half of the 1980s, Japanese manufacturing firms increased their presence significantly in US and European industries through foreign direct investments (FDI). Japanese firms entered a large cross-section of US and European industries by investing in green fields, acquiring local concerns and forming joint ventures. They entered into these industries horizontally, vertically and through diversification (Yamawaki, 1994a and b).[1] While the explosive increase in the flow of FDI from Japan to the United States and Europe is still a recent phenomenon, this flow had already reached its peak by 1990. More recently, a small but growing number of Japanese manufacturing firms that entered US and European industries during the 1980s have left these markets.

The purpose of this chapter is to provide a first picture of the pattern of Japanese exit from US and European manufacturing industries during the early 1990s[2] by addressing the following questions: What are the distinctive characteristics of exiting subsidiaries and parents? Is the pattern of Japanese exit from US industries different from the pattern in European industries? Is the exit behaviour related to the way in which Japanese firms entered the US and European markets? This chapter thus examines the pattern of Japanese exit by using unique data constructed at the subsidiary level and identifies the factors that explain the observed pattern by applying a statistical model to the data.

After describing the data set used, the next section presents some descriptive evidence on the pattern of Japanese exit by comparing the characteristics of exiting and non-exiting subsidiaries and parents such as size, age and the level of ownership control. It also provides some preliminary statistics on exits and entry mode. The analysis of the third section uses a Logit model to identify the factors that explain the probability of exit of Japanese subsidiaries from US and European manufacturing industries. The chapter ends by summarizing the major findings and providing some conclusions. The most important results that are produced in the statistical analysis are that the probability of exit of Japanese firms is related to the way in which they entered, and in particular that firms that entered through diversifying acquisitions are more likely to exit from the United States. It is also found that the exit behaviour of Japanese firms in the United States is different from that in Europe.

THE DATA AND DESCRIPTIVE STATISTICS

The Data

The data base for the present study is constructed from the individual subsidiary level data collected in Toyo Keizai, *Kaigai shinshutsu kigyo soran* (Directory of Japanese Multinational Corporations). This annual corporate directory lists an extensive number of Japanese firms that own subsidiaries and affiliates in foreign countries for which Toyo Keizai conducts an annual survey. For example, the 1993 survey covers 3300 firms and their 15 100 subsidiaries distributed around the world. While the Ministry of International Trade and Industry (MITI) conducts a more detailed survey on the behavioural pattern of Japanese firms operating abroad and publishes a summary of this survey every three years,[3] the original information on individual firms and subsidiaries collected for this survey is not easily accessible. For this reason, the Toyo Keizai survey data are used in this study, as in the previous empirical literature on Japanese multinational firms (for example, Hennart and Park, 1993; Yamawaki, 1994a, 1994b).

In the analysis that follows, an exit is observed at the subsidiary level and identified if a subsidiary that was established during the period 1980–90 disappears from the list of subsidiaries of its Japanese parent firm during the subsequent period 1991–3. With this definition of exit, we confine our sample of exiting subsidiaries to ones that entered during the 1980s, and exited during the first three years of the 1990s. While this procedure identifies subsidiaries that exited, it is not able to distinguish the ways in which these exits occurred. For example, we are not able to answer the question of whether the firm exited by closing its foreign subsidiary or by selling off the subsidiary. The information on the mode of exit is not available in the data base used in this chapter.

The sample of Japanese subsidiaries is generated by the following criteria: (1) the subsidiary is in manufacturing; (2) the Japanese parent firm is in manufacturing; (3) the subsidiary was established during the 1980–90 period; (4) the subsidiary was in operation in 1990; and (5) the subsidiary is controlled more than 10 per cent by the Japanese parent. These criteria and an additional criterion on availability of data on subsidiary, parent and industry characteristics produce the sample of 371 subsidiaries in the United States and 198 subsidiaries in Europe. The sub-sample of exiting subsidiaries is further generated by imposing the following criterion: the subsidiary is not listed in the directory during the 1991–3 period.

Patterns of exit

Table 11.1 reports the number of exiting Japanese subsidiaries in the United States and Europe during the 1991–3 period. Of the 371 US subsidiaries in operation in 1990, 34 subsidiaries exited by 1993, accounting for 9.2 per cent of the sample in 1990. In Europe, of the 198 subsidiaries in operation in 1990, 15 exited by 1993, accounting for 7.6 per cent of the sample in 1990. In both regions, a majority of exits occurred in 1991; exits slowed in 1992 and increased again in 1993.

Table 11.1   Exit of Japanese subsidiaries from US and European manufacturing industries, 1991–3

	United States	Europe
Number of exits		
1991	19	9
1992	2	1
1993	13	5
Total	34	15
Number of subsidiaries in 1990	371	198
Percentage of subsidiaries exited	9.2	7.6

To examine the characteristics of exiting subsidiaries and surviving subsidiaries, Table 11.2 compares subsidiary, parent firm and industry characteristics across the two sub-samples. For the US subsidiaries, the sample means for exiting and non-exiting subsidiaries are statistically different at the 10 per cent level for subsidiary size (measured in employment) and the level of ownership control.[4] The average size of exiting subsidiaries is 907 employees, while the average size of surviving subsidiaries is 504 employees, which is 55 per cent as large as the size of exiting subsidiaries. The average level of ownership control is lower for exiting subsidiaries, at 73 per cent, than the level of ownership for non-exiting subsidiaries, at 83 per cent.

Table 11.2   Sample means for exiting and non-exiting subsidiaries

Variable	United States		Europe	
	Exiting subsidiaries	Non-exiting subsidiaries	Exiting subsidiaries	Non-exiting subsidiaries
Subsidiary size	907.1	503.6	165.2	590.5
(Employment)	(3 127.9)	(1 273.3)	(271.8)	(1 795.0)
Parent firm size	13 150.9	10 986.2	9 519.7	13 315.9
(Employment)	(19 444.6)	(15 781.0)	(12 409.4)	(18 242.3)
Ownership level	72.6	83.0	67.6	78.9
(%)	(34.1)	(23.9)	(28.8)	(25.3)
Age in 1990	3.7	4.0	3.7	4.7
	(2.1)	(2.5)	(2.7)	(3.0)
No. of countries	9.1	10.3	10.5	12.9
Previously entered	(7.2)	(8.3)	(10.2)	(9.2)
Host industry	0.06	0.07	0.13	0.11
annual growth	(0.05)	(0.07)	(0.07)	(0.06)
No. of observations	34	337	15	183

Notes:
1. Standard deviations are in parenthesis.
2. The growth rate for the US sample is for the 1982–7 period, and the growth rate for the European sample is for the 1981–8 period.

For European companies, the average size of exiting subsidiaries is smaller than that of surviving subsidiaries, but the difference is not statistically significant. The statistically different means are observed for the level of ownership control and the age of subsidiaries in 1990. As observed for the US subsidiaries, the average level of ownership control is lower for exiting subsidiaries than for non-exiting subsidiaries. The European subsidiaries that are surviving have a higher mean value of age in 1990, 4.7 years, than the exiting subsidiaries, 3.7 years.[5]

Table 11.3 provides additional statistics on the number of exits, classified by entry mode. Of the 34 exiting subsidiaries in the United States, 15 were established through acquisitions, thus accounting for 44 per cent of all exiting subsidiaries. In Europe, of the 15 exiting subsidiaries, five were established by acquiring local concerns, which account for 33 per cent of all exiting subsidiaries. While the number of observations on exit is still too small to make any conclusive remarks, it is interesting to note that these percentages of exiting subsidiaries that entered by acquisitions are disproportionately high compared to the percentage of entry by acquisition in total entry. In the United States, 25.9 per cent of subsidiaries in the sample joined Japanese firms through acquisitions, and in Europe, 27.8 per cent of subsidiaries in the sample joined Japanese parents through acquisitions (Yamawaki, 1994b).

Table 11.3   Number of exits, entry mode and years between entry and exit

	United States	Europe
Number of exits	34	15
Number entered by acquisitions	15	5
Percentage entered by acquisitions	44.1	33.3
Average years between entry and		
exit: all exits	4.5	4.4
Entry mode:		
Acquisitions	3.3	3.6
Start-ups	5.4	4.8

The bottom half of Table 11.3 shows the average years elapsed between entry and exit and compares them by entry mode. The average lag for all US exiting subsidiaries is 4.5 years and for European subsidiaries 4.4 years. However, when the difference in entry mode is taken into account, a clear difference in the average lag between entry and exit emerges. In the United States, the average lag between entry and exit is 3.3 years for subsidiaries entered by acquisitions but 5.4 years for subsidiaries entered as start-ups.[6] Thus the decision to divest the acquired subsidiaries comes on average two years earlier than the decision to divest or close down the subsidiaries established as start-ups. The same observation can be made for European subsidiaries, though the difference in the mean lag between the two sub-samples is much shorter.

One of the most interesting findings that emerged from the descriptive statistics presented above is that more than 40 per cent of exits in the United States are identified with subsidiaries that entered by acquisitions. While this percentage is calculated on the basis of the sample of exiting subsidiaries, a similar observation can be made when the percentages of exiting subsidiaries are calculated for the sample of subsidiaries that entered by acquiring local concerns and for the sample of subsidiaries that entered by greenfield investments. In fact, when the US sample is divided into the group of subsidiaries entered by acquisitions and the group of subsidiaries entered by greenfield investments, the mean exit rate is higher for the acquisition sample (14.4 per cent) than for the greenfield sample (7.1 per cent), and these two means are statistically different at the 5 per cent level of significance.[7] Thus 14.4 per cent of the acquisitions completed by Japanese multinationals in the United States between 1980 and 1990 had been divested by the end of 1993.

While this is a new finding for Japanese multinationals, the previous literature on corporate divestitures has found that, in the United States, divestitures of acquisitions are observed rather frequently. Indeed, Kaplan and Weisbach

(1992) find that 43.9 per cent of the large acquisitions completed between 1971 and 1982 had been divested by the end of 1989. In a study using the FTC Line of Business data, Ravenscraft and Scherer (1987) estimate that the sell-off rate for acquisitions made during the 1960s and early 1970s was in the range of 19–47 per cent. By examining the 1950–86 diversification histories of 33 large US corporations, Porter (1987) finds that over 50 per cent of diversifying acquisitions in new industries were later divested.

In comparison to these divestiture rates observed for US corporations, the 14.4 per cent exit rate for acquiring Japanese multinationals is rather modest. However, this rate is likely to be an underestimate because of the short length of the post-entry observation period used in this study, which spans only three years. For the European sample of acquisitions, the exit rate is found to be 8.2 per cent, lower than for the US sample. The exit rate for the European sample of start-ups is 7.3 per cent and is not statistically different from that of the sample of acquisitions.

ANALYSIS OF EXIT

While the existing stock of research on exit of multinational firms is relatively small (see Caves, 1994 for a survey), Caves (1994) seems to have shown that divestment and exit decisions of multinationals could be explained by various firm characteristics and in particular by organizational factors.[8] By examining divestment decisions of US multinational firms, Wilson (1979) found that a subsidiary that sells little of its output to other members of the multinational system, that produces only a few products, and that is incorporated through acquisition is more likely to be disinvested.

The findings from the descriptive analysis given in the previous section suggest a pattern similar to the Wilson's finding that entry by acquisitions is likely to be an important cause of exiting for Japanese multinationals. The descriptive statistics indicate that this is especially the case for US subsidiaries of Japanese multinationals. In this section, this point is elaborated further by using a statistical method to identify factors that influenced Japanese multinationals' decisions to divest individual subsidiaries. To evaluate the effect of acquisition entry on exit, additional factors that measure the characteristics of subsidiary, parent firm and entered industry are controlled in the statistical analysis.

As noted earlier, the data used in this study do not distinguish different forms of exit. Therefore the phenomenon to be explained here is exit, which includes divestitures or sell-offs and plant closures. The dependent variable is a dummy variable that equals one if exit occurred, and zero otherwise. Since this is a dichotomous variable, a Logit analysis is used here to estimate the probability that the subsidiary will exit. The samples used in the regression analysis are equivalent to the samples presented in the previous section. Thus the US sample has 371 observations and the European sample has 198 observations.

Entry Mode

The main hypotheses to be tested here are that (1) the probability of subsidiary exit is high when the subsidiary was established by acquiring a local concern; and (2) the probability of subsidiary exit increases especially when the subsidiary joined the parent firm through diversifying acquisition.

A previous study by Yamawaki (1994b) on the choice of entry mode by Japanese multinationals in the United States, which employed the same data set as the present study, found evidence that Japanese multinationals are motivated to acquire local concerns especially when they diversify into new industries and when they lack technological and comparative advantages. Thus it is important to examine the influence of acquisition entry on exit in conjunction with the firm's diversification strategy. While such diversifying acquisitions are far more common among US corporations (Odagiri, 1992), it is also common to find that diversifying acquisitions tend to result often in divestitures. Indeed, previous empirical studies have found that divestiture rates are significantly high for diversifying acquisitions in the United States (Porter, 1987; Ravenscraft and Scherer, 1987; Kaplan and Weisbach, 1992). Standard explanations for this pattern include the management of the parent firm lacking the skill and competence to operate in unrelated new industries and the firm's organizational structure is not being well adapted to coordinate acquired and ongoing units (Porter, 1987).

Such evidence on the high propensity for divestitures of diversifying acquisitions of US corporations, along with the doubly difficult task for Japanese multinationals to manage acquired foreign subsidiaries in new industries, suggest surely that the subsidiary that joined the Japanese parent through diversifying acquisition is more likely to be divested. To test this hypothesis and the general hypothesis on the effect of acquisition on exit, the following three variables are used:

ACQUI = dummy variable equal to one if the subsidiary is established through acquisition and zero if it is established through greenfield investment.

DIVENTRY = dummy variable equal to one if the subsidiary's principal two-digit industry is different from the parent's principal two-digit industry and zero otherwise.

DIVACQUI = dummy variable equal to one if the subsidiary's principal two-digit industry is different from the parent's principal two-digit industry and the subsidiary is established through acquisition, and zero otherwise.

ACQUI identifies entry by acquisition, and its coefficient is expected to have a positive sign. *DIVENTRY* is constructed to examine whether the subsidiary shares the same two-digit industry as the parent and therefore to identify unrelated diversification. In the US sample, 78 subsidiaries are classified as diversifying entry, while in the European sample, 18 subsidiaries are diversifying entries. Of the 78 diversifying subsidiaries in the United States, 33 are established by acquisitions, representing 42 per cent of the sample of diversifying subsidiaries. In contrast, diversifying acquisitions are very rare in Europe, and only one case is identified out of the sample of 18 diversifying subsidiaries. To the extent that *DIVENTRY* represents diversifying acquisitions, its coefficient is expected to have a positive sign as well. However, this effect is expected to be present only for the US sample and not for the European sample because of the infrequency of diversifying acquisitions in Europe.

To evaluate the effect of diversifying acquisitions on exit more directly, *DIVACQUI* is constructed to identify entry through diversifying acquisitions. This variable is defined as the interaction of *ACQUI* and *DIVENTRY*, and is included only in the statistical specification using the US sample. The coefficient of *DIVACQUI* is again expected to show a positive sign.

While diversifying acquisition is frequently used to enter a new industry, the multinational firm that is entering a new country as well as diversifying into a new industry where it lacks some competence to operate successfully tends to use a joint venture with local partners. Kogut and Chang (1991) have found that Japanese firms are motivated to form joint ventures in the United States when they are lagging behind their US rivals in R&D expenditure. However, in separate studies, Kogut (1988, 1989) showed evidence that joint ventures formed in the United States were instable, and a significant number of joint ventures were terminated in the early years because of business failures. To control the possibility of terminating joint ventures, the following proxy is used:

OWNERSHIP = percentage share of the subsidiary's equity held by the Japanese parent.

OWNERSHIP measures the level of ownership control of the subsidiary by the parent. While this variable does not distinguish joint venture and capital participation when control is less than 100 per cent, the 1990 MITI survey shows that capital participation is a relatively uncommon mode of entry by Japanese multinationals.[9] Therefore *OWNERSHIP* with a value less than 100 per cent is likely to represent the subsidiary established by joint venture. If joint ventures are prone to fail, and the probability of failure is influenced by the level of ownership control, *OWNERSHIP* will then have a coefficient with negative sign.

Additional Explanatory Variables

Previous studies based on US data have addressed the question of whether firm size affects the probability of exit. Mansfield (1962) first discovered evidence that smaller firms are more likely to exit than larger firms. In more recent studies using larger samples, Evans (1987) and Dunne *et al.* (1988) found that small, new firms have high mortality rates, and thus the probability of survival increases with size and age. Dunne *et al.* (1989) further uncovered evidence of the tendency for plant failure rates to decline with size and age.

Empirical studies based on declining industries have found a similar pattern of plant closure. By examining exit decisions in the US steel industry, Deily (1991) concluded that steel firms were more likely to close small plants. In a study that tests the hypothesis proposed by Ghemawat and Nalebuff (1985, 1990) that the probability of plant closure increases with firm size, Lieberman (1990) presented evidence that in the US chemical industry, smaller plants had higher rates of closure, and most exiting firms were small. Lieberman found further that, after controlling for plant size, large multiplant firms were more likely to close.

To test the hypothesis that smaller plants have higher exit probabilities, the following two variables are included:

SIZEIND = employment of the subsidiary, divided by the total employment of the three-digit industry entered.

SIZEPAR = employment of the subsidiary, divided by total employment of the Japanese parent.

SIZEIND measures subsidiary size and is defined as its share in the industry entered. *SIZEPAR* measures subsidiary size and is constructed as its ratio to parent size. If smaller subsidiaries were more likely to exit, the coefficients of *SIZEIND* and *SIZEPAR* would have negative signs.

To control for subsidiary age and parent experience, the following two variables are included in the specification:

AGE   = subsidiary age in 1990.

EXPERIENCE = number of countries in which the Japanese parent firm owns subsidiaries.

AGE measures the subsidiary's age in years of operation and *EXPERIENCE* is a proxy to measure the extent of the parent's previous experience abroad. If older subsidiaries and more experienced parents have higher probabilities of survival, *AGE*, and *EXPERIENCE* will have coefficients with negative signs.

Additional factors that have been suggested by previous studies as becoming barriers to exit and thus influencing the firm's exit decision include the extent of diversification/specialization of the parent firm (Caves and Porter, 1976). Baden-Fuller (1989) showed that diversified firms were more likely to exit than specialized firms in the UK steel castings industry. Lieberman (1990) found evidence that single-product chemical firms were less likely to close their plants. However, Deily (1991) did not confirm this relationship for US steel producers. To control for the extent of parent diversification,

SPEC = proportion of the Japanese parent's total sales classified to its principal two-digit industry

is included in the statistical model. The smaller the value of *SPEC*, the higher is the extent of diversification.

Finally, the entered industry's growth rate is expected to determine the firm's decision to exit by influencing its calculation on potential profits. The industry growth variable is defined as:

GROWTH = rate of growth of shipments in the three-digit industry to which the subsidiary's primary product is classified.

GROWTH is constructed for the 1982–7 period for the US sample and for the 1981–8 period for the European sample because of the availability of industry censuses in these two regions. The coefficient of growth is expected to have a negative sign.

Table 11.4 shows that means and standard deviations of the variables explained above. Owing to the discrepancy that exists between the US and European data sources, the years of observation used to construct *SIZEIND* and *GROWTH* differ between the US and European samples. A European industry is represented by four member states, Germany, France, the United Kingdom and Italy, because of the unavailability of complete industry data at the three-digit level for the rest of the member states. This procedure certainly creates an upward bias for the subsidiary's employment share in the European market (*SIZEIND*).

Table 11.4   Independent variables and their means and standard deviations

Independent variable	Sample	
	United States	Europe
Subsidiary characteristics		
OWNERSHIP	82.008	78.045
	(25.120)	(25.660)
DIVENTRY	0.210	0.096
	(0.408)	(0.295)
ACQUI	0.280	0.308
	(0.450)	(0.463)
DIVACQUI	0.089	0.005
	(0.285)	(0.071)
AGE	3.978	4.652
	(2.434)	(2.964)
SIZEIND	0.005	0.003
	(0.019)	(0.008)
Parent firm characteristics		
SIZEPAR	0.095	0.089
	(0.170)	(0.135)
EXPERIENCE	10.181	12.677
	(8.195)	(9.282)
SPEC	84.197	89.288
	(19.298)	(16.244)
Industry characteristics		
GROWTH	0.350	0.801
	(0.327)	(0.457)
Sample size	371	198

STATISTICAL RESULTS

Table 11.5 reports the Logit results to explain the probability of subsidiary exit in the United States. A test using the chi-square distribution is applied, and all equations are significant at the 1 per cent level. All equations correctly predict at least 90 per cent of the choices made.

In all the three equations presented in Table 11.5, the variables that measure the influence of entry mode on exit have significant coefficients with expected variables included. The coefficient of *OWNERSHIP* is statistically

Table 11.5   Logit analysis of exit: the United States

Independent variable	5.1	5.2	5.3
CONSTANT	−0.950	−1.160	−1.078
	(0.817)	(0.980)	(0.922)
OWNERSHIP	−0.017	−0.016	−0.016
	(2.484)^a	(2.424)^a	(2.292)^b
DIVENTRY	0.797	0.659	
	(1.753)^b	(1.403)^c	
ACQUI		0.492	
		(1.203)	
DIVACQUI			1.439
			(2.931)^a
AGE	−0.027	−0.013	−6.005
	(0.332)	(0.161)	(0.313)
SIZEIND	−3.825	−5.316	−6.005
	(0.350)	(0.459)	(0.535)
SIZEPAR	0.870	0.665	0.927
	(0.981)	(0.721)	(1.027)
EXPERIENCE	−0.023	−0.019	−0.022
	(0.824)	(0.694)	(0.780)
SPEC	0.004	0.003	0.004
	(0.396)	(0.329)	(0.356)
GROWTH	−1.040	−0.916	−0.895
	(1.730)^b	(1.487)^c	(1.489)^c
Log. likelihood	−107.55	−106.838	−105.23
No. of observations	371	371	371

Notes:
1. Numbers in parenthesis are t-statistics.
2. The levels of significance for a one-tailed test are: a = 1 per cent; b = 5 per cent; c = 10 per cent.

significant at least at the 5 per cent level and has a negative sign, suggesting that the subsidiary established by joint venture and controlled less by the parent is more likely to exit. In other words, the subsidiary controlled 100 per cent by the Japanese parent tends to stay in the US market.

The variable that identifies a diversifying subsidiary, *DIVENTRY*, also has a statistically significant coefficient, with a positive sign. This result suggests that the subsidiary that does not share the same two-digit industry as the parent has a higher probability of exit. When the choice of entry mode between acquisition and greenfield investment is controlled in equation 5.2, the effect of *DIVENTRY* becomes weaker, while the coefficient of *ACQUI* has the expected positive sign, though it is not quite significant. Equation 5.3 disentangles the effects of diversification and acquisition on exit by replacing *DIVENTRY* and *ACQUI* with *DIVACQUI*. The coefficient of *DIVACQUI* is highly significant at the 1 per cent level and has the expected positive sign, indicating that the probability of exit is high for diversifying acquisitions. The US subsidiary that joined the Japanese parent through diversifying acquisition is more likely to be divested than the subsidiary which entered through greenfield investment.

While the coefficients of *SIZEIND*, *AGE* and *EXPERIENCE* have the expected negative signs, they are not statistically significant. The remaining two firm variables, *SIZEPAR* and *SPEC*, are also not significant. The entered industry's growth rate, *GROWTH*, has a significant coefficient with negative sign, suggesting that the probability of exit is high for the subsidiary in a slow-growing industry.

Table 11.6 presents the Logit results of the probability of subsidiary exit in Europe. A chi-square test shows that all equations are significant at the 1 per cent level, and all correctly predict at least 92 per cent of the choices made. The results obtained for the European subsidiaries, however, differ from the results for the US subsidiaries in the effects of the entry mode variables and the size variables on exit.

Among the entry mode variables, the coefficient of *OWNERSHIP* remains significant in the European sample and has the consistent negative sign, confirming the result obtained for the US sample that the probability of exit is high for joint ventures and decreases with the level of ownership. The discrepancy between the US and European results, however, appears in the coefficients of *DIVENTRY* and *ACQUI*, as expected from the discussion in the previous section. In the equations using the European sample, the coefficient of *DIVENTRY* is not significant at all, while the coefficient for *ACQUI* tends to be marginally significant with positive sign. This result most plausibly reflects the difference in the frequency of diversifying acquisitions existing between the US and European samples. As mentioned earlier in the chapter, the European sample contains only one case of diversifying acquisition out of the sample of 18 diversifying subsidiaries, while the US sample observes 33 diversifying acquisitions out of the sample of 78 diversifying subsidiaries. Therefore the European result is not contradictory to the US result, but suggests consistently that diversifying entry, if not through acquisitions, does not affect the probability of exit. The positive coefficient on *ACQUI* then confirms that the subsidiary established through acquisition is more likely to exit.

Another difference between the US and European results emerges in the coefficients of the two size variables. The coefficients of *SIZEIND* and

Table 11.6   Logit analysis of exit: Europe

Independent variable	6.1	6.2	6.3
CONSTANT	−0.965	−0.953	−1.173
	(0.465)	(0.467)	(0.581)
OWNERSHIP	−0.020	−0.019	−0.021
	(1.799)[b]	(1.766)[b] .	(1.855)[b]
DIVENTRY	−0.439	−0.362	−0.553
	(0.374)	(0.310)	(0.480)
ACQUI	0.841	0.579	0.798
	(1.282)[c]	(0.929)	(1.118)
AGE	−0.105	−0.097	−0.119
	(0.989)	(0.915)	(1.118)
SIZEIND	−494.67	−767.10	
	(1.215)	(1.872)[b]	
SIZEPAR	−8.340		−14.123
	(1.210)		(2.094)[b]
EXPERIENCE	−0.014	0.005	−0.036
	(0.375)	(0.149)	(0.989)
SPEC	0.005	0.0002	0.009
	(0.224)	(0.011)	(0.457)
GROWTH	1.006	0.913	1.052
	(1.494)[c]	(1.354)[c]	(1.642)[c]
Log. likelihood	−44.93	−46.06	−46.18
No. of observations	198	198	198

Notes:
1.   Numbers in parenthesis are t-statistics.
2.   The levels of significance for a one-tailed test are: $b = 5$ per cent; $c = 10$ per cent.

SIZEPAR are significant at the 5 per cent level when they are included in the equation separately (equations 6.2 and 6.3), but their significance deteriorates when they are included jointly (equation 6.1).[10] However, the signs attached to the coefficients of these two size variables remain negative in any specification. Thus, on the basis of these results on the effect of subsidiary size on exit, one may conclude that the probability of subsidiary exit decreases with greater subsidiary size: smaller subsidiaries are more likely to exit than larger subsidiaries in Europe.

As in the case of US subsidiaries, *AGE* and *EXPERIENCE* have coefficients with negative signs, though they are not significant either. Nor does the extent of parent diversification, *SPEC*, have any significant coefficient either. Finally, the coefficient for *GROWTH* is significant but has an unexpected positive sign.

CONCLUSIONS

This chapter has examined the pattern of the Japanese subsidiary's exit in the United States and Europe by using newly constructed data at the subsidiary level. The statistical analysis of this chapter appears to have produced evidence that the probability of exit is influenced by entry mode, and especially that the probability of exit is high for the subsidiary established through diversifying acquisition as well as for the subsidiary established through joint venture. And this pattern was found more clearly for the US subsidiaries of Japanese multinationals. This finding of the high probability of exit for diversifying acquisitions is consistent with the existing literature that finds evidence on high divestiture rates of diversifying acquisitions in the United States (Porter, 1987; Ravenscraft and Scherer, 1987; Kaplan and Weisbach, 1992). The finding on the effect of entry by joint venture on exit is also consistent with the evidence presented by Kogut (1989) on the instability of joint ventures.

The statistical analysis found some discrepancy between the US and European results. In particular, subsidiary size was found to be more significant in influencing the probability of exit in the European sample, than in the US sample. The most plausible explanation for this result is that the pattern of entry mode represented in these two samples differs in important respects. Japanese multinationals more often used acquisitions to enter unrelated industries in the United States than they did in Europe (Yamawaki, 1994a). Since there was but one diversifying acquisition in the European sample, the representative cause of subsidiary failures is naturally different between the US and European samples. In Europe, the more standard factor, subsidiary size, therefore appears to have come forward. In contrast, in the United States, when entry by diversifying acquisitions is controlled, the size effect disappears.

This final point leads us to make some qualifying remarks on the research design of this chapter, which future research in this area should overcome. The first qualification concerns the data on exit. As mentioned repeatedly, owing to the unavailability of information on the form of exit, an exit is identified when the subsidiary is dropped from the list of subsidiaries of the parent. It is, therefore, not known whether this corresponds to plant closure or divestiture. Thus the empirical results in this chapter are not able to set out clearly the factors that explain the decision to close the subsidiary and the

factors that explain the decision to divest the subsidiary. The second qualification is that the post-entry observation period is relatively short. This was
inevitable, given the exit phenomenon of Japanese multinationals in the United
States and Europe, which occurred in more recent years. Finally, again owing
to the lack of data, variables that measure the subsidiary's financial state,
such as profitability, are not included in the statistical analysis.

NOTES

1. For a survey of economic analysis of Japanese foreign direct investment in the United
   States, see Caves (1993).
2. There exists a previous empirical study that examined the exit behaviour of Japanese
   multinationals using the data on exit during the 1981–6 period. See Horaguchi (1992).
3. MITI, *Kaigai jigyokatsudo kihonchosa: kaigai toshi tokei soran.*
4. The t-statistics for subsidiary size and ownership level are 1.45 and 2.28, respectively.
5. The t-statistics for ownership level and age are 1.65 and 1.34, respectively.
6. The 3.3 year lag is quite short compared to the mean lag observed for the US corporations
   (9.75 years) studied by Ravenscraft and Scherer (1987). The short lag observed in this
   chapter is surely an underestimate because of the short observation period.
7. The t-statistic is 2.19, and the sample sizes are 104 for acquisitions and 267 for greenfield
   investments.
8. Boddewyn (1983) provides some theoretical basis to explain the exit behaviour of foreign
   multinationals.
9. The percentages of firms which entered the US and European markets through capital
   participation are 3.8 per cent and 6.0 per cent, respectively. See MITI (1991).
10. The simple correlation of *SIZEIND* and *SIZEPAR* is 0.30.

REFERENCES

Baden-Fuller, C.W.F. (1989), 'Exit from Declining Industries and the Case of Steel
   Castings', *Economic Journal*, 99, December, pp. 949–61.
Boddewyn, J.J. (1983), 'Foreign Direct Divestment Theory: Is it the Reverse of FDI
   Theory?', *Weltwirtschaftliches Archiv*, 119, pp. 345–55.
Caves, R.E. (1993), 'Japanese Investment in the United States: Lessons for the
   Economic Analysis of Foreign Investment', *The World Economy*, 16, pp. 279–300.
Caves, R.E. (1994), 'Stasis and Flux in Multinational Enterprises: Equilibrium Mod-
   els and Turnover Processes', paper presented at the PAFTAD Conference, Hong
   Kong, June.
Caves, R.E. and M.E. Porter (1976), 'Barriers to Exit', in R.T. Masson and P.D.
   Qualls (eds), *Essays on Industrial Organization in Honor of Joe. S. Bain*,
   Cambridge, MA: Ballinger.
Deily, M.E. (1991), 'Exit Strategies and Plant-closing Decisions: The Case of Steel',
   RAND Journal of Economics, 22, 250–63.
Dunne, T., M.J. Roberts and L. Samuelson (1988), 'Patterns of Firm Entry and Exit
   in U.S. Manufacturing Industries', *RAND Journal of Economics*, 19, Winter, pp. 495–
   515.

Dunne, T., M.J. Roberts and L. Samuelson (1989), 'The Growth and Failure of U.S. Manufacturing Plants', *Quarterly Journal of Economics*, 104, November, pp. 671–98.

Evans, D.S. (1987), 'The Relationship Between Firm Growth, Size and Age: Estimates for 100 Manufacturing Industries', *Journal of Industrial Economics*, 35, June, pp. 567–81.

Ghemawat, P. and B. Nalebuff (1985), 'Exit', *RAND Journal of Economics*, 16, Spring, pp. 184–94.

Ghemawat, P. and B. Nalebuff (1990), 'The Devolution of Declining Industries', *Quarterly Journal Economics*, 105, February, pp. 167–86.

Hennart, J.-F. and Y.-R. Park (1993), 'Greenfield vs. Acquisition: The Strategy of Japanese Investors in the United States', *Management Science*, 39, September, pp. 1054–70.

Horaguchi, H. (1992), *Nihon kigyo no kaigai chokusetsutoshi: Asia eno shinshutsu to tettai* (Foreign Direct Investment of Japanese Firms: Investment and Disinvestment in Asia, Tokyo: University of Tokyo Press.

Kaplan, S.N. and M.S. Weisbach (1992), 'The Success of Acquisitions: Evidence from Divestitures', *Journal of Finance*, 47, March, pp. 107–38.

Kogut, B. (1988), 'A Study of the Life Cycle of Joint Ventures', in F.J. Contractor and P. Lorange (eds), *Cooperative Strategies in International Business*, Lexington, Mass.: Lexington Books.

Kogut, B. (1989) 'The Stability of Joint Ventures: Reciprocity and Competitive Rivalry', *Journal of Industrial Economics*, 38, December, pp. 183–98.

Kogut, B. and S.J. Chang (1991), 'Technological Capabilities and Japanese Foreign Direct Investment in the United States', *Review of Economics and Statistics*, 73, August, pp. 401–13.

Lieberman, M.B. (1990), 'Exit from Declining Industries: "Shakeout" or "Stakeout"?', *RAND Journal of Economics*, 21, Winter, pp. 538–54.

Mansfield, E. (1962), 'Entry, Gibrat's Law, Innovation and the Growth of Firms', *American Economic Review*, 52, December, pp. 1023–50.

Ministry of International Trade and Industry, Japan (1991), 'Dai 4 kai kaigaijigyokatsudo kihonchosa no gaiyo' (The Summary of the 4th Survey of Foreign Operations of Japanese firms), MITI, January.

Odagiri, H. (1992), *Growth Through Competition, Competition Through Growth: Strategic Management and the Economy of Japan*, Oxford: Oxford University Press.

Porter, M.E. (1987), 'From Competitive Advantage to Corporate Strategy', *Harvard Business Review*, 65, May–June, pp. 43–59.

Ravenscraft, D.J. and F.M. Scherer (1987), *Mergers, Sell-offs and Economic Efficiency*, Washington, D.C.: Brookings Institution.

Wilson, B.D. (1979), 'The Disinvestment of Foreign Subsidiaries by U.S. Multinational Companies', DBA thesis, Harvard Business School.

Yamawaki, H. (1994a), 'Entry Patterns of Japanese Multinationals in U.S. and European Manufacturing', in M. Mason and D. Encarnation (eds), *Does Ownership Matter?: Japanese Multinationals in Europe*, Oxford: Oxford University Press.

Yamawaki, H. (1994b), 'International Competitiveness and the Choice of Entry Mode: Japanese Multinationals in U.S. and European Manufacturing Industries', mimeo, Université Catholique de Louvain, April.

APPENDIX

The information on subsidiary exit was obtained from Toyo Keizai, *Kaigai shinshutsu kigyo soran* (Directory of Japanese Multinational Corporations), Tokyo: Toyo keizai shinposha, various years. Entry mode (*ACQUI*), subsidiary employment (*SIZEIND* and *SIZEPAR*), the subsidiary's line of business (*DIVENTRY* and *DIVACQUI*), the number of countries in which the parent owns subsidiaries (*EXPERIENCE*), age (*AGE*) and ownership level (*OWNERSHIP*) were all taken from this data source. To construct *SIZEPAR* and *DIVENTRY*, the data at the subsidiary level were matched with the data on the individual subsidiary's parent firm domiciled in Japan. The major source of the parent data was Nihon keizai shinbun sha, *Nikkei kaisha joho*, Tokyo: Nihon keizai shinbun sha, various years. *SPEC* was also constructed from this data source on Japanese firms. The industry variables, *SIZEIND* and *GROWTH*, were constructed from US Bureau of the Census, *Census of Manufactures*, for the US sample, and Statistical Office of the European Communities, *Structure and Activity of Industry*, for the European sample. Aggregation used for these variables is at the three-digit level for both samples. The parent's primary industry is chosen according to the share of sales accounted for by its primary product.

12. Some concluding remarks

John H. Dunning

It is, I imagine, a consequence of growing older that one has an increasing sense of 'déjà vu' at conferences such as this. Many of the issues, which have been raised over the last two days I first came across when I was writing my own PhD thesis on American investment in British industry in the 1950s; and some of the policy prescriptions which have been advanced by the participants here are very similar to those offered by scholars like Ed Safarian, Art Stonehill, Donald Brash and others, who investigated the impact of foreign direct investments (FDI) of a number on host countries in the 1960s.

Then, and now, the most appropriate answer to the questions: What are the costs and benefits of inbound FDI to the host country?' and 'What are the consequences of the activities of MNEs on the relocation of economic activity?', was (is) that 'it all depends'. This is, of course, a typical economist's answer, and one which is both unsatisfactory and frustrating to policy makers, but it is, nevertheless, one which many of us who have advised governments on their policies towards FDI have repeated *ad nauseam*.

There *are* no easy solutions to any of the problems we have been considering over these past two days. The consequences of inbound MNE activity will vary according to the countries making and receiving the FDI, and according to the size, product structure, degree of multinationality, experience and strategy of each firm undertaking the investment. The consequences will also vary according to MNE motives for foreign production and the kinds of value added activity in which MNEs engage. If anything has changed over the last 30 years, it has not been the questions, or even some of the answers, of interest to the economist, but rather the nature of MNEs, and the global economic and political environment in which they operate. So there is no cause for the contemporary researcher to be dismayed if many of the problems he or she is seeking to deal with have already been tackled – and sometimes, at least, with a degree of success.

The present-day milieu for international business is one in which economic activity is being either regionalized or globalized. How different this is from the late 1950s, when US direct investment was beginning to penetrate European markets. Then Europe was divided into a number of segmented economic fortresses. There was little integration of European production or markets by the MNEs of the time. Investments by most firms outside their national boundaries accounted for only a small fraction of their domestic operations. Foreign affiliates usually engaged in relatively low value added activities and sold their products mainly to domestic markets. They found that they could serve foreign markets more effectively through FDI than through exports. Sometimes, indeed, this was the only route to serve the European consumer, because exports were frozen out by tariff and non-tariff barriers. In other cases, particularly in developing countries, FDI was undertaken to obtain primary products which firms could not obtain, or obtain as economically, at home. Most of the theory of FDI – certainly up to the 1960s – was concerned with explaining the determinants and consequences of these two types of investment.

Regional integration in Europe signalled the emergence of a rather different kind of MNE activity, the purpose of which was designed to rationalize and restructure portfolios of FDI initiated in a more restricted trading environment. Moreover, while most of the early theories of FDI were concerned with explaining the initial foray of firms into foreign production, over the last two decades much more attention has been given to the growth and composition of existing MNE activity. In his presentation, Peter Buckley reminded us of the different modalities by which firms might service foreign markets and, in doing so, made the point that, initially, these were largely substitutes for one another. But today we are increasingly thinking of FDI, exports and collaborative alliances as being complementary modalities of exploiting firm competitive advantages and as being components of integrated and holistic MNE strategies.

The formation of the European Common Market in 1957 eventually removed all tariffs between the member states and this enabled foreign MNEs – and particularly US MNEs – to reappraise the structure of their value added activities in Europe. Now, instead of viewing each country as a separate market, they could treat the European Union (as the Community is now called) as a single market. As a result, they initiated programmes of product and process rationalization. This had a marked impact, not only on the trading patterns of MNEs, but also on the characteristics of their investments, their responses to the locational attractions offered by the member states, and the consequences of their value added activities for European economic welfare.

Several speakers in the conference observed that, over the last two decades or more, the determinants of MNE activity have changed and, certainly, my own work on intra-Triad FDI lends credence to this view. The main reason for this, I believe, is that the character of this activity, and thus the need for complementary location-bound assets, has changed. Today, one of the 'buzz words' in the vocabulary of international business is globalization. The word is much used, and frequently abused. It has spawned its own variations, one of which is 'glocalization', which is supposed to imply a situation in which a firm is exploiting the advantages of global integration, but is cognizant of the need to adapt some of its activities and functions to take account of the unique characteristics of the countries in which it is investing. Like it or not, however, globalization is changing the name of the game of international commerce in a number of ways. In particular, it is both widening and deepening the *structural* integration of economic activity between countries and is leading to new organizational modes of inter- and intra-firm production and transactions.

The papers presented at the conference seem to fall into three groups. The first are those which essentially represent an extension and refinement of the kind of research on FDI which has been conducted by economists and business scholars since the 1950s. They add value to our perceptions and understanding of MNE activity in that they consider well rehearsed problems from a different perspective and/or use upgraded analytical and statistical techniques to do so. What explains the impressive rate of growth of Italian multinationals over the last few years? Why has the geographical structure of French FDI undergone a major shift, and why? What impact has the change in the policy of the French government towards inward investments had on the destination of foreign MNE activity in the European Union?

Several of the papers in this first group focused on Japanese FDI. To what extent, and in what way, is such investment different from its European and US counterparts? Is it simply that Japanese firms are at an earlier stage in the internationalization of their production and markets?[1] Or is there something unique about the location-bound endowments in Japan, and about the competitive advantages of Japanese firms which explains why the ratio between Japan's outbound and inbound FDI is so much higher than that of other industrialized countries?[2] The answer is most surely multifaceted, but what is especially interesting is that at least some of the characteristics identified with the Japanese economy and with Japanese firms in the 1970s and 1980s are now being disseminated across national boundaries, and are at the forefront of the globalization process.

Globalization is, of course, the outcome of both technological and political change. Viewed from the perspective of firms, globalization is a necessary strategy for capturing additional markets in order to recoup the escalating costs of research and development (R&D). R&D, in its turn, is the engine driving firms to compete in world markets. We are in an innovation-led, globalizing economy and upgrading of the core competencies of firms and of the location-bound resources and capabilities of countries is a feature which differentiates the current state of technoeconomic production from the mass production – or the Fordist – era of the last century or more. Increasingly, commentators are distinguishing between a trajectory of capitalism dominated by large hierarchies – which reached its peak with the mass production of standardized cars by the United States in the motor vehicle sector in the 1950s – and one that is emerging which is based on a new type of micro organization, that of innovation-led flexible manufacturing, which, since the late 1960s, has been increasingly associated with the Japanese industrial machine and institutional framework.

This leads us on to a discussion of the second group of papers presented at this conference, of which that by Terutomo Ozawa is particularly interesting. Ozawa writes a great deal about lean production. In Chapter 9, he distinguishes between the age of scale production and the age of lean production. He observes that, although the latter mode of production is a Japanese phenomenon, it is one which is spreading to other industrialized countries, and it is most pronounced in those sectors in which, until very recently, Japanese firms have had a marked competitive and comparative advantage.

There is accumulating evidence that at least some American firms, particularly in the motor vehicle sector, are very quickly learning the lessons which the Japanese forcibly taught them. According to the *World Competitiveness Report* for 1994 (World Economic Forum/IMD, 1994), the United States, for the first time in ten years, replaced Japan as the world's most competitive nation in 1993.[3] Here, then, we have an example of an organizational system which was originated in America, was taken up by the Japanese, was exported by them back to America, and is now enabling US enterprises to regain many of the competitive advantages they earlier lost to their Japanese counterparts. And we do well to remember that in several other industrial sectors, in which the techniques of lean production offer fewer competitive advantages, American and European firms remain ahead of the Japanese.[4]

The point to be made, however, is a more general one. It is that the introduction of lean and flexible production is requiring a reappraisal of the technoeconomic paradigm which, up to now, has dominated our thinking about both the determinants and the impact of FDI. If we look at the extant literature on FDI, it tends to assume that most MNEs are products of hierarchical capitalism, and hierarchical capitalism is very much an American product. Much of the early FDI by American corporations represented a territorial expansion of Chandlerian-type capitalism (Chandler, 1962,1990). Essentially, it was a response to the failure of cross-border intermediate product markets. At the same time, the internalization of these markets was, itself, an extension of hierarchical capitalism. Such hierarchical capitalism – which was later embraced by European firms – continued to be the main form of the transnational involvement by firms right up to the 1970s.

Today we are seeing the emergence of a new sort of capitalism. Without pronouncing on how pervasive it is, or even on how far it is going to go, it can be said that it is requiring us to rethink some of our cherished notions of economic organization, both at a macro and a micro level. Scholars have variously described this phenomenon as 'collective', 'relational' and 'cooperative' capitalism, but the most apposite term may be taken from the title of a book by Michael Gerlach on *Alliance Capitalism* (Gerlach, 1992).

Alliance capitalism is different from hierarchical capitalism both in its character and in its effects, and certainly in its implications for FDI and transborder value added activity. Its essence is that, instead of internalizing market failure through hierarchical operations, firms are increasingly seeking to improve the organization of arms'-length markets by establishing cooperative relationships with other firms. This implies that, in considering the activities of MNEs, it is no longer appropriate to focus on majority-owned FDI. Increasingly, MNEs are being viewed as orchestrators of a plurality of organizational forms of intra- and inter-firm economic activities. Increasingly, too, inter-firm alliances are becoming more important features of cross-border production and transactions.

At the same time, these relational forms are very different from hierarchies. For one thing, their success rests on the presence of trust, mutual forbearance and reciprocity between the participating firms, rather than on administrative fiat. There are various forces making for inter-firm cooperation. One is the increasing pressure on firms to reduce the scope of their value activities and to concentrate on those based on their core assets. The competitive imperatives of globalization are forcing firms to reappraise their product and process portfolios and, in so doing, to engage in vertical or horizontal disinternalization. At the same time, the disinternalizing firms have not resorted to arms'-length relationships with their new suppliers and/or industrial customers. Instead, in order to protect and best exploit their critical assets, they are attempting to ensure that the other assets, with which they need to be combined, are of the appropriate quality and price and that they are continuously upgraded along with their own assets.

In short, whereas the competitive advantages of firms in hierarchical capitalism rest on their abilities to create and sustain their particular proprietary rights and core competencies, in alliance capitalism, a firm's advantages also depend on the extent to which it can draw upon (and influence the quality and supply conditions of) the complementary assets of other firms – and particularly those of its suppliers and industrial customers – and can efficiently coordinate these assets with its own. The interaction of firms in the Japanese motor industry is a very good example of alliance capitalism, dominated as it is by a variety of *keiretsu* relationships. As Ozawa points out in Chapter 9, the Japanese success is due, not just to the competitive advantages internalized by Toyota, but also to the way Toyota relates to and influences its suppliers in order to upgrade the quality and design of components and parts, which can then be used to advance Toyota's own core competencies.

The concept of alliance capitalism can also be used to explain some of the current developments in *intra*-firm relationships. In the case of hierarchical capitalism, succeeding stages of the value chain were largely independent of each other, albeit they were centrally organized. Today, however, the work of the R&D department is likely to be highly integrated with that of the manufacturing department, while each area, in turn, needs to be increasingly tuned to the work of the sales and the marketing departments. At the same time, the contribution that all grades of workers make to the continuous improvement of products and production processes is becoming increasingly recognized by managers. Thus the interface between competition and collaboration runs right the way through alliance capitalism, and takes many forms. It follows from this that scholars interested in evaluating the determinants and effects of FDI need to consider the extent and character of both inter-firm and intra-firm relationships as variables influencing the modality of cross-border economic activity.[5]

It has also been argued that the advent of alliance capitalism has important implications for the competitiveness of firms and the competitive advantages of countries. In the former case, the competitive advantages of firms need to embrace those which arise from the participation of those firms in alliances and networks (including business districts). The concept must also embrace the extent to which firms may be able to influence the effectiveness of these non-equity organizational forms. Economic gains (such as the economies of synergy, information sharing and risk pooling), which are external to the firm but internal to cooperative arrangements, seem to be evolving as more important components of the competitive advantages of firms.

What, finally, does alliance capitalism imply for governments? It implies that they have to take into consideration their roles as providers of critical complementary assets for their own and foreign firms, and as facilitators of efficient market systems. For, in spite of the removal of many structural market distortions, there is still a great deal of endemic market failure, which requires government to play a supervisory or monitoring role in order to ensure that the social costs and benefits of economic activity are equalized with private costs and benefits.[6]

The above points need to be taken into account by scholars dealing with the kinds of issues addressed by the third group of papers presented at the conference. These are essentially issue-oriented or impact studies, and deal with the consequences of FDI. But, apart from some discussion of the restructuring of North–South economic activity, the papers use extant analytical tools, and make no attempt to modify these to take account of the advent of alliance capitalism. This, for example, is the case of the contributions on the impact of FDI on the balance of payments and on the transfer of technology.

However, it seems clear that we should now be considering whether or not the growth of inter-firm alliances and flexible production makes a difference to the impact of FDI. Is it likely to create more or fewer jobs in host countries? Does it aid or inhibit industrial restructuring? Does it make the cross-border transfer of technology a more or less viable proposition? Does it lead to greater or less industrial concentration? Does it lead to more or fewer industrial linkages? Does it affect the balance of payments and, if so, in what way? And what, if anything, does alliance capitalism mean for government policies towards MNEs, and for competition, technology and FDI policies in general?

In short, we are moving into a new paradigmatic phase of our hypothesizing about the determinants and consequences of MNE activity, and it is a phase which will make new demands on our intellectual capabilities. It is also likely to require that such capabilities should be just as lean and flexible as the firms we praise! At the same time, we must accept that international business research is increasingly crossing disciplinary boundaries. For example, much fruitful research on alliance capitalism is being undertaken by geographers, sociologists, political scientists and organizational theorists. As economists and business scholars, we really do have to extend our intellectual horizons if we are properly to appreciate and understand what is really going on in our global village; and it is very much to be hoped that all of us interested in the subject of FDI and MNEs will be prepared to examine – and, where appropriate, to embrace and exploit – some of the rather exciting ideas and concepts that are now emerging from disciplines other than our own.

NOTES

1. As shown, for example, by their lower ratio of foreign assets or employment to worldwide assets and employment, than those of European or US MNEs.
2. In 1990, it was 16.9, compared with 1.1 in the case of the United States, 1.2 in the United Kingdom and 1.7 in Germany (Dunning, 1996).
3. The *World Competitiveness Report* presents a series of statistical indicators and perceptions by business executives on the competitiveness of both industrialized and industrializing countries (44 in 1994). No less than 381 criteria covering a wide range of competitiveness-related issues are embraced in the report, and from these overall ranking indices are derived. Further details on the methodology used to obtain these indices are given in the 1994 report, pp. 24–6.
4. More than two-thirds of the trade gap between the United States and Japan in 1993 was within the motor vehicle and electronic product, camera and office machinery sectors.
5. I have tried to examine the consequences of alliance capitalism for our theorizing about the determinants of MNE activity in Dunning (1995).
6. For an examination of the way this might be accomplished, see Dunning (1994).

REFERENCES

Chandler, A.D. Jr (1962), *Strategy and Structure: The History of American Industrial Enterprise*, Boston: Harvard University Press.

Chandler, A.D. Jr (1990), *Scale and Scope: The Dynamics of Industrial Capitalism*, Cambridge, Mass.: Harvard University Press.

Dunning, J.H. (1994), *Globalization: The Challenge for National Economic Regimes*, Dublin: Economic and Social Council.

Dunning, J.H. (1995), 'Reappraising the Eclectic Paradigm in an Age of Alliance Capitalism', *Journal of International Business Studies*, 26(3), 461–91.

Dunning, J.H. (1996), 'Explaining Foreign Direct Investment in Japan: Some Theoretical Insights', in M. Yoshitomi and E.M. Graham (eds), *Foreign Direct Investment in Japan*, Cheltenham: Edward Elgar, 8–63.

Gerlach, M.L. (1992), *Alliance Capitalism: The Social Organization of Japanese Business*, Oxford: Oxford University Press.

World Economic Forum/IMD (1994), *World Competitiveness Report*, 14th edn, Geneva: World Economic Forum.

Index